THE EAGLE AND THE STONE

A Stone Laid in Zion

The Story of Pilate, Claudia, and Jesus

Ellen Whitman Bynum

Copyright © 2003 by Ellen Whitman Bynum

A Stone Laid in Zion
by Ellen Whitman Bynum

Printed in the United States of America

Library of Congress Control Number: 2002117688
ISBN 1-591604-41-9

All rights reserved. No part of this publication may be reproduced or transmitted in any form or by any means without written permission of the publisher.

Unless otherwise indicated, Bible quotations are taken from The King James Version and Revised Standard Versions of Layman's Parallel Bible. Copyright © 1980 by Zondervan Publishers.

Xulon Press
10640 Main Street
Suite 204
Fairfax, VA 22030
(703) 934-4411
XulonPress.com

To order additional copies, call 1-866-909-BOOK (2665).

Pontius Pilate Dedication

Child of my soul and spirit,
I send you on your way,
Not knowing who will hear it—
This word I have to say.

As Hannah in God's temple
Was then, so I am now—
One woman, plain and simple,
Who made an earnest vow.

For what God did to save me,
My thanks, long over-due:
"This precious child You gave me
I now give back to You."

Ellen W. Bynum
February 12, 1992

Table of Contents

Part I	At Caesarea by the Sea	9
Part II	The Trip to Jerusalem	95
Part III	Promise and Compromise	161
Part IV	The Cost of Compromise	249

Part I

At Caesarea by the Sea

Table of Contents

Chapter 1	Thunder at Dawn	13
Chapter 2	Sebastos	15
Chapter 3	Man and Governor	17
Chapter 4	Religion, Disillusion, and Philosophy	23
Chapter 5	The Fates and Fortune	29
Chapter 6	Heroes, Gods, and Poetry	33
Chapter 7	The Perfect Woman	37
Chapter 8	On Marriage and the Almost Perfect Wife	41
Chapter 9	Between Sea and Harbor	47
Chapter 10	At Dockside	51
Chapter 11	The Temple and the Gods	53
Chapter 12	The Bride of the Jealous God	55
Chapter 13	The Episode of the Ensigns	59
Chapter 14	A Cornerstone that Bears the Name of Pilate	63
Chapter 15	Harbor Entrance and Aqueduct	65
Chapter 16	The Imitator of Herod the Great	67
Chapter 17	The Water Project and the Secret Agreement	69
Chapter 18	The Dedication and the Interrupted Tour	75
Chapter 19	The Aqueduct Affair	79
Chapter 20	Two Views on Parenting	83
Chapter 21	The Disillusioned Wife	85
Chapter 22	The Threat of the Messiah	89
Chapter 23	The Barabbas Case and the Nazarene Contigency	91

CHAPTER 1

Thunder at Dawn

"*D*oom!" Turning pale, my augur shook a warning finger at me as he pronounced the dreadful word. Three hours later, I can still hear him.

This is what provoked his extreme reaction: When I sent for him early this morning and told him about the thunder that wakened me at dawn, he voiced his objections to the trip I had planned for today. What clinched it for both of us was the highly unlucky sighting of the birds which followed my hearing the thunder. (Obviously the man didn't want me to go; he knew he would be following close behind me.) This is why I now find myself a little before noon, walking along the waterfront toward the harbor of Caesarea instead of riding cross-country toward Jerusalem.

As far as my augur and I are concerned, it is an inauspicious day for any enterprise outside of this city which is protected by the gods of Rome—but a good day to do what I am doing now. I am safer here in Caesarea, my home away from home, than in the rest of Judea. I look like any other citizen of our city, except for one of the Jewish minority, who hold to themselves. Most of the people I meet as I pass the workshops and warehouses do not recognize me; the few who do, keep it quiet. At least nobody stares at me with hatred and fear.

At this hour of a busy workday, the activity in the dock area ought to occupy my mind and help me keep it off those bad omens earlier in the morning...

I wonder what disasters lurk between here and Jerusalem. Could it be a rockslide in one of those narrow passes? More likely, a band of Zealots lying in wait for me in such a place, where they can hide out behind the rocks and suddenly descend on our party? Perhaps some friends of that Barabbas we captured, who is now locked up, awaiting my arrival in Jerusalem, which is sure to result in his trial, condemnation, and death by crucifixion?

Of course a group of terrorists like the Zealots could not hope to defeat a cohort of Roman soldiers in open country, but in the hills, they could bide their time until they spotted Claudia and me in our carriage, then jump us and cut us down before being cut to pieces themselves. They hate me—and the empire for which I stand—enough to lose their own lives in an attempt to put an end to mine.

Approaching the harbor...

Oh-oh! Watch your step, man, you need to keep your mind on where you're going! (I almost tripped over a coil of rope back there, and that would have been another bad omen. Could have caused me to twist or break an ankle, even a leg.) And now, entering the harbor...

Maybe, like my augur, today I should have stayed behind stone walls and barred doors, thus avoiding all possibility of accident. But I will not allow myself to become a prisoner of fear.

I walk out on the slim spit of land at the southeast end of the harbor, now built up with dock facilities. Before Herod built the breakwater which constitutes the rest of it, this is all there was.

CHAPTER 2

Sebastos

"Oops! Sorry, gov'nor!"

He practically runs into me as I cross his path between the storage vault and loading area at the southeast end of the harbor.

"No problem—you're a man in a hurry, and you have work to do, while I have time on my hands."

He obviously has something else on his hands. A short, burly, bow-legged man, he is wearing a stevedore's harness. One of the hundreds who do the manual labor in this huge port which is on a major east-west trade route—a vital link between Rome and the caravans of Asia. At the moment he is carrying a large bale on his back, probably flax for export. As soon as they finish loading the hold of that boat drawn up dockside, he and others like him will be pulling it toward harbor mouth by a towrope which will be attached to their harnesses.

"Sebastos..."

"For a moment his Semitic features take on a puzzled expression.

"My name is Aram."

"Might as well be Sebastos—you do the work of this port. You aren't Jewish...?"

"Samaritan, sir."

That figures. You wouldn't catch these Caesarean Jews sweating under the harness. Thousands of them, rich shopkeepers and landowners and moneylenders. Live in town but own lands in territory donated to them by Herod the Great when he founded the city. Get tenant farmers to work the land for them. Lots of Samaritans, people like this man.

"Where are you from?"

"Maioumas, sir."

One of the city's subject towns in the rich hinterland. Located about two miles to the northeast just below the slopes of Carmel.

"Maioumas... Fine theatre there."

"Suppose so. No time for theatres, though. Have a job to do."

"I won't keep you. Get back to your work, Sebastos."

"Aram, sir."

"As you will." (They're all Sebastos to me.) "Have a nice day."

"You too, gov'nor."

He ducks his head courteously and goes on with his business of loading the ship. And I continue my way out toward the breakwater.

If the man only knew—*I really am his governor!*

Once in a while, I have to leave the governor's headquarters and all insignia of office behind me. Then, looking like any ordinary Gentile citizen of Caesarea, I walk out here to talk to people and get the feel of this great harbor which Herod called Sebastos as a tribute to his imperial patron Augustus. In the common Greek, *Sebastos*, translating the Latin *Augustus*—a concession to a population largely Gentile and Greek-speaking.

The harbor functions like a single living organism such as the stevedore I just spoke to. And in selecting a model for the little god who personifies the harbor, the sculptor must have chosen one like him: For Sebastos is represented as a little half-man straining in harness at the feet of the much larger goddess who personifies the city of Caesarea Maritima, Caesarea by the Sea.

CHAPTER 3

Man and Governor

Crossing over from what must have originally been a rocky spit of land to the man-made facilities beyond... A little hump-backed bridge spans the narrow channel connecting the south bay area with Sebastos. In fine weather ships can anchor there and unload their cargoes, using rowboats which pass under the bridge into this larger harbor.

Walking across the loading platform toward the two-story building of the harbormaster who controls such operations... Climbing up the exterior staircase to the flat roof, one of my favorite spots out here when I want to meditate... I can't pursue a connected line of thought in a closet away from everyone; my mind soon goes blank. And I can't concentrate in a crowd where I must constantly interact with others. But this is an ideal place, close to bustling human activity and yet not a part of it.

To think that I am standing on the roof of a building erected atop a single huge concrete block, one out of several which make up this loading platform. From what I have been able to learn, boatmen towed huge wooden forms out here and sank them on the site, filling them with rubble and a special mortar mixed with lime and a volcanic ash imported from Italy. The result, concrete that hardens under water, was not unknown at the time but was the largest wide scale application of the concept. Awesome, truly awesome. Workmen then laid paving blocks of the local limestone from which much of both harbor and city were built.

All alone up here, the way I want and need it for my purposes today...

"I, Pontius Pilate, in my seventh year as prefect of Judea..."

No, that sounds too pretentious. I am not addressing a public gathering of my subjects, trying to impress them. I am not speaking to the Roman Senate, trying to defend myself before them. At this point in time, I am simply reviewing in my mind things that have happened to me here and things that have happened in the outside world that affect my tenure of office. For this may prove to be a crucial moment in my career.

I tend to become too self-important in my administrative headquarters, with everyone running around at my bidding and saying, "Your Excellency." (My wife calls it "obnoxious.") Claudia would have liked to see me a couple of minutes ago, chatting with the stevedore who was unaware of my identity. She likes me to keep the common touch, yet at the same time she fears for my safety when I go forth like this without an armed escort. Irrational, typical of her sex. It's scarcely a half-mile here from the governor's palace on the promontory beyond the south bay. There are warehouses on the land side and open paved dock side area. And I always pass my soldiers. Most of them recognize me, but I have instructed them not to salute me. They are to intervene only if they see someone giving me trouble.

The sight of the sea and the harbor helps me to get in touch with who I am and what I am, man and governor. I need this from time to time, especially today when I must be ready to leave for Jerusalem as soon as the auspices prove favorable. It is a week till the Jewish Passover, one of their greatest feasts, and I must make an enforced pilgrimage there to conduct necessary business and to maintain public order. At this time when the population of the city is swollen to nearly four times its normal size, rioting is likely to break out. Even a minor disturbance could lead to a general uprising. This is a duty which I still dread after seven years, perhaps even more than at first when I still had dreams of Romanizing Judea and its population. It will be less unpleasant because for the first time in several years Claudia will go with me.

Who am I? A middle-aged man with a much younger wife but no children after ten years of marriage. I am getting bald in back in spite of sniffing portions of the flowering cyclamen everyday as my barber has prescribed. I depend increasingly on his art to conceal my hair loss. I am developing a paunch in spite of the daily sessions with my masseur and my exercise at the gymnasium. If I am lucky, I have perhaps ten more years to make my mark in life before retirement. I must make no further mistakes.

For I am a governor on probation, serving under Flaccus, acting prefect of Syria, under an absentee emperor, the aging Tiberius, who for the past six years has shut himself off on the island of Capri, from whence he governs this empire. I am in the bad favor of a suspicious, depraved, and possibly senile ruler. In more senses than one, I stand here alone.

Behind me lies Caesarea Maritima, built forty years ago by Herod the Great beside the Mediterranean. Caesarea—a typical provincial capital of the empire, the seat of the political power in Judea and Samaria, though Jerusalem is the religious capital of the former and the city called Sebaste, of the latter. Judea and Samaria, commonly called simply Judea, a small and relatively unimportant dependency of Syria, the easternmost province in the Roman Empire. I am far removed from Rome, and yet I am controlled by her.

It takes forty days for the imperial post to travel overland in the winter. It takes half that time or less in the summer when travel by sea is safe and speedy. But whether the mail arrives sooner or later, I am controlled by the messages I receive from Tiberius. A stroke from his pen in Capri can replace me here and send me home packing to face charges of maladministration. Yet in spite of warning letters in the past, he has chosen to leave me here these seven years. Although I am heartily sick of this land with its exasperating people and their incomprehensible God, I do not wish to leave under a cloud of suspicion. Man and governor, I stand alone.

It is true that I made a serious blunder at the very beginning of my administration, but my real troubles did not begin till a year and a half ago, when Sejanus' high treason was discovered—when Tiberius had him strangled and his body thrown down the Steps of Mourning into the Tiber River. Sejanus, prefect of the Praetorian Guard, my commanding officer in Rome the year I completed my military service. Sejanus, to whom I owe my present office. Since his death and the subsequent executions of his wife and family, his friends and supporters, I have felt most insecure in my position here. Though I was innocent of complicity in Sejanus' plot to gain control of the empire, that makes little difference to a vicious, doddering old emperor.

Being the governor oneself is not like serving under someone else as governor. A few years before I came to Judea, when I was a tribune serving under the governor of Syria, I had comrades I could trust—fellow officers who were in the same situation as myself—men who would not turn me in for some indiscreet remark made while we were in our cups. I have no social equals here in Judea. I am at odds with Herod Antipas, tetrarch of Galilee and Perea and my political rival.

He would like to get back for himself the throne of Judea which, along with the surrounding provinces, was all intended for him according to the terms of his father's first will. Herod the Great later altered this so that on his death, the land was divided between Antipas and his brothers Philip and Archelaus, the last being named to rule over the largest and most important parts, Judea and Samaria. Archelaus proved to be so unpopular that after ten years, the Jews prevailed upon Caesar Augustus to depose him and place Judea under the direct rule of Rome. Since then, Judea and Samaria have been governed by a succession of knightly governors serving under the legate of Syria, while Antipas and his brother Philip have retained their former holdings.

I associate with Herod officially, but even when we met socially, I was never at my ease with him. You cannot trust a man who is culturally half a Jew and half Hellenized eastern potentate. You never know at any given moment which half of him you will be dealing with. I have trustworthy aides and an adequate staff of advisers, composed of senior officers and prominent citizens of Caesarea who are experts on the Jewish nation and its culture. They will tell me what I ask them—but no more. In the beginning, I did not know the right questions to ask, and after seven years, at times I still do not know. Sometimes I do not ask because I can anticipate their answers and do not wish to hear them.

When all is told, I can confide only in my wife. But you cannot tell a woman everything you would tell a man, not even when the woman is your wife. Claudia and I are closer here in Judea than we would have been in Rome where most marriages these days do not last for ten years. I can tell her many things because I love her and trust her. But precisely because I love her, I do not wish to tell her everything. And I cannot get rid of the fears and tensions and hostilities that are building up inside me. So I stand here essentially alone.

CHAPTER 4

Religion, Disillusion, and Philosophy

I have no personal gods to turn to. Like most Roman men, I had lost my belief in the gods long before I put on the toga and was given my first shave. In my career as a soldier, I have seen people worship many strange gods in widely separated lands as far apart as Germany and Syria. Other people's gods may have different names, but in their nature, they are the same as ours—gods of warfare and procreation, gods of the sky and the earth and regions beneath it. We Romans have a tendency to pick up the gods of the people we conquer and to identify them with our own. Even the gods of Egypt, those beings with the heads of birds and animals, we have made our own—for example, Jupiter-Ammon.

I distrust these foreign cults, even ones which have been in Rome for centuries, like that of the Asian fertility goddess Cybele, and if I could, I would keep them out of Caesarea. However, with our auxiliary troops drawn from every Middle Eastern people except the Jews, worship of foreign gods is infiltrating the army. Moreover, with the commerce of many nations passing through this great port, it is hard to keep out their gods, too. And here I run into real problems. Is the cult of a deity popular in Rome the same as that which is practiced in other parts of the world—specifically, here in Caesarea?

A good case in point is the cult of the Egyptian deities Isis and Osiris. Isis is popular in all ports as the patroness of seamen, and every year at the beginning of the shipping season here, there is a big parade here down to the waterfront for the launching of her sacred ship. Priests, mummers, followers and initiates of both sexes take part in these apparently harmless rites. Now this presents me with a real problem. What if the worship here should degenerate into the kind of fraudulent farce which entraps silly women in Rome? Women like my wife? I keep telling myself sailors have more sense than to be so misled. Unsure of the best course of action, so far I have done nothing to prevent these parades.

Always in the back of my mind is Claudia's experience with this cult when she was in Rome last year. She wrote me she had become a member of the cult of Isis and the dead Osiris, very popular especially among women. Knowing her susceptible religious nature and her desire to be healed of her barrenness, I was not surprised. She assured me the cult of the fertility goddess Isis involved no such objectionable features as the orgies of self-mutilation associated with the cult of Cybele. From her account, it seemed as if the ritual had been purged of its grosser elements, discreetly Hellenized, and infused with some mystical emotional appeal. She said many Roman matrons were fellow devotees, including several influential people among her acquaintance, one of them a senator's wife.

But when she returned to Caesarea with broken health and disappointed hopes, I realized she had not been telling me the whole truth—and my old suspicions of half-naked priests with shaven heads and "gods" wearing animal masks have revived in full force. I heartily approve of the restrictions which the emperor periodically places on the activities of such pernicious cults in Rome, and if they try any such antics here, I shall make an example of them.

Gods and goddesses—who needs them? Uneducated people, simpletons, and of course, women. The fiction of the gods is man's attempt to deal with the uncertainties of life. I am an educated Roman man, and I do not need gods. I am schooled in philosophy and the classics. In the plot of the classic Greek drama and the even older epic poems of Homer, gods have their place. And there the interaction of gods with each other and with mankind may really be important. But in our life today, gods are completely irrelevant. There may be deities with distinct personalities, but if there are any such, they matter very little to the individual.

One must pay lip service to the gods as a soldier or as a servant of the state or as a citizen of Rome. One must make the proper sacrifices to the gods. This is the essence of the civil religion which binds our empire together. When I was a younger man, if I worshiped any god, it was Roma, the personification of our empire. When I served in Germany under the command of Germanicus Caesar, I would gladly have died for Rome and for Emperor Augustus. But Tiberius Caesar, his heir, is no Augustus, and Roma has fallen from the high position she held at the beginning of the empire. Rome is still great, but she is no longer good.

I was profoundly disillusioned by the treachery of my former patron Sejanus. I was thoroughly disgusted by the revelation of adultery, intrigue and murder employed by him to get rid of legitimate heirs to the throne and to place himself in the direct line of succession. If the plot had not been discovered, Tiberius himself would have been the next to die. I cannot criticize our emperor for executing Sejanus. Although I have no love for him, I cannot but admire the ingenuity and thoroughness with which he disposed of the second man in the nation, separating Sejanus from his Praetorian Guard, secretly obtaining the cooperation of the senators—keeping Sejanus in the dark until, literally and figuratively, the noose was around his neck, It was a masterful scheme, perfectly worked out.

But I am completely revolted by Tiberius's conduct since—by the indiscriminate blood bath which has ensued and which still continues—by his treatment of Agrippina, the unfortunate widow of Germanicus, whom he has exiled to the island of Pandateria. It is rumored that he has ordered her to starve herself to death. I thought it was Sejanus who had turned the emperor against Agrippina, but apparently Tiberius was suspicious of her all along, jealous of her popularity with the people, distrustful of her favor with the senators who backed her in her ambitions for her sons. Strangely enough, Tiberius is now grooming as his successor her youngest son Caius.

May he walk warily!

The philosophy I have learned in the schools does not give me much comfort. I suppose I am an eclectic in my beliefs, neither a Stoic nor an Epicurean—a little of both, but I cannot go to the extremes of either. Stoicism is a noble ideal—virtue as its own reward—but it is too ascetic for most Romans. We enjoy the good life too much to be thorough Stoics. Of course I heartily disclaim the view of the Cynics who despise pleasure and show contempt for all material things. To deny yourself something good because you would feel pain if you had it and then lost it sounds like lunacy to me. At the opposite extreme, I loathe the excesses of the wealthy profligates who make a god of their appetites and declare themselves Epicureans. True, Epicurus taught that happiness is the highest good. Yet the happiness he taught his followers to seek after is not produced by sensual enjoyment but by the cultivation of all the virtues.

Now the practice of moderation in all things sounds like a good idea, but I do not believe as Epicurus taught that all human conduct can be regulated by what gives pleasure to oneself and at the same time, to others. For philosophers teaching under the porticos, this is all very well, but it will not work for soldiers or statesmen. To secure the good of the state and the empire, these have to do things that are unpleasant to others. Soldiers do not look forward to being killed in battle, but they must either kill others or be killed themselves. And surely no people as a nation wish to be subjugated by another power.

If I have a personal deity, it is duty. My philosophy is living up to the standards which our noble ancestors have set for us. As a governor, my first duty is to keep the peace; second, to collect the taxes; and third and last, to administer justice. These three take precedence over everything else. I would like to be remembered as a benefactor through monuments that bear my name, but this is not number one on my list of priorities. I will be faithful to duty. Perhaps I am more of a Stoic than I think.

Yes, I like to think of myself as being faithful to duty. But at times like this when I ponder the meaning of my life in its larger context, I wonder where the limits of my duty lie. I would have fought to the death at the command of General Germanicus, but he is dead now. Do I have a duty toward his family? Where does duty end and self-interest begin?

If someone else should start a revolution to overthrow Tiberius, recall the family of Germanicus and set one of his sons on the throne, I would not hesitate to join him—after the fact. But till someone else makes the first move, I shall devote myself to a narrower concept of my duty and to personal survival. Some might call me an opportunist; I prefer to consider myself a realist. The people who start revolutions are the first to die, and death ends all things. My choice is to wait on the sidelines until the winner emerges from the conflict and then to join him. The spirit of our times is expediency, not self-sacrifice. I will do the expedient thing, and I will survive.

CHAPTER 5

The Fates and Fortune

For I do believe in the Fates and in Fortune. Consequently I consult our military augurs about nearly everything I do. But to me the Fates are not female deities—they are faceless powers, forces unmoved by the prayers and tears of men. Nothing can cause the Fates to change their minds. Yet Fortune may be propitiated by ceremonies, gifts, and sacrifices. Up to a certain point, men may use Fortune to their advantage. For instance, it was luck that put me here. Who would have thought Sejanus would pick me for prefect of Judea? Now all is told, I wonder why he did so, for he knew of my former loyalty to Germanicus. Perhaps it was his anti-Jewish bias. It might have been some chance remark against the Jews which I tossed off carelessly at a party of the Praetorian Guard. When I am drinking, I lose some of my inhibitions but not my ability to tell a joke. Perhaps he thought he could insure my loyalty to him by recommending me to Tiberius for this job. Clearly, there were many others he could have chosen who were as ambitious and as qualified as I.

Whatever it was, I'm sure of one thing: When I got this assignment to begin with, someone or something was working in my favor—the supernatural power which men call luck. At that time, I paid my respects to the goddess Fortuna at Antium in Italy, and I have continued to send her occasional votive offerings. But since my arrival in Caesarea, I have chosen to deal mainly with Tyche, the local goddess of luck and the Divine Patroness of Caesarea. Her image is seen here on everything from pottery lamps to marble statues, including the one in the center of my pool at the governor's palace. Oddly enough—or perhaps quite understandably—she looks very much like the colossal image of the Patroness of Rome in our Temple of Augustus and Roma. Even her attire, her posture, and the emblems of authority she holds are similar.

In one thing, however, the goddess Tyche is different; she is represented with Sebastos at her feet. And though of course I must pay my tribute to Roma, I can't afford to neglect the power protecting this harbor in which I stand. The goddess Fortuna looks like neither of these two ladies, and the symbols of her divine attributes which she holds are also different. But it doesn't matter to me what luck or Fortune looks like—it can be a divine lump, for all I care. I just want it on my side. If it's all one entity, very well, but if it's differentiated among Fortuna, Tyche, and whatever, I want to stay in good with all of them. I just know I need all the luck I can get.

I know I am a good soldier, a good administrator, and a good magistrate, but as Claudia tells me, I am no diplomat. Apparently Sejanus did not want a diplomat. He wanted a man who could keep the Jews in line, a man who would put up with no nonsense—and that is what he got. But Sejanus is gone now. The times have changed, and I must change with them. Now Tiberius makes it known throughout the empire that we must conciliate the Jews and protect their institutions. This is why I am nervous about going to Jerusalem. It is as hard for a man of middle age to change his mind-set as it is for him to change his daily routine. And as my wife says, I have a tendency to be abrupt, to speak and act on impulse without due reflection.

I shall take my official augur to Jerusalem with me. He is at least as important as my barber. I need Fortune on my side. The things which happen between the birth and death of little men occur by chance at the caprice of Fortune. But the rise and fall of great men who bring about the rise and fall of nations—these are decreed by the Fates. No one can change them.

I am reminded of a fowling expedition on the Nile seven years ago when Claudia and I stopped at Alexandria, the capital of Lower Egypt. We spent a week there as guests of Governor Galerius before the last lap of our long sea voyage from Rome to Caesarea. I remember how Galerius took me back into the region called the Delta, where the Nile fans out into many tributaries that make their way toward the Mediterranean. The marshes there are filled with thickets of papyrus, havens for all kinds of water birds. Since the prevailing wind is from the north, all we had to do on the way upstream was to raise our sails. Then the wind blew us to our destination. Once there, we furled our sails and dropped anchor while we hunted. The Egyptians demonstrated their ancient skill with the throwing stick and brought down many ducks and geese. A fine day's sport, but I wondered how we should return.

I found out how the river flows against the wind. On the way back to Alexandria, the current bore us swiftly downstream, assisted by slaves at their oars. Wind and current against each other. Can it be that Fate and Fortune also are sometimes in opposition? When there is chaos on earth, are there also conflicts in heaven? Surely the ancients thought so. I do not know. Perhaps a man cannot row unaided against his Fate, but he can assist Fortune to do so by plying his oars well. Fortuna, Tyche, whatever, be with me! I need all the help I can get when I go to Jerusalem this time. And I repeat—I shall take my augur with me.

I needed to come out here today to look at the earth, the sky, and the sea—to remind myself of who I am. Though I am a big man in Judea, I am a little man in the Roman Empire. I am a little man in the natural world. The Fates are very likely unconcerned about what I do, and so I must court Fortune. I consulted my augur this morning about something I saw when I rose at dawn and looked outside my window. It was four birds on my right, heading landward from the sea. A bad omen, he agreed. To make doubly sure, he performed a sacrifice. The animal's entrails proved to be abnormal. Today was not a good day for our trip to Jerusalem. So instead I followed my usual routine of official duties, doing things that my aides could have done just as well without me. Perhaps tomorrow will prove more auspicious.

I took time to jot down a pleasing thought I had this morning. It occurred to me when I opened the casement window to check on the weather, which can go either way at this time of the year. And inclement weather is a bad omen also.

> A dull-looking day. A brisk wind sending the clouds scudding into little drifts, piling up like gray tufts of wool tinged with the blood of a sacrifice. The same wind combing up little waves on the sullen surface of the sea. The winds of Fate drive gods as well as men; all are subject to the winds of Fate.

CHAPTER 6

Heroes, Gods, and Poetry

As I wrote this down, I thought of Claudia; perhaps she will like it when I share it with her tonight. She usually says she likes my poems, though she may disagree with the ideas behind them. Now it helps me to find parallels between the natural world and man's condition, to put into words the way I think and feel. Like Germanicus, my ideal, I am something of a poet. He was a great man who wrote and fought equally well. I am a lesser man with lesser gifts, so I must remain a closet poet. I am conscious of the distance I must maintain between myself and my subordinates. I cannot afford to show my heart to them, lest it give them an undue advantage over me. So only Claudia will hear such words as these.

Germanicus, my great general, the man who almost conquered Germany—he would have finished the job if our jealous emperor had given him another year to do it. But Tiberius recalled him to Rome and shifted him to the command of the eastern provinces. And there, in Syria, he came to grief—felled, it is said by poison, at the age of thirty-five. We soldiers who served under him were stunned. Everyone suspected Piso, the commander of the Syrian forces. On his return to Rome, the people, who had idolized Germanicus, demanded a senatorial investigation. Though Piso took the blame, it was widely rumored he had done the deed at the order of Tiberius. Impossible to prove, for before the investigation came to an end, Piso was found one morning with his throat cut and his sword lying next to him. A suicide? Perhaps. Or was it also done by order of Tiberius? In Greek mythology the god Saturn devouring his own sons—Tiberius causing the death of his own heir, his nephew Germanicus...

Then there is Caius, the youngest son of Germanicus. I think of him as a tiny boy in Germany, wearing that miniature soldier's uniform and strutting around his father's camp in those little boots, those *caligae*-"Caligula," as we soldiers fondly called him. If he is anything like his father, he will make a good emperor—that is, if Tiberius allows him to survive. We are at the mercy of the winds of Fate....

The winds of Fate, controlling sea and sky. If there are gods, they are driven, too. They are not separate entities but spirit forces presiding over the affairs of men. When I look out my window daily just before sunrise, I see white mists rising from the salt marshes to join the clouds above. They are like the souls of the dead rising to join the elemental spirits. The lesser powers below rising to join the greater powers above—the *numina*, the divine presiding spirits that rule the world of men. These, like the clouds, are constantly changing, assuming shapes which the imaginative may see as giants, heads of men or animals, mountains or fortresses. So men have seen and marveled at the numinous power milling above them in the heavens. Men have imagined Jupiter with his rain and his thunderbolts. The Fates determine whether men will receive from heaven the fire that destroys or the water that gives life. The clouds are a spirit-filled canopy covering the earth. From them come both good and evil. But it is the winds of heaven that drive the clouds.

Is this a religion, a philosophy, or a poem? Does it come from my head or from my heart? Claudia calls me an unofficial atheist, which I suppose I am. But she is religious by nature, and if there were no gods, she would invent them. She was looking for new gods to worship while she was back in Rome. She may even be interested in the God of the Jews, for she asks frequent questions about their religion and festivals. I will not tell her how I feel about the God of the Jews, although it is a part of the imagery of my poem. He is like a dull and threatening bank of clouds above the mountains behind me. His form never changes. No winds seem to move him. He is the mountain God whom people fear, and he controls them from his home in Jerusalem. I do not understand him, and what you do not understand, you fear. Definitely I shall not tell this part to Claudia. Where women are concerned, about some things, the less said the better.

Walking up and down, trying to keep warm and dry on this open roof top in this damp stinging wind blowing from the south... Wrapping around myself the old brown cloak which I wear when I do not wish to be recognized... An angry froth of waves churning up below on the south bay side of the loading platform, bursting through the sluiceway... Not a day when ships could ride at anchor and unload there. But then, so early in the season, there is plenty of room in the main harbor. Now from what I understand, the chief reason for such sluiceways to begin with is in order to force water from the tops of the waves into the harbor and flush out the sediments which collect on the bottom. Blamed clever man, this Herod.

The works of his genius are all around me, behind me and before me. From right to left, starting with the palace, the sight of each recalls something special that happened to me there. I remember Claudia's pleasure when she first glimpsed the inner court of the Promontory Palace and experienced the wonder of a man-made pool of fresh water in the middle of a flowery courtyard with the waves of the sea crashing only a few feet away. We were still newly married, and she thrilled at the thought of summer evenings together in the garden beside the pool. (Thank you, great Herod!) And I dashed off a few romantic lines for the occasion.

Claudia liked what I wrote for her then because it was so sentimental. What I wrote this morning was actually more poetic. And she'll smile and say she likes it, but she'll prefer the other one. That's the way wives are.

CHAPTER 7

The Perfect Woman

She did not appreciate my poetic attempts the first time we were alone together—in a smaller garden with a fountain but no pool. We had not seen each other during all the years I served in the army under Germanicus. Now I was home on leave, awaiting reassignment to Syria, and we were soon to be married. Our parents had been planning for us to marry almost from the day she was born. Of course I had seen her once or twice before. The last occasion I remember was when she was a skinny child with unpleasant staring eyes, and I had lately donned the toga of manhood. At that time I was thinking a lot about girls but not about marriage. I was glad I would not have to marry this strange little creature for a long time. And now, fifteen years later, I thought it was perhaps still too soon. But she had changed. Her beauty startled me and caught me completely unprepared.

As a soldier I had been with many women, and I knew how to talk to the kind of girls who beckon in the streets; but this was the woman I was going to marry, and I wanted to make a really good impression. I was not worried about my appearance, for then I had a flat belly and a full head of hair; but how was I, a professional soldier of thirty-five, to talk to this slip of a girl scarcely more than half my age? This girl who was going to be my bride?

My parents and hers were talking in the master room off the partially open-roofed reception area of her father's house. They had presented us to each other, and they had turned us out into the inner garden court to get better acquainted. I was really apprehensive. After some small talk about ourselves, I attempted to pay her a compliment.

I said, "You have beautiful hair."

She looked me full in the eyes. I did not find that steady gaze unpleasant now. There was a roguish gleam in her eyes, an odd little lilt in her voice. She was delightful.

She said, "Thank you. You say you are a poet; tell me what my hair is like. What does it make you think of?"

From my neck up, sudden fire. On the outside, I felt my face burning. On the inside my brains were melting like wax. Finally I blurted out, "The dregs of wine!"

The moment I said it, I knew I had ruined our relationship before it had even started. And I felt completely wretched until I saw the expression on her face—a bit amused, a bit curious, with the trace of a frown between her eyes. She was more composed than I, the man of the world.

I tried to explain myself. "I meant that your hair is an interesting shade of dark reddish-brown."

She laughed. "Then why didn't you compare it to something pretty like a chestnut?"

"I was nervous."

"Why should you be nervous?"

"Because I wanted to make a good first impression."

This time she and I both realized how ridiculous this sounded, and we both laughed. Now I grew bold enough to take her hand.

I said, "You are so beautiful that when I look at you, I turn to mush inside, and I say the first thing which comes into my head. But at least the comparison was original."

Now she was the one to blush; I could see I had pleased her. I took her arm as we strolled around in the patio. She said she would not judge my poetic ability by my first attempt. I told her I need time to connect my thoughts and weigh my words, for whenever I speak right out, I come to grief. I recited one of my poems for her. She said she liked it and would put it to music, if I would give her the words. We sat down on a stone bench beneath an arbor of flowering vines. While I wrote, she was humming and singing a few words together. Her voice was entrancing.

I said, "I can't wait to hear you sing and play *our song*...." And after a slight pause, I added significantly, "*I can't wait for a lot of things.*" I ventured to run my fingers through one of the little curls that fell in front of each of her ears.

She looked up at me archly and said, "Pilate, I like your hair, too. Do you want to know what it reminds me of?"

"Yes, go ahead."

"Seaweed, seaweed growing on the rocks."

"Come now—seaweed? Slick, smelly seaweed?" Had I overdone the olive oil pomade?

She gave her head a toss which caused the ringlets to jiggle in a tantalizing manner. "No, none of these," she said coyly. "We spend every summer on the coast of Campania, and while we are there, we frequently visit my uncle at his cliff-side villa. Ever since I was a little girl, I have liked to go walking on the rocks along the shore when the sea is out. Then there are little tidal pools in the hollow places. I have always thought the seaweed in these pools looked like a sea god's hair—short but wavy and luxuriant. That is how I imagine your hair—like a sea god's."

I liked her poetic associations, and I liked her roguish wit. She was irresistible. I took her hand again. I said, "You are perfect, absolutely perfect. Will you let me be your sea god and lay my head in your lap so you can run your fingers through my hair?"

"I will, after we are married."

I said nothing, but I gave her hand a squeeze which I hoped was eloquent. I was glad she found me physically attractive. I was sure I had found the perfect woman, ideally suited for my lover and my companion.

CHAPTER 8

On Marriage and the Almost Perfect Wife

Now ten years later I know I was right—or almost right. For Claudia is a perfect wife, or as nearly perfect as a woman can be. If only she were not so religious! In a man I would consider that a defect, but in a woman perhaps it is a virtue. It tends to keep them faithful to their husbands and devoted to their children. I would rather have her running after strange gods than strange men....

I would not have believed it could be so chilly up here at the end of March. I have been standing in one place on this roof too long. It's no patio in Rome in the springtime, and I don't have Claudia and my love to keep me warm. I should have put on an extra tunic before I came out here. They say our first emperor was cold-natured and sometimes wore two or three. If Augustus Caesar could get away with it, why not Pontius Pilate? I shall move on and that will warm me. I'll go below. I'll walk out on the breakwater, on the long arm which encircles the harbor on the south and the west. Sea wall behind harbor facilities will cut the wind... Broad promenade ideal for walking, and I can keep a brisk pace...

Men at work moving back and forth on the breakwater between the red-roofed arches of the storage vaults and the stations for the ships... Oh-oh! If I stay down here and keep up this pace, I'm putting myself on an immediate collision course with some other Sebastos. But if I go up on the sea wall behind the vaults, I can walk all around the south arm of the breakwater without interference. The parapet on both sides of me will protect me from much of the wind without obscuring the view. And the only people I'm likely to meet will be up there for the same reason I am.

Steps are slick... Mustn't risk a fall on this last day...

Claudia would be clucking over me like a mother hen if she knew I was out here like this. If she had a houseful of children, she would not always be fussing over me....

If only she could bear children. She would be in her element if, like Agrippina, she had nine of them. If she could have only one! That desire for motherhood nearly led to her undoing in Rome. It made her believe the lying priest of Isis who promised her life in her womb. It made her willing to endure outrageous things. If she had stayed in Rome another six months, she would have starved herself to death.

I believe she wants a child as much for me as for herself. Perhaps I talk too much about Germanicus and Agrippina, too much about little Caligula. Of course it would be nice to have a son and heir. However, I have got used to the idea that I shall never have a son by her to inherit my name and estate. It would have been pleasant, but I must content myself with having a nearly perfect wife. She is beautiful, talented, congenial, affectionate, faithful, truthful—to a point. As truthful as a woman can be, for women are manipulative by nature. They twist the truth to suit their purposes. They will get their way, if necessary, by underhanded means.

My wife is a daughter of the Claudians, which I should never forget. The Claudia *gens* have always been leaders. The noble Claudians—unscrupulous, considering themselves above the plebeians and above the law. The commoners of the clan, like the Marcelluses, distinguished as military officers and public servants. All of the Claudians are accustomed to command, and Claudia is no exception. She likes to have her way, but usually her little deceptions issue from her desire to prepare some surprise for me. She is completely unselfish. She rarely asks me to buy her anything. Of course I give her an unlimited allowance. You do not stint the spending of a wife who brought you the dowry her parents gave me. But gifts are different. I should like to give her a truly special gift, but the one thing she really wants, I am unable to give her. I am unable to give her a child.

At the age of forty-four, have I lost my procreative powers? Why a healthy young woman like Claudia cannot bear a child is a mystery to me—unless I myself have become sterile at a comparatively early age. It is the fault of our social system, the reason for the decline of our upper classes. We Roman men of the nobility marry so late in life that by the time we settle down to the serious business of producing an heir, we find we have lost the ability to do so. We have already sown our best seed. I can think of many noble families who are dying out, or who at best produce weakling sons or just daughters. A noteworthy example is Julius Caesar, who bore no legitimate male heir. And my wife's family, the Proculuses—she is an only child.

The only way a soldier can be assured of many legitimate children is to marry young and take his wife with him to the wars, like Germanicus. Although he died younger than I at the time of my marriage, he left behind him nine children to carry on his name. But he was an exception. Army regulations and the conditions of a soldier's life keep most of us from marrying during our years of service. So we carelessly scatter our best seed, enriching the stock of the peoples we conquer, leaving little to sow at home. Rome is left with the few and the weak, and the stock of noble Roman families is dying out....

Air full of spray, even at this height, and the parapet doesn't shield my upper body from it... Claudia would be really upset if she could see me clutching my cloak about my head and shoulders. She would scold me for not thinking ahead and putting on my oiled cloth cloak with the hood to avoid catching a spring cold. Well, I suppose I could take temporary shelter in one of these towers which provide lodging for the seamen. Their top floors serve as covered extensions of the walkway around the wall. My wife would say that's the only sensible thing to do. And people will scarcely notice me huddling in my old cloak by this open window....

In a way, I rather enjoy her attentions. If we had nine children, she would not be so solicitous, so intent upon pleasing me, so concerned about her appearance. She would always be pregnant, always occupied with her motherly duties. The children would be her first concern. I suppose she has spoiled me for lack of children to indulge.

On the other hand, does she think I cannot take care of myself? And if so, how did I ever get along the year she went home to Rome? It had been five years since she last saw her parents, and her aged father was ill. I urged her to go. I knew I should miss her, but I had no idea I should miss her so much. While I was here in Caesarea, my days were bearable. I had my administrative duties to perform and the cultural activities of this bustling port city to occupy my afternoons. In my spare time I would visit the theater and the amphitheater and the hippodrome, not so much for entertainment as to put off going back to rooms empty of her presence. In my evening hours, I thought I would read books, perhaps write poetry, but I found I had no desire to do these things. I wrote many letters to Rome and a few short poems, pouring out my heart to her—and I drank more than usual to dull the pain.

I missed her embraces. Duty is an impersonal ideal and Roma is a cold, remote goddess. When I would wake up lonely in the middle of the night, I had no wife of flesh and blood beside me, warm and responsive. Strangely, I missed her companionship even more than her arms around me—her chatter and her laughter and her singing—her wifely solicitudes and her understanding silences—her often sensible advice and her restraining influence on my own headstrong tendencies. Perhaps I am getting to the age when a man needs a woman more for a companion than a lover. I would be ashamed to admit this to another man, but while Claudia was gone, I felt no strong temptation to turn to other women. I was faithful to Claudia. At the age of forty-four, am I losing my virility?

Need to start moving again, stay active ... Sit too much, stay inside too much ... Getting soft ...

If Claudia could see me now, she would call me crazy for walking unprotected up here in this weather. She would say, "A man of your age should take better care of himself." Do I look so old to her? At twenty-nine, she still looks the same, but I am changing. Yet I am not so old that I need a nurse, as she seems to think. I do not need a mother to wipe my nose and tell me what to do....

CHAPTER 9

Between Sea and Harbor

Pausing to look through openings in the parapet at sea, harbor, and city, first on one side and then on the other... Never cease to marvel at the creative vision of Herod and the technical skill of his engineers... I'm approximately midway on an artificial breakwater eighteen hundred feet long and two hundred feet wide. Of these two hundred feet, the half on the harbor side is taken up with a broad semicircular promenade for passengers who are disembarking in the boat slips. And also with the adjacent storage vaults. Long and narrow, their scalloped tile roofs lie just beneath me and between me and the people.

The other hundred—the seaside—includes the part above water, finished off with the stone sea wall (on which I stand) with its towers at intervals. but there is just as much under water—the real structure that breaks the force of the waves. This largely unfinished outer barrier consists of rubble rising in a sort of terrace to the surface. Furthermore, on the southeast there is a secondary barrier which extends at broken intervals and parallel to the main one for perhaps a hundred feet. It further reduces the impact of the waves.

On the harbor side, the few boats that ride at anchor in the landing places are rocking in a gentle swell. But on the seaside, the wind is strong, and the waves are pounding hard against the Great Mole. Just as I feel the years pounding on me.

Remarkable ingenuity, to construct an artificial harbor where nature has placed such obstacles—a comparatively straight coastline with dangerous unmarked reefs that have deep channels between them—to build jetties on top of these reefs and use them to divide the inner harbor into more stations for shipping! If one includes the small harbor to the north and also the south bay area, this Sebastos compares favorably even with Pireus, the port of Athens.

Still more ingenious to me, the sewage system devised by Herod to flush out the waste of the city. To the north, just outside the city wall, I can see one of the drains. There is another one farther south between the palace and the theatre. These are connected to a network of channels running under the streets. Herod contrived to have these cleansed twice daily by the tides in a truly amazing manner. It is no less remarkable than the fabled labors of Hercules when he cleaned the Augean stables by harnessing the waters of two rivers. The tides of the sea–man cannot go against such mighty forces, but sometimes he can bend them to his purposes.

Next month there will be calmer seas and more favorable winds, and ships from all parts of the empire will enter this harbor. We can depend on a change in the weather with the changing seasons. But what of the seas of our lives and the winds that chafe them? When will they change? No breakwater can keep out the waves that roll from Rome. So long as Tiberius lives, nothing will change for the better. I must hold on and wait for a savior to come to Rome. Will it be Caius, son of Germanicus?

The pressure of the wind against my back, the pressure of the sea against the mole... How long will it last? A hundred years? Five hundred? A thousand? Will the relentless sea tear down the breakwater? Will relentless forces from the land tear down things which have been built upon it? And what of the Roman Empire? How long will it stand? With emperors like Augustus, it could easily last a thousand years, but if we have many like Tiberius...

Eyes dry, smarting... Need to get out of the wind again for a little while... The towers have no windows opening on the sea. But I can look out of an opening on the harbor side.

Fine view of the city here. I'm up high enough to see the boundaries of the city, the buildings outside the walls and the countryside beyond. But I'm not as high as the temple of Augustus and Roma—at least outwardly, the most impressive building in Caesarea. Directly in front of me, it rises to awesome heights on its vaulted platform, with the waters of the innermost harbor practically lapping at its base.

I see the market place flanked by stately columns and enclosed on three sides by temples, public buildings, and shops. On this large square converge the streets of the town, laid out at right angles in the Hellenistic manner. All municipal and some of my provincial government offices are located here or close by. (Tax records alone would use up all available space in the administration area at the governor's palace.) I see a few private homes and many tenements, everything built of local white stone or faced with imported marble. The whole city is surrounded by a semicircular wall which forms an arc extending from the small northern harbor as far south as the governor's palace, where it adjoins and strengthens the fortifications on the land side. On the seaside, sheer walls and surf furnish all necessary defense.

Just south of the walls and my palace, I see the theatre seating between three and four thousand. Claudia and I often enjoy plays and concerts from our place in the middle, in the governor's box. The concave fan of the seating, hidden from my view by exterior walls... Farther to the southeast, the U-formation of the hippodrome... Both of these are situated so as to have a prospect of the sea. The latter has a seating capacity of perhaps thirty thousand. It isn't the Circus Maximus, but it will have to do until some benefactor presents the city with a better one. I relish the excitement of chariot racing though Claudia says she dislikes the heat and the dust. Farther north and nearer the coast, the egg-shaped amphitheater where men fight beasts or each other for the enjoyment of the masses—it isn't far from where the aqueduct transects the walls at a point near the north harbor.

Looking north, south, and east of the city, I see small villages, isolated villas, and the lush spring green of rectangular plots of farmland. They are part of the extensive territory given to Caesarea by its founder. All of this is familiar, pleasing, and prosperous. Beyond it, the foothills of the Carmel range... And behind the hills, the bank of cloud which always look the same.

CHAPTER 10

At Dockside

I smell something—sausages cooking, steaming hot sausages. My stomach knows it's lunchtime; it growls in response. I know what is down there on the lower level—the stalls where snacks and beverages are sold. (I made the rule myself so that the food services would not spread throughout the area, taking vital space from those services involved with shipping.) I could descend here through this tower at the first angle where the sea wall starts turning north. The stalls directly below are set up so close to the storage vaults that they are invisible to me from here, but any fool can follow his nose. I go down the tower staircase to the dock area and take the only possible route (the narrow passage between two long vaults) coming out among the stalls. Aha! Now for one of those sausages, a piece of bread, and something to drink...

"Man, are these beef or pork?"

"Friend, this is Judea, and there isn't a herd of pigs this side of the Jordan. So what do you think?"

"I think I'll have one of—whatever. I was just hoping maybe these were imported from some place where pigs are raised for food."

"If so, I couldn't let you have one at this low price...."

Holding in one hand the hot sausage wrapped in a piece of flat bread, I move over to the drink line. A female vendor is ladling into cups the wine from a large earthen bowl which a small girl is stirring as a male slave periodically adds more wine and water.

"Woman, where do you get your wine from?"

"From Piraeus, the port of Athens."

"Then it's Greek wine, fortified with resin?"

"Yes, sir."

"Well, give me a cup."

Ugh—it may be bitter, but at least it's wet. And it isn't sour, like that vinegar our soldiers on duty have to drink.

I stand aside, holding in one hand the sausage sandwich, and in the other, the cup of

wine mixed with water. Between munching and swallowing and sipping and swallowing, I find time to chat with the people around me. I let my eyes wander, scanning the adjacent dock areas where the real business of the harbor goes on. Nothing must be allowed to interfere with men and their work. I see boats towed into and out of boat slips, cargoes being loaded and unloaded, sailors and passengers boarding and de-boarding.

Many of them are joining the lines on either side of me. As long as they keep moving, fine. I look out for people who attract small groups around them; I wish to prevent solicitation of all kinds in the harbor area. We don't need peddlers of charms and trinkets here, any more than we need promoters of taverns, inns, and brothels. Let them advertise their wares and services in the marketplace, where they belong.

Having finished my snack, I return my cup to the female vendor (who at least for the moment is selling only a beverage) and move on, picking my way through the area next to the storage vaults and heading for the tower at the second angle where the breakwater takes a north-northeast turn. I go down the passageway between the vaults and I enter the door. I take the staircase to the upper floor of the tower. There I'll have a window-seat for observation and meditation.

CHAPTER 11

The Temple and the Gods

I feel better. My stomach is full, occupied with the digestive process, and all seemed to be going well below as far as I was able to determine. So I shall return to my observing and meditating from another window-seat in an identical tower.

From this location, I have a picture-perfect view of the city and directly in front of me, the temple which dominates it. Now I am not religious, and temples as such leave me cold; but as a building, this one is remarkable for its beauty and its grand proportions. It contains a colossal statue of the late Emperor Augustus and another of Roma. The one of Augustus, modeled after that of Olympian Zeus, and in no wise inferior. Zeus, whom we Romans borrowed from the Greeks, adding his epithets and attributes to those of our own Jupiter. And now Zeus, extended to the deified Augustus. On merging with them, our Caesar has lost his own face and personality, but he has gained in power. The other statue, also of heroic size, the goddess Roma, made like the famous Hera of Argos. The names of the gods change, but their faces remain the same. It matters little. What is important is their numinous power concentrated in this place. It is the worship of men which gives the gods their worth.

I must grudgingly admit that temples are necessary. Just as a burning glass concentrates the sun's heat on one particular spot until it starts a fire, so a temple and the images it houses concentrate the spirits' power. They set up a protective barrier against unfriendly spirits. Those gilded shields I originally placed in the governor's palace in Jerusalem now decorate the walls of the temple here. Although they bear only lettering and no images, there is as much spirit power in them as there is in the forms and faces of the colossal statues. First we create our own gods and then we worship them. And last of all, most irrationally, we ask them to grant our requests!

Most gods are a reflection of the people who create them; people make their gods in their own image. Hence we have gods who war against each other and steal each other's wives. Gods with human virtues and human foibles equally magnified. Gods who can be fooled and manipulated into doing what men want them to do.

My stomach knows there is an exception to such a sweeping statement, and it is already starting to rebel at the very thought of the Deity with whose worshipers I shall have to deal while I am in Jerusalem.

Quiet, below! Ha! All I need now is indigestion. I've enough problems without one more.

CHAPTER 12

The Bride of the Jealous God

But the God of the Jews, the God who broods in the clouds behind the mountains, is the opposite of all these. He is intolerant of other gods, impossibly demanding of his people and unreasonably jealous of their love. His people are his creation, and he constantly tries to make them conform to his image. He is an interfering God who claims his part in everything they do and his share in everything they have. He is not like most gods, content with a pinch of incense and the sacrifice of a pair of doves. He demands a tenth part of all their worldly goods. In addition he requires a half shekel every year from every Jewish male in all the world, so that the Temple treasury stays full to bursting.

He has no tangible presence, no face or body for men to behold and worship. No one has ever seen him and no one knows what he looks like. In the Holy City he permits no images of men or animals that men might bow down to. Yet he makes his presence felt throughout the city, from the sacrificial altars in the Temple to the stones trodden underfoot in the streets.

I feel uneasy whenever I am in Jerusalem. To combat the power of their God, I feel the need to surround myself with the symbols of

Roman sovereignty. I draw renewed strength from their numinous aura of power. Perhaps that is why I changed my mind about the shields and placed them in Jerusalem instead of Caesarea. Outwardly I did it to honor Tiberius, but I could have honored him as well in Caesarea, thus avoiding a conflict with Herod and an imperial reprimand. With Claudia gone and no one to restrain me, I acted on an impulse which I would later regret.

But you never can tell about these people. Who would have thought that a simple inscription dedicating the shields to Tiberius would cause such a stir. I could anticipate the objections of the scribes and Pharisees—they object to nearly everything we Romans do—and I reasoned they were most unlikely to enter a Gentile palace. But for Herod Antipas and his family to object to something so petty! He is Jewish only when it serves his own interest to be Jewish. (I wonder if Tiberius has received the gift of the five identical shields which I sent him. It will be anticlimactic after my humiliation to receive a thank-you note from Tiberius.)

The Jewish people are outraged by everything that could draw away the faithful from the worship of their God. They equate their relationship to him with that of a wife to a husband, and infidelity to him is classed with adultery.

There are strict controls on their sexual behavior. Men do not mix with women socially; when they go to banquets, they leave their wives at home. A woman always covers her head in public and sometimes veils her face. You can see nothing of her body except for her hands and feet—little to entice a normal man—especially since the penalty for adultery is death by stoning, an excessive punishment which could effectively wipe out half the population of our Rome in a single night. Of course the Jews are not allowed officially to execute anyone, but sometimes the crowds take matters into their own hands, and the priests give tacit approval. Then later they disclaim any responsibility.

These Jews are not free sexually though any dog is free to pursue a female in heat. They are not even the masters of their own bodies. To become a Jew, a man must submit to the cutting of the foreskin, a barbarous practice usually performed on the males soon after birth. All a man needs to do to remind himself he is not his own is to look down at his circumcised flesh. He is the property of his God. He is not allowed to forget it even when he takes his private pleasure.

Jews marry as young as they are able, both males and females. When you see a young woman in public, she is usually pregnant, accompanied by several children. Procreation must be the husbands' only recreation.

Their demanding God allows them no other pleasures. Gambling is forbidden, also eating and drinking to excess. In fact the ultra-pious fast several times a week. And when they do eat, they will touch no food that they consider ritually unclean or any meat that has been sacrificed to idols. They will not eat with Gentiles; they consider us to be the ultimate uncleanness. They do not participate in sports or attend sports events because they abhor nakedness. They do not go to the theatre. They do not celebrate our Roman holidays. Instead they have their own which they observe scrupulously.

Unlike the Roman plebs, they do not have to be compelled to worship their God. There is no need among them for free bread and circuses as a motivating factor. From sundown on Friday night to sundown on Saturday of every week they observe their Sabbath. They attend their synagogues and listen to the reading of their law, which they believe was handed down to them by their God through a man named Moses. This law is a set of rules impossible to follow perfectly, yet they spend their whole lives and all their energies trying to follow it. Jews will do no work on their Sabbath, nor will they take a journey as long as a mile. They will not even cook food. They attend their synagogue two other days each week, as well as on the Sabbath. And to top it all, they pray three times a day, wherever they are. You can see them praying in any public place.

There is a large Jewish colony in Rome, but you seldom see Jews in numbers unless you travel to a run-down district across the Tiber where they first settled over a hundred years ago. (Pockets of more recent immigrants are located in the slum areas to the east of the forums.) Nevertheless from my early childhood I heard tales of them. I knew Jews were different and I was afraid of them.

I am no longer afraid of them, but because they are different, I am uneasy around them. The men do not shave their beards but let them grow long. They let their hair grow to shoulder length. They keep to themselves and avoid social contact with outsiders. They will not even enter a Gentile's house for fear of defilement. I cannot stand a person who thinks he is better than I, especially one who belongs to an inferior breed like the Jews.

They will not socialize with us Gentiles, but they will do business with us. Since outside of worship, they are allowed to do little but work and procreate, some of them grow quite wealthy. Jews will lend money at interest to Gentiles though they are forbidden to do so among themselves. The Temple in Jerusalem is the focus of their worship. If they are financially able, they will go there every year for one of the three great feasts, preferably at Passover time. They will come from all over the world because they are forbidden to offer sacrifice in any other place.

The Jews are intolerant, and I cannot tolerate intolerant people. We Romans are tolerant. In our empire, we permit the practice of all officially recognized religions including Judaism. In fact, the Jews have been given special dispensations. They are not required to join the provincial armies since they could not keep their Sabbath or follow their dietary restrictions. Yet they refuse to associate with us except in the marketplace. Strangely, it does not defile them to accept our money although our coinage bears the images of gods and men.

Jews are incomprehensible. Unlike their leaders of the upper classes, the common people do not seem to be motivated by self-interest. They would rather die than submit to the slightest infraction of their law. Their God is incomprehensible. They claim him to be all-powerful, yet he has let them be defeated time and time again and taken into captivity in foreign lands.

I do not like the Jews. I am not afraid of them, as I was when I was a child, but I do not like them. No special edict from Tiberius can make me like them. I will deal justly with them, but I do not like them.

CHAPTER 13

The Episode of the Ensigns

The Jews are incomprehensible, as I have said. I realized this very early in my administration—only a few weeks after my arrival from Rome. Initially I had been lulled into security by the familiar character of life in this bustling port city, its similarity to capitals in other Roman provinces. These left me unprepared for what would soon happen....

I'm looking at the marketplace, bearing left from the Temple of Augustus and Roma to the basilica beside it. Unlike the lofty temple on its platform, even from this distance, the low building doesn't show up at all well. But in my opinion, it is beautiful because it fills human needs. This structure is employed for public meetings and for lectures by visiting philosophers. The townspeople use it as an indoor market in bad weather. Its arches give them shelter from wind and rain and from the heat of summer. There are probably citizens resting there today.

But the most important use for such a basilica is as a court of law. I am reminded of this whenever I look at the *bema* in the square out front. It is a place where traditionally magistrates have been able to address the people and make semi-official pronouncements. I can't see the stone platform from here, but I shall never forget what happened—or rather, what nearly happened—the day I first sat on it.

When I arrived here as governor of Judea, I was duly installed as judge of both the ordinary civil suits and the criminal cases. I could, if I chose, impose the death sentence. Sitting in my judgment seat on the dais in the semicircular apse, I felt proud yet nervous, very conscious of my responsibility. But it was outside on the stone platform that I had my first clash with this incomprehensible people. I shudder to think of it.

In my imagination the stalls and booths and the crowd of busy shoppers fade away, and the square is once again filled with fanatical Jews—praying, chanting, gesticulating—single in their purpose like a mob and yet non-violent. Most alarming in their non-violence because as the representative of Roman justice, I had no recourse against it. Not fickle like our Roman populace, who can be bribed and manipulated by clever orators. It was a confrontation I had never expected to occur.

It all began with a well-intended plan that did not work out as I had hoped. Now I realize I should have assembled my civilian advisers and consulted them, not just my military leaders. But to tell the truth, I had already made up my mind what I would do, and I probably would not have listened to negative criticism. I wanted to set myself up in Judea—and particularly in Jerusalem—as the one in command here. I wanted to establish my ascendancy over their ruling class and their religious establishment. I particularly wanted to show the High Priest he must yield to my authority.

It was time for the semiannual changing of the guard at the Antonia Fortress in Jerusalem. This always occurs early in November before the outset of the winter rains makes troop movements slow and difficult between Caesarea and the Holy City. The second rotation takes place after the letup of the spring rains at Passover time in late March or early April.

I hit upon the idea of sending the Sebastinian Cohort to Jerusalem because of the unusual emblem on their standards—an image of Augustus Caesar, for whom Herod the Great named the city of their origin. *Sebaste*, which means "Augustus" in Greek, is the current name of the capital of the province of Samaria. As a mark of his

A Stone Laid in Zion

special favor, the emperor had granted to this body the right to bear medallions engraved with his image on their standards. I was informed by them that they had never before carried these standards into Jerusalem because the human effigies would be offensive to the Jews. This might be the very occasion I was looking for—my chance to impress the High Priest, Joseph Caiaphas, before our first meeting.

So I gave orders for the cohort to march into Jerusalem with their special standards, but to do so by night in order to avoid unduly arousing the people. I instructed them to install the standards on the ramparts of the Antonia in full view of the Temple below. When it was day, this excited a great turmoil among those in the Temple. The outcry was not limited to the Temple crowd, as I had expected it to be, for the people who were close enough to see were astonished at the sight of them and angry at this flouting of their law, which forbids any sort of image within the walls of the Holy City.

The people, the unconsidered element in my plan! As a measure of the extent of their indignation, a crowd of citizens came running out of Jerusalem toward Caesarea. They were joined by a multitude of country people along the way. By the time they reached Caesarea and came together in the public square in front of the basilica, they numbered in the thousands.

They sent a delegation to meet with me inside. Their leaders zealously besought me to remove the offending ensigns, this flagrant violation of their ancient law. I denied their request. When my refusal was reported to the people, they fell prostrate on the ground and refused to be moved. They remained in their attitude of grief, outrage, and supplication. They encamped in the square that night, and the next day they resumed their posture of self-abasement at regular intervals. Thus they continued for five days and nights.

Although they did not attempt to interfere with my movements, I felt like a prisoner. I was afraid to leave the heart of the city and return to the governor's palace. I either stayed in the basilica or slipped out back to the barracks of the Caesarea Cohort several blocks away.

Even when I could not see them, my ears were constantly assailed by their chant, "Remove the abominations!" Their monotonous oriental wailing got on my nerves until I could take no more. Thoroughly exasperated, I decided to make my move. On the sixth day I had my judgment seat moved to the *bema* in front of the basilica. I mounted the platform and announced to the multitude that I was ready to give them an answer. Unknown to them, I had made plans and taken steps the night before.

During the dark hours, my troops from the barracks had secretly entered the spacious hall and some adjoining public buildings. Fully armed, they were lying in wait. At a signal from me, these immediately poured out with their weapons. The Jews were surrounded on three sides, and they had the harbor at their backs.

The people were in the utmost consternation at this unexpected sight. I announced to them that they should be cut into pieces unless they would agree to the presence of Caesar's images. I intimated to the soldiers that they should draw their swords. As though at one signal, the Jews fell down in vast numbers together. They bared their necks and cried out that they would rather be slain than have their laws broken. I was greatly surprised at their unheard-of superstition.

Although in my anger and extreme frustration I felt tempted to give the order for attack, I realized it would gain me nothing to kill all these people. Such an unwarranted slaughter would probably cost me my governorship before it had really started. At the same time I was deeply affected by their firm resolution to keep their law inviolate. So I gave an order for the ensigns to be carried out of Jerusalem.

This incomprehensible people had won without striking a blow, and I had experienced the humiliation of defeat. But I had learned something valuable: These people have minds of their own. Their action was a response to inner conviction, rather than to the incitement of their leaders. For the Jerusalem authorities never became involved, and when I met Caiaphas later, neither he nor I even mentioned the episode of the ensigns.

CHAPTER 14

A Cornerstone that Bears the Name of Pilate

I was determined to rise above this temporary setback. I would find a way to regain the favor of the emperor in case he should hear of this potentially dangerous confrontation—and also the favor of my citizens, especially those in Caesarea. Although for the most part they had not been actively involved in the protest, they were quite disgruntled after five full days of chaos. The disturbance in the city's public square had caused an almost complete shutdown of business for Jew and Gentile alike, not to mention interference with the normal activities of the harbor, which is the lifeline of this whole province.

I decided to follow the example of Herod the Great—to become a pious and loyal benefactor. He dedicated a huge magnificent temple to Augustus and Roma. I was unable to copy him on a large scale, but I could certainly dedicate an exquisite small temple to Tiberius. I would present it to the citizens of Caesarea and give them the chance to show their own piety and loyalty whenever they passed it by.

But where to put it? Certainly not near the far larger and grander temples already in existence. That would be to make Tiberius look small and mean in the presence of the now divine Augustus and other gods and goddesses. After some thought, I decided to put it in front of the theatre just south of the governor's palace. Whenever the patrons entered, they would be able to burn a pinch of incense to the divine genius of Tiberius, to the guardian spirit protecting our emperor and our institutions.

I got in touch with Herod's architects and had them design a *tholos*, a little round jewel of a temple in the style of one that is located at the sanctuary of Apollo in Delphi. Give them quality if not quantity, I say. How proud I was when I stood with Claudia at the formal dedication which marked the laying of the cornerstone. "Pontius Pilate, Prefect of Judea, Presents This Tiberieum to the Caesareans." A gift to the people of Caesarea which is at once a compliment to the emperor and a declaration of allegiance to Rome.

My gesture seems to have achieved its effect. I received a nice commendation from Tiberius although—true to his reputation for stinginess—he did inquire if this use of the tribute money was really necessary. And at least the Gentile population of the city seems to have forgotten my initial blunder.

Whatever else I may accomplish here in Judea, this Tiberieum was certainly a good beginning. Perhaps a thousand years from now when people have forgotten my name and everything about me, someone will discover the cornerstone and think, "This Pontius Pilate must have been a good governor and a pious and loyal Roman."

CHAPTER 15

Harbor Entrance and Aqueduct

I am ashamed to sit here any longer. Will move on. The closer I get to the end of the long extended left arm of the Great Mole, the more people I meet, going and coming. The view at the end is most spectacular, for Sebastos holds in his hand, like a flaming torch, the Drusion. This tower must be close to three hundred feet high. Its massive base supports a smaller second level on which rests the lantern, where a beacon fire is kept burning night and day. Herod had an eye toward the future when he named the lighthouse for the stepson of Augustus, a popular general who at the time seemed likely to succeed him as emperor.

Won't attempt to enter the great tower, but I'll go around it, following the walkway which joins the smaller towers. No danger of feeling cold here, with the flames and the smoke hanging overhead. From my place on the sea wall, I look out and up at the six gigantic bronze statues gleaming dully atop six lofty columns, three on each side of the harbor entrance. They represent members of Herod the Great's family. The three nearest me, on the west side, are supported by two upright blocks of stone clamped together; those on the east, by a massive tower. An imposing sight for passengers entering or leaving the harbor on ships, sails furled, towed by oarsmen in small boats.

To pursue my imagery, on the opposite side of the channel, Sebastos holds the customs house in his right hand. This arm of the breakwater is shorter and straighter than the other, only three hundred feet in length. It, too, is lined with arched storage vaults, backed by a sea wall, and topped with towers connected by a broad walkway.

The northern wall of the city is intersected by a Roman-style aqueduct, useful and beautiful. Looking north, I can see it extending along the coast for a good mile and a half. When Herod the Great built the city and the port around fifty years ago at a small place called Strato's Tower, he had to drain the coastal swamps and bring in fresh water via tunnel and aqueduct. This stone-built channel, supported on masonry arcades, is today the most prominent feature between the Carmel Range and the northern confines of the city.

It brings water from Shumi Springs located near the village of Maioumas at the foot of Mt. Carmel, a bit more than three and a half miles to the northeast. It does not follow a direct route to the city. It heads nearly due west across the plain for a mile and a half. Then for nearly a quarter of a mile, it tunnels through a ridge paralleling the coast. It emerges, heads southwest for nearly a half mile, and then turns south for the final leg, a straight shot to Caesarea.

What could be more worthwhile than to supply a thirsty city with abundant water? More than an architectural achievement, it is almost a gift of life itself. Now this inspired me to do for the Holy City what Herod did for Caesarea.

CHAPTER 16

The Imitator of Herod the Great

In my third week as governor, I made an unofficial visit to Jerusalem to assess its needs, particularly in regard to the water supply. I found it to be woefully deficient on a year-round basis. Jerusalem has only one source of living water, a spring called the Gihon. This served the city well during its early years, but it is quite inadequate for present-day Jerusalem. The main source of water today seems to be the numerous cisterns throughout the city, in which they collect the runoff from their roofs during the winter rains. In fact, even the Herodian Palace receives most of its water from a huge storage tank on top of one of its towers that was build expressly for this purpose.

Immediately I compared the parched city with water-rich Rome. I envisioned Jerusalem with abundant water, perhaps provided by aqueducts like those which supply Rome with water for her public baths and fountains and for the private use of her citizenry. Why could not Pontius Pilate be a public benefactor to the city of Jerusalem, as Herod the Great was to Caesarea? Why could not I construct a system bringing water to the Holy City?

I planned to revisit the city in late fall before the start of the rainy season. The unfortunate episode of the ensigns did not deter me. I realized that it might actually even help me to achieve both of the following objectives. Number One was to make a thorough survey of the existing water systems and of the possibilities for improving them. For this I would need the cooperation of the High Priest. This led to Number Two—to meet with Caiaphas and establish a working relationship with him. It seemed to me an auspicious time for our meeting. I needed to impress him with my Roman benevolence, as well as with my firmness, after my first blunder. He had won the initial round and we both knew it. Perhaps this fact would predispose him to cooperate with me in my plans for improving life in his city.

CHAPTER 17

The Water Project and the Secret Agreement

Right after this episode, I took my corps of engineers and my financial advisers to Jerusalem. We met with their counterparts there. We inspected the Pool of Siloam, which is connected to the Gihon by an underground tunnel. We found the water level disappointingly low. My engineers and I followed the tunnel to the source of the spring. Local advisers told me about the construction of this tunnel. It had been accomplished in a few months' time by a Jewish king named Hezekiah. He was anticipating an invasion by Assyria and needed to assure the water supply in case of a siege of the city.

I conceived a grudging but sincere admiration for this man and his remarkable achievement of engineering, accomplished about seven hundred years ago, at the time of the founding of Rome. Using primitive techniques, he made his measurements so accurately that he was only five feet off. His men started working on both ends of the tunnel. Using picks and shovels of brass. They had to dig through seven hundred fifty-two feet of solid rock to connect Siloam, this specially constructed reservoir inside the city walls, with the Spring of Gihon, exposed and vulnerable, outside the walls. We saw the spot where the two work teams met, a short dogleg marked by an inscription describing the event. They could actually hear each other through a hollow in the walls and made haste to join the two ends of the tunnel. A truly outstanding accomplishment, one that saved the city then and still serves it today.

We went on to the source of the Gihon. To further his secretive purposes, Hezekiah had walled off and camouflaged the outside entrances to the grotto in which the Gihon is located. We found the spring still flowing but hardly capable of emitting a greater flow of water. The impending outset of the winter rains postponed further investigations until the spring of the following year.

In regard to my second objective, I believe I succeeded in convincing Caiaphas of my good intentions for Jerusalem. I got his assurance of complete cooperation in the ongoing project with only one stipulation: That the tax load on the citizens would not be increased. We both knew it would be a costly undertaking. I already had in mind a possible solution, but at the time, I said nothing about it. I purposely deferred my confirmation of Caiaphas as High Priest until after he should demonstrate this cooperation.

In the late spring of my first year in Judea, I returned with my work team to Jerusalem. This time we diverted our attention to water sources outside the city in the surrounding hills. My consulting local experts told me about a pool attributed to King Solomon, a little more than six miles southwest of the city. It seems Herod the Great built two lower reservoirs and connected all three with his nearby fortress, the Herodium, by an intricate system of channels. After the fortress was converted into a mausoleum for the remains of Herod, water was no longer needed, and these had been allowed to fall into disrepair. My engineers and I visited these three pools, which are located on an elevation at the head of the Artas Valley. They made successive sightings through a viewing tube, first of the Temple Mount in Jerusalem and then of the elevation on which the pools are located. The Temple Mount is nearly the highest spot in Jerusalem. By their computations they were able to determine that the lowest pool is eighty feet higher than the Temple Mount, thus assuring the flow of water to the city. From this moment on, my mind was made up as to how I would pursue my project. Now my fiscal advisers and I sought a means of financing it.

There were no provisions in the annual budget for such a great expenditure. I learned the citizens of Judea were already taxed to the hilt. In fact, under the Gratus administration, they had appealed to Tiberius Caesar to lower the tribute—the taxes paid to Rome. Their request was not granted. I learned the Jews must also pay their synagogue tithes and their Temple dues. I remembered Caiaphas's one stipulation and decided it was futile to consider an increase in taxes at this time. Moreover it seemed unethical to add to the burdens of the whole country to supply a local need. Then I thought of the Temple treasury and the surplus funds which are said to accumulate yearly.

I consulted first with my advisers on Jewish affairs. Afterwards I called in Caiaphas, who arrived with the Temple treasurer, Rabbi Helkias. My engineers described to them the means by which we proposed to convey water to the city from the Pool of Solomon by utilizing the already existing watercourses above the pools and constructing some lower courses to follow the natural contour of the ridges as far as the Valley of Hinnom. Between this point and Jerusalem, it would be necessary to build an aqueduct similar to the high level one in Caesarea. This water bridge would enter the city through the southern wall.

The High Priest was enthusiastic. He said when they have their great festivals and the population swells to nearly four times its normal size, the need for additional sources of water becomes acute. Then Rabbi Helkias remarked that the project would be very expensive and inquired how it would be funded. I told him I was as strongly opposed to a raise in taxes as they were themselves. Rabbi Helkias seemed momentarily relieved. He asked about any surplus funds at my disposal. I told him how after I met my local budget for protecting and administering the province, I was required to turn over any surplus to the emperor. So I had no local funds at my disposal. I presented them with two alternatives: Double the tribute money for several years or pay for the project out of the Temple treasury. A third alternative would be to forget the whole thing. We had just agreed that the first was out of the question, and they were most reluctant to forget the project; but their reaction to the second choice was nearly as violent as that of the citizens to those offensive effigies on the standards. It would be an understatement to say they were extremely upset.

Rabbi Helkias protested that the Temple funds were sacred in their tradition and could be used for no secular purpose, only for religious expenses like paying the salaries of the priests and the upkeep of the Temple. I told them I knew they had a big surplus after they paid their obligations each year. I proposed their using this surplus to benefit the city and its citizens instead of letting it lie unproductive in their treasury. I pointed out their self-interest in the matter, since the Temple is easily the largest consumer of water in Jerusalem. They both insisted that the provision of water was a secular affair and should not be funded by the *Corban*.

When I saw they were set against me, I decided it was time to outflank them with what seemed to me an ingenious maneuver. I told them my expert on Hebrew affairs had discovered a little-known law which states that any surplus in the *Corban* may be used for the upkeep of the city wall and towers and all the city's needs. I pointed triumphantly to this last phrase: Certainly water was one of the city's most pressing needs. In fact, maintaining the water channels was one of the items specifically sanctioned as a proper expenditure.

The High Priest hesitated and whispered to Helkias. I had Caiaphas in a tight place, and he knew it. I had delayed confirming him as High Priest until this spring meeting. He must have realized his confirmation was conditional on his accepting my terms. He and Helkias found their voices again. They protested that the people would never permit the *Corban* to be used for this purpose. I answered that the people need not know. And besides, if the secret should leak out, only the ultra-orthodox would raise serious objections. The majority would simply be grateful for the increase in their water supply. Then Caiaphas speculated that the Sanhedrin might refuse to confirm the agreement. I retorted that if Caiaphas was the right man for the office, he would surely find ways to bring his people into line. He said he would do his best.

Two days later he told me the Sanhedrin would permit the use of the *Corban* to help defray the cost of the aqueducts under the following conditions: First, that the Temple fathers agreed only under protest; second, that it would be a private agreement between the governor and the Temple authorities, and the financing of the aqueduct must be kept in confidence by both parties; third, that if the public should learn that the sacred treasury had paid for the aqueducts, Temple authorities would state that their hands were forced in the matter; and fourth, instead of constructing a new reservoir in Jerusalem, the aqueduct would lead directly into cisterns already existing under the Temple. This would reduce the cost of the total project.

I was agreeably surprised at this last revelation and at the High Priest's concession. I had not known previously about the existence of such cisterns. He permitted my engineers to inspect them. The men reported back to me how some are of great depth, fifty to sixty feet. One which is called the Great Sea has an estimated capacity of two million gallons. They were only partly full and could be easily expanded without weakening the substructure of the Temple. And since the Temple is nearly the highest point in the city, there would be sufficient water pressure to supply the fountains in Jerusalem.

I commended Caiaphas for this common-sense offer and countered it with a concession of my own: If the Temple authorities would underwrite the full cost of the underground systems and three-fourths of the estimated expenditure for the rest of the aqueduct, Rome would take care of the remaining one-fourth. I reasoned that the Jerusalem Cohort could provide the labor, making up the difference. After all, the emperor likes to keep our armies busy with public works when they are not occupied with military matters. We made a bargain. As soon as I was sure of his cooperation with my unfolding plan, I would confirm him as High Priest. We came to an understanding that he would not interfere with politics and I would not interfere with religion. So the work on the aqueduct was already in progress when I left Jerusalem.

The project was completed in the late spring of my third year as governor four years ago.

CHAPTER 18

The Dedication and the Interrupted Tour

Claudia and I made plans to attend the dedication. Proud of my accomplishment, she was, like me, eagerly anticipating this triumph. I had not told her about the financing of the aqueduct, and I considered the chances minimal that this secret would ever leak out. Who of those involved would have anything to gain by such a revelation? We would make this dedication in the Holy City the first stage in a tour which would be partly pleasure, partly public relations. From Jerusalem we would travel north through Samaria and then through Galilee to its capital city, Tiberias, where we would pay a long-delayed visit to the Tetrarch Herod and his wife Herodias. We would return to the coast by a roughly western route to Ptolomais and then head due south for Caesarea. Taken in leisurely stages and allowing some extra days for official and social visits, the whole trip should take about three weeks.

For a long time Antipas had been asking us to visit him. I could hardly refuse any longer without insulting him, for we had already entertained him and his wife on several occasions when they were passing through Caesarea. And frankly, I was eager to compare his architectural achievements in Tiberias, the capital city which he himself had built, with those of his famous father in Caesarea.

Claudia and I set out for Jerusalem in high spirits. We arrived in the early afternoon of the day before the dedication. As we approached the city, we admired the new Hinnom water bridge, its graceful proportions and solid construction. It would be a lasting contribution from Rome to the city's welfare. As usual, we installed ourselves and our retinue at the Herodian Palace. Its spacious, richly-decorated rooms and sumptuous apartments surpass even those of our palace in Caesarea.

The next morning, with Claudia at my side, I stood at the point where the conduit penetrated the south wall of Jerusalem. We were accompanied by my aides and the Temple authorities. At high noon I flashed a signal which would be transmitted to the reservoir in the distant hills. An answering flash confirmed that six miles away they were opening the valves to the aqueduct. We waited for an hour in eager anticipation. Fortune was with us—there were no hitches. At last the water was overflowing the conduit and spilling down the sides of the city wall before us. To the accompaniment of a trumpet fanfare, I opened the valves of the sluice gate, and the waters flooded into Jerusalem.

That afternoon Claudia and I toured the city. At the street corners we saw fountains gushing with unaccustomed water. For the first time in Jerusalem, I heard the sweet sound of popular applause. Perhaps now they would forget the earlier episode of the ensigns.

The next day we left on the second leg of our journey. It took us a full week to get to Tiberias, allowing for two stopovers. The first was at Sebaste, the capital of Samaria, a large and well-built city, another of Herod the Great's accomplishments. As governor of this province, I had been there on various previous occasions. It is a city where I feel right at home, for the architectural style is Hellenistic and the population is mostly non-Semitic. A generation ago the Emperor Augustus settled here six thousand veterans of the Roman legions and set aside a large district for their support. The city fathers entertained us suitably.

After a day dedicated to administrative details, we resumed our tour, crossing through the Esdraelon Valley into Galilee. It was the first time I had visited this province and its former capital, Sepphoris. This is the largest city in Galilee, with some fifty thousand inhabitants—the seat of Herod Antipas before he built Tiberias. I learned that while he was here, he embellished the city with a theatre and other Greco-Roman institutions. I made a mental note to compliment him on these attainments.

The next night we arrived in Tiberias, thus completing the second week and the second stage of our extended tour. Although smaller than Sepphoris, the new capital is equally impressive for its architecture and clearly superior in its natural attractions. It has a perfect setting with the green hills of Galilee in the background and the beautiful lake called the Sea of Tiberias in the foreground.

Claudia and I had planned to spend our third week here with the Herods. We were looking forward to a pleasant stay. Though neither of us really liked the couple—especially Herodias—we would enjoy the amenities of the palace and the city. And our visit would build a better relationship with a neighboring ruler.

On the afternoon of our second day, when I was relaxing with Herod at his luxurious spa, in the bathing pools of the famous hot mineral spring, our plans suddenly changed. I received an unwelcome message from the High Priest. It seems as if our secret had leaked out—he did not know how—and Jerusalem was teeming with unrest. He urged me to return to the city as quickly as possible. We expressed our thanks to the Herods for their hospitality, and they expressed their regrets at our untimely departure.

That afternoon Claudia and I and our retinue started back to Jerusalem. We took the shorter route skirting the Jordan valley and approached the Holy City from the east, coming up from Jericho. We made this journey in three days over rough and often arduous terrain. If it had not been for Claudia, I would have been able to travel much faster. So within two weeks we were back in Jerusalem where we had started—although on this return trip, instead of arriving by daylight among crowds of cheering people (as we had done before) I planned to slip in after dark when the streets would be deserted. What an ironic contrast! And we did not head for the Herodian Palace, as we had done before. Instead we entered through a gate in the wall of the Upper City near the sheep pool and market, and we went directly to the nearby Antonia Fortress. If there should be an open rebellion, I could hold out there longer than in the

Herodian Palace on the other side of the city where I would be separated from the Jerusalem Cohort. Despite the late hour, I sent a messenger to Caiaphas, informing him of my arrival and assuring him that under my direction everything would work out all right.

CHAPTER 19

The Aqueduct Affair

If there should be trouble in the morning, we could handle it, for during the last three days I had devised a plan. I communicated my instructions to the commanding officer of the Antonia, and he made his preparations. Then we all bedded down for a few hours of sleep. I did not want to burden Claudia with the details of my plan, but I wanted to reassure her. I told her I would have to confront the crowd in the morning, but despite appearances, I would be safe. I told her not to worry. Neither one of us slept much.

I awakened to tumultuous shouts from the plaza in front, of the fortress: "Pilate! Pontius Pilate!" Somehow the whole city had caught wind of our arrival overnight. When I opened the casement and looked out at the square, it seemed as though half the city was milling below waiting for my appearance. I sent out a herald to announce to the people that I would ascend my tribunal shortly. As I dressed, I urged my wife to stay in bed and close her eyes and ears to what was going on outside. If there should be trouble, I did not want her watching. I was sure my plan would work. I told her to trust me. As I breakfasted hastily, I purposed in my heart to make a sacrifice at the four-pillared Temple of Tyche on my return to Caesarea if my mission succeeded—and also to send an offering to the Temple of Fortuna at Antium.

I had given orders for two hundred soldiers to arm themselves fully with swords and cudgels and to disguise themselves in the flowing robes of the local citizenry. They were to intermix with the assembling people. If the crowd should become unruly, they were to club the most clamorous into submission. Thus I hoped to avoid unnecessary bloodshed and stave off a full-scale rebellion. I had considered one alternative—to disperse my cohort visibly throughout the city as a warning to the people—but I decided against it. I remembered the crowd's fanatical reaction to the sight of armed soldiers in the square at Caesarea, and I decided on my first plan. I had arranged with my men that, at a given signal from me, they should simultaneously start local skirmishes. The night before, I had ordered my men to set up my tribunal, just outside the fortress gate. All was now in readiness.

Escorted by an armed guard, I walked out and mounted my tribunal. This time I had to win a victory over the people in the battle of the wills. Rome and I could not afford another humiliating defeat, like the one I had suffered in the matter of the ensigns.

My heralds called for silence. When the crowd had quieted down, I began to speak. I told the people I would consider their complaints and answer their questions if they would state the case in a calm and reasonable manner. I went on to explain how I had built the water system for their benefit and how lacking the funds necessary to finance it, I had turned to the Temple authorities, who had agreed to pay for the project out of the Temple treasury. There were angry cries and a rumble of mounting disapproval. The heralds again called for order.

I was determined that the people should hear me out. I told them I had no other choice unless they wanted me to double their taxes for several years. I told them this use of their *Corban* was in total compliance with one of their ancient laws, as their priests could verify. I asked if any priests were present. No one stepped forward. The catcalls, insults, and obscenities were becoming louder and bolder. I called on them to hush their outcry voluntarily and to clear the plaza promptly, or I should summon my auxiliary troops and clear it by force. I told them I would have my trumpeters blow two blasts. The first would be a warning. I advised them, if they valued life and limb, not to wait for the second blast.

At the first blast some left, but the majority held their ground. They were in a defiant mood and they needed to be taught a lesson. I could no longer brook their insults to Rome and to me as Rome's representative. I signaled for the second blast. Thereupon the men I had caused to infiltrate the crowd pulled out their cudgels and began to break the heads of the riotous. Some of my soldiers were so incensed at the insults of the mob that they attacked them with much greater force than I had intended. They exceeded my commands and laid about them with great sweeping blows which struck down the innocent as well as the guilty. True, the crowd was unarmed, but my soldiers were vastly outnumbered. The people fought back with their bare hands. Some of my soldiers drew their swords and cut and slashed their way through the crowd, driving them backward.

Their retreat became a hysterical stampede toward a few narrow side streets, the only exits from the square. Some ran away wounded, many died because of the blows, and many were trodden to death by their own countrymen. In a few moments it was all over except for one or two local brawls. Thus an end was put to their sedition. The spirit of the multitude was broken; they made no further protest. They willingly made use of the new water supply to cleanse the wounds of the living and to wash the bodies of the dead.

My part in all of this I saw as regrettable but unavoidable. I tried to explain it later to Claudia. In spite of my advice, she had watched from the window of our room. She could not see what was going on close to the gate because of the intervening exterior wall of the fortress. However, she saw and heard enough to alarm her thoroughly. She was visibly shaken by the violence she had seen and by her fears for my safety. She was not herself again for several weeks. She could not wait to leave Jerusalem, and she vowed she would never go back. This is why her present eagerness to return is so hard for me to comprehend.

CHAPTER 20

Two Views on Parenting

I'm tired of sitting in one place. Have noticed people entering this tower from the walkway, then going up inner stairs to the roof. Think I'll follow them to where there will be no solid walls—only a low railing—between me and the view, which is truly spectacular.

Leaning on the railing, looking across at the rigging of a boat being towed out of the harbor by one of the many skiffs constantly busy with the sailing vessels which come and go all day long....

Hot up here so close to the Drusion, hot and smoky, due to the fires burning in the lantern many feet above... People coughing—no place for anyone with a breathing problem... However, there is no actual danger to those of us here below, for the wind carries away both sparks and soot. I become aware of distracting sounds nearby.

I turn and notice slightly behind me on my right a man with a small boy riding on his shoulders. He is whimpering and clutching his father around the neck. Some people! Though I lack experience with children, I've enough common sense to realize that all of this must be frightening to a young child.

As I look on in dismay, the man takes his son off his shoulders and carries him in his arms toward the railing. The child struggles and screams, holding on for dear life. What is this father about to do?

I can't believe it: He's actually leaning over the railing and holding his son out at arms' length, so that there is nothing between him and the water many feet below! Naturally the poor child is yelling his head off.

"Man, are you crazy?" I tap the fellow on the shoulder. He looks around at me as if he thinks I'm the crazy one.

He says quite seriously, "I wanted to give him a real thrill."

"Well, you're overdoing it—you're scaring him to death."

"Old man, what I do with my son is my affair. So why don't you mind your own business?"

I have made the fool angry; I could care less. At least he now straightens up and moves backward. The child clings to the bosom of his father's robe, rigid and speechless with fear.

"Who do you think you are anyway—*the governor?*"

(Ha!)

"That's not important. You have a fine boy there. I'm a man who has never been so fortunate as to have a son. My wife and I would give almost anything to have one of our own."

"So what?"

"So I can't stand to see a father acting like you just did."

"The child needs to get used to being scared so that he'll grow up tough enough to take whatever the Fates throw at him."

"While he's young, he needs to be able to depend on his father to protect him from danger, not expose him to it unnecessarily."

"Not so: One day when he's older, he'll thank me for all this."

"One day when you're both older, he may repay you for it with hatred and neglect. That is, if he lives so long—you too. Think it over, man. The child is helpless now, but some day the tables will be turned. Do you want to be remembered with hate or with love?"

The man shrugs his shoulders and moves away wordlessly, leaving me alone in my corner. He must think I am a self-righteous busybody.

One thing for sure—if I had a son, I would probably spoil him.

CHAPTER 21

The Disillusioned Wife

Two years ago I stood on the loading platform on the opposite side of the channel, watching the departure of a ship bound for Rome. As it slipped through the entrance of the harbor, I waved at Claudia. She waved back at me from the deck. I hoped the visit with her family would bring her inner healing, but the political upheaval in Rome which soon followed dealt her another devastating blow. After all she has been through, why should she want to accompany me to Jerusalem now of all times? I turn my back on the harbor entrance and the aqueducts which remind me of proud and painful moments, and I retrace my steps along the sea wall in the direction of my palace. Before I go on to the baths, I shall send my wife a message that I may be a little late for the evening meal. By the time I reach the palace, I will have spent three hours out here, walking and meditating. It is something I needed to do, and I hope Claudia will understand.

I wish I could understand her better. If I knew what is going on behind that pretty face, I would feel more at ease. I want to avoid another crushing experience for her, and who knows what may happen in Jerusalem at Passover time, given the present uncertain religious and political situations. But she insists on going with me and even talks positively about staying at the Antonia Fortress, the scene of her previous trauma. Now this is the first time in months that she has shown an active concern about going anywhere and doing anything. I fear she may return to the deep depression which settled upon her several months after her return from Rome.

When she first arrived, I was shocked to see how thin and pale she was. I assumed her poor health was due to the rigors of the ocean voyage. Despite her weak physical condition, she seemed strangely elated, buoyed up by her nervous energy. And her mind was set on only one thing—procreation. After a year of continence, I was hardly unwilling to oblige her. Yet it grieved me to see her so confident because I knew that in due time she would be disillusioned. We had tried for eight years to have children, with no success. Why should she expect to get pregnant now, especially when she was in such poor shape?

I soon learned she had been hoodwinked by some priest at the Temple of Isis into believing she was now fertile. The shaven-headed rascal had actually promised her she would bear a child a year from that day. The reason for her ill health was the fasting and purging and self-denial which he had enjoined. I would like to get my hands around the scoundrel's scrawny neck! If she had stayed in Rome six months longer, she would have starved herself to death.

After her return, I coaxed her with her favorite foods and she started to put on weight. At first she thought she was actually pregnant, but when after two months she realized she was not, she sank into apathy. She knew the priest had lied to get her money, for there was no way she could bear a child by the date he had promised. She still performed her wifely duties, but her heart was not in them. She was like a body with no spirit. I cast about in my mind for some expedient to reawaken her desire to live.

We had always discussed current events and matters affecting my administration, but now I would go further. I decided to make her my closet counselor, and I began to read her the dispatches which I receive almost daily from my envoys and informants in Samaria and Judea. I wanted to make her feel important. When she started to show some interest, I continued, even asking her opinion about developing situations. She has become so involved in these matters that I wonder if I may not have overdone the treatment, especially in regard to these two Jesuses, for all we have discussed in the past few months concerns either Jesus Barabbas or Jesus of Nazareth.

CHAPTER 22

The Threat of the Messiah

First I briefed her on the difficulties of my task as governor of Judea, where every spring brings forth a new crop of candidates for the Messiah. It is as though they issue like thorns from this forbidding soil. The Messiah, I told her, seems to be the Jewish version of one of the mythical god-kings or hero-gods in the common culture of Rome and Greece. As I see it, he is to start out as a man sent by their God and will end up, I suppose, as another God. The Jewish people believe his main purpose in coming is to kick out us Romans and restore Judea to the fabled glory it enjoyed under their kings David and Solomon. The Messiah is supposed to be a descendant of King David. When he appears, he will first announce himself to his people and perform signs and wonders to prove his claims. Then he will get down to his real business—the business of high treason. Naturally I get edgy when I hear talk of all these Pseudo-Messiahs.

I asked Claudia if she remembered any discussion about John the Baptist when we visited the Herods at Tiberias. She said she had talked to one of Herodias's ladies, a woman called Joanna, who had told her a lot about him and his ministry. She said Joanna feared that Herod might arrest John because he had spoken openly against Herod's divorce and remarriage to Herodias, the wife of his brother

Philip. I asked my wife if Joanna considered John to be the Messiah. She said she and many others considered him to be a great prophet, but he had denied being the Messiah.

This tied in with reports I had received from soldiers and other informants about John's activities in the wilderness beyond the Jordan. Some had heard him tell representatives of the chief priests he was not the Messiah—he was only the forerunner—and the real Messiah was in their midst. Scarcely a comforting report to carry back to Caiaphas. He and the Sadducean party do not want a political Messiah any more than Rome does. They want to maintain the status quo for political and economic reasons, both to their benefit. Therefore since John did not identify this man—this Messiah, as John called him—he must still be at large.

So far as the man John is concerned, he eluded Herod for a year, but finally he was captured and imprisoned by Herod. After John's execution, I expected problems with his followers, but many of them switched their allegiance to somebody else who rose to public attention about that time—perhaps to one of the two named Jesus. Could one of them be the Messiah of whom John spoke? For nearly three years I have combed the country for reports of any activities which would point to a Messiah. Each year has brought forth its own. Most of them have fallen, a fact which proves they were false ones. The current survivors are these two men named Jesus—and one of them has already fallen, for all practical purposes.

CHAPTER 23

The Barabbas Case and the Nazarene Contingency

Strange that two men who bear the same given name should be so different—the first, a rebel and a murderer caught in the act. He is safely locked away in the Antonia pending my arrival. Half Jerusalem will be eagerly awaiting the outcome of his trial, and my courtroom will be packed. Since the man has a following among the young hotheads of Judea, this Barabbas case must be handled prudently.

Now the other Jesus—the man from Nazareth—has committed no crimes so far as I know. He is a former carpenter turned teacher and is said to be a worker of miracles. He has never been arrested although Caiaphas would like to lock him up and silence him. The reason? Ostensibly some matters of their religion which I do not presume or care to understand. I think it must all boil down to jealousy on the part of Caiaphas, for this Jesus is said to have unusual power to stir men's hearts and command their allegiance. His main emphasis seems to be moral or spiritual rather than political. Yet a man like him is subject to be used by the unscrupulous for political purposes. The matter of the Nazarene is not a case at this time; it is hardly more than a contingency. However, if he comes to Jerusalem for the Passover

Feast, it could rapidly develop into a full-fledged case.

Since Claudia showed eagerness to hear more about this Jesus, I dug into my files and pulled out everything I had on him from the beginning of his ministry. I tried to use Jesus as another example of the kind of charismatic personality that attracts and deceives many people, especially impressionable women. In a public gathering, either by magic, chance, or collusion, he performs a so-called "miracle," and henceforth the people flock to him. From that time forward they believe he can do anything, even things against all reason, and they will do anything he asks of them. Claudia is not the first or the last to be taken in by a smooth-talking charlatan. It seems as if her priest of Isis has his Judean counterpart in this Jesus.

I read to her my reports about his healings and his exorcisms, his stilling of the storm and his walking on the water. I read to her about his feeding thousands of people with one person's lunch. In all of these, I tried to point out what might really have happened, how the people saw only what they wanted to see. I had trouble in explaining well-authenticated reports like that of one of Herod's centurions who is stationed in Capernaum. He related to my informant how Jesus healed his sick slave without even seeing the man, without even entering the house and the room where he lay. A most unlikely chance—that a desperately ill man should recover at the very moment when Jesus, at some distance, should say the word. But then this Gentile centurion is a Jewish sympathizer, possibly an actual convert. He even has the Jewish mindset and is ready to see miracles where none exist. I suspect him of exercising in this instance both imagination and a certain amount of exaggeration.

There is one thing which I cannot explain in all of this, one outstanding difference between Jesus and the religious fakers like the priest of Isis: Jesus is never reported to have asked for anything as a reward for his service. If not money, what does he gain from it? He is never reported to have promoted himself as a political Messiah, and so it cannot be power. I would like to meet this man and pass judgment on him. Of course I mean this only in a figurative sense. May Fortune forbid that I should ever see him standing at my judgment seat. If he has done no more than is indicated in my reports, he is certainly not worthy of the death penalty.

On my way home by the most direct route... Approaching the land, cutting around the south bay side of the wharf... Walking briskly along the waterfront toward the palace....

Just thought of something—when I go through the administrative area, I must stop by the governor's office and pull out my dossiers on the matter of these two men. Otherwise I might forget them in the morning. I shall find time for extra study along the way when and if Claudia's babble will permit it....

Checked the water clock when I passed it in the outer courtyard... It's late, nearly five. Entering the promontory part of the palace... Guards here salute me openly. They're familiar enough with my face, whatever rag they may see me wearing.

First of all, I must stop by Claudia's quarters to let her know I'm back. She can quit worrying about me. I'll tell her to have the cooks hold our evening meal. Then I'll go directly to the baths. I am looking forward to the steam room especially. Due to the lateness of the hour, I'll pass up my usual visit to the gymnasium. And I think I can do without the offices of my masseur. If luck is with me, tomorrow my backside will be well pommeled, slapping against the seat of our carriage, as we jog along the road toward Jerusalem.

Part II

The Trip to Jerusalem

Table of Contents

Chapter 1	Good-by to the Gods	99
Chapter 2	On Self-Control and Discretion	101
Chapter 3	A Friend Who Brings New Hope	103
Chapter 4	A Lack of Sensitivity	111
Chapter 5	Defending a Friendship	117
Chapter 6	At the Post in Antipatris	121
Chapter 7	A Wild Ass and a Lost Ark	123
Chapter 8	A Priest Who Gets His Way by Doing Nothing	131
Chapter 9	Jesus Will Come	139
Chapter 10	A Devious Daughter of the Claudians	143
Chapter 11	At the Way Station	147
Chapter 12	A Complaining Camel and a Wild Ride	149
Chapter 13	A Most Uneasy Seat	155
Chapter 14	A Singing Serpent	157

CHAPTER 1

Good-by to the Gods

It is early Friday morning, and I am ready to set out on the greatest adventure of my life. Last night I supervised the packing of my husband's things and my own, enough for two to three weeks in Jerusalem. Now our whole company of wagons and carriages and our cavalry escort are drawn up in the square fronting the Temple of Augustus. We cannot leave without first making sacrifice and consulting the augurs.

While the sacrifices are going on at the base of the main staircase, Pilate and I are walking around on top inside the portico and gazing up at the gilded shields which have caused such needless trouble. To the left and the right, at the head of the columns and just under the roofline, they now decorate the formerly blank spaces in the frieze. Looking through the doorway of the inner chamber, we view on raised platforms at the rear the gigantic cult statues of Augustus and Roma.

I no longer believe in any of these things. They were all made by men and they give glory only to man's skill. These statues can do nothing for me in themselves, and the glory they once stood for has ceased to be. How can Augustus dead do more for me than Augustus living? And Augustus living never even saw me, for when he died, I was a girl of ten. Now that he is dead, how can he know me and answer my prayers? Just because the Roman senate has declared him to be a god, does that make him a god? How can a human being make another human being into a god? Senators are noble, but they are not divine. In the reign of terror in Rome, I saw them die like ordinary men. The senators may be able to make a man into an emperor by voting him into office, but how can they make a man into a god? Only a god can make another god, if indeed it can be done. This now seems like nonsense to me.

If I should express such thoughts around most Romans, I know they would label me an atheist and recoil from me in horror. They would consider such talk unpatriotic, even treasonous. Therefore I shall keep my thoughts to myself, at least for the time being.

Pilate does not believe in the fiction of the gods any more than I do but he is superstitious. He will not undertake any action without first checking the auspices. He is even taking one of his augurs with us to Jerusalem. He believes in spirit forces that dwell in nature, amoral and impersonal. He says they are like clouds which give you rain or thunder and lightning—good or evil—depending on your luck. If you know the right things to do and the right words to say, you can get these forces to help you.

I do not want a god like that. A god you can control is no god at all; he can do no more for you than the man who made him. I need a god I can touch, a living god who can reach out and touch me. I need a god who cares, one who can relate to human needs. Give me a real live god with a human face but more than human power—a god who can heal my infertility. Augustus and Roma cannot do that, for they are just impressive statues. But this Jesus, whom I hope to meet secretly in Jerusalem—perhaps he will prove to be everything I need.

My husband says, "The auspices are favorable. Let us be going."

CHAPTER 2

On Self-Control and Discretion

We have a long day's trip ahead of us, as far as Antipatris. The procession takes off with a rumble and a clatter, the cavalry leading and also bringing up the rear. Pilate and I are in the middle in our two-wheeled carriage drawn by two horses. Behind us are the other carriages and carts with our servants and our luggage. At a time like this, it is exciting to be seen and known as the wife of Pontius Pilate, governor of Judea. Here in Caesarea most people seem to like us. They are lining the streets, watching us as we pass. They are waving their hands and hailing us. We nod back gravely. A small boy waves at me. He has chubby knees and a head full of dark curls. I smile and wave back at him.

My husband frowns at me and says, "Restrain yourself, Claudia. Show some discretion. We have to keep our distance from these people, or they will not respect us."

"But Pilate, did you see that precious little boy waving at us? Wouldn't you just love to have him for your own?"

"Not if he's a Jew. But you—you want every child you see."

It is true. Whether it is a Syrian child, an Egyptian child, a Greek or a Roman child, it doesn't matter. Even a Jewish child. I can have no children of my own, and I want every child I see.

I have lived through the horror of seeing my countrymen killing indiscriminately the families of those suspected of treason. They killed even the helpless young children of Sejanus. They executed them with the same strangling rope, his little boy and his girl scarcely more than a baby. Either our gods do not care, I thought, or else they can do nothing.

In desperation I turned to new gods, to the cult of Isis and the dead Osiris. Isis, whose temple in the Campus Martius draws many Roman women. Isis, the Egyptian goddess of the earth and fertility. Osiris, her husband, murdered by his evil brother Tryphon. His body cut into pieces and thrown into the Nile. Isis, the faithful wife, searching tirelessly for the pieces of her husband's body in the river. Isis, with the aid of their son Horus, finding Osiris' body parts. Isis, through the intensity of her grief, achieving the resurrection of her husband. I went through the emotional initiation rites lasting for ten days and ending with a nightlong dramatization of the death and rebirth of Osiris. I was led to believe that I, too, was being reborn, that I had gained immortality by purging myself and fasting and subjecting my body to painful discipline—and also by paying a large sum of money to the priests. When I left Rome, I confidently believed what the priests had assured me—that I could now bear a child. Although my body felt weak and sick, I believed because I wanted to believe.

After my return to Judea, I tried to get pregnant. When I began to gain some weight, I was hopeful. But after a few months' time, I realized I had been deceived; Isis and Osiris could do no more for me than Augustus and Roma could. They are not real gods, for they do not have the power to fulfill their promises. I will worship any god, I will undergo any suffering to be able to bear a child. And my husband has the audacity to say I do not exercise self-control! Now as for discretion, I am discreet enough not to tell him what I plan to do in Jerusalem, or he would certainly not be taking me with him.

CHAPTER 3

A Friend Who Brings New Hope

Once out of the city gates, we cross the Plain of Sharon, heading for the foothills. At this time of the year, the low coastal plain is subject to flooding and the roads are muddy. Therefore we take the inland route to Antipatris. I love the springtime here when the hills are green, dotted with grazing cattle, and the wheat and barley are already growing tall in the little terraced fields. Later in the season, everything will be parched and brown except around the waterholes in the valleys.

Pilate does not respond to my comments about the pretty countryside. He seems to be sulking, giving me the silent treatment. It will take time for him to work out of this sullen mood. I might as well be thinking about something pleasant. I know—I will think about my Jewish friend Joanna. Joanna, whom I met three years ago but have not seen since. We have kept our friendship alive and growing through our correspondence. This has become really heavy in the past few months. If Pilate were less occupied with his official duties or if he were more curious about women's matters, he would not have allowed my friendship with a Jewish woman to go so far. If he had any idea of what was in those letters, he might have started to monitor my mail.

I met Joanna when Herod Antipas invited us to visit him in Galilee at Tiberias, the new capital, which replaces the old one, Sepphoris. It is on the Sea of Tiberias, that lovely fresh-water lake which the Jews call the Sea of Galilee or the Lake of Gennesaret. I knew he invited us because on several previous occasions when Antipas and Herodias were in Caesarea, Pilate and I had entertained them at the governor's palace. We accepted their invitation, and we planned to visit them after attending the dedication of the aqueduct in Jerusalem.

Tiberias reminds me of Caesarea because it is relatively new—about the same age as our city—and because it fronts a body of water. But since it is built several hundred feet below sea level, in the great depression which extends as far south as the Red Sea, the climate is mild year-round. The hills facing the lake stay green all year, and the valleys running down to it are extremely fertile. Picture a pleasant garden with fruit and nut trees, grain and vegetables. Where man has planted nothing, the wild flowers in their season splash the landscape with color. But the lake itself is like an eye which gives expression to the face of the land. The lake changes its appearance from morning to evening. The surface is always flecked with the sails of the fishing boats that ply it night and day.

It soothes me to remember this lovely spot, a perfect setting for Herod's capital. Here he has all the pleasant features of Greco-Roman culture—a luxurious palace, a stadium—and nearby he has built baths over hot mineral springs reputed to have great curative powers. Pilate spent some time in them with Antipas, but we ladies were occupied with other things. I believe Herodias did not want to spoil her coiffure so early in the day.

I felt sorry for Joanna when I first met her. She had an obvious visual problem. Instead of calling on other ladies-in-waiting, Herodias seemed to pick Joanna to do things which would draw attention to her handicap so she could mock her or scold her for clumsiness. On one occasion Joanna dropped and broke an expensive cup. Herodias remarked crossly that she would tell Herod to deduct the price of the cup from the generous salary he paid Joanna's husband. As Herod's head steward, manager of all his estates in Galilee and Perea, Chuza must be quite wealthy. But this does not excuse Herodias' spitefulness and pettiness.

I was to find out later the reason for her dislike of Joanna and Chuza. It was because of their devotion to John the Baptist. Herodias despised him for his outspoken criticism of her marriage to Antipas. (Herodias was formerly the wife of Herod's brother Philip, and according to Jewish law, such a union is incestuous.)

Shortly after her peevish outburst, Herodias tried to make half-hearted amends. She said, "Joanna, you really ought to try to do something about your eyesight. With all Chuza's money, he should send you to some of those doctors at the medical school of Laodicea in Phrygia where they specialize in anointing the eyes with their secret salve. I hear they have accomplished some amazing cures."

Herodias was obnoxious even when she was trying to be nice. Joanna's eyes were snapping, but not because of her ailment. The statuesque Herodias would make two of this little bird-like creature who reminded me of one of my aunts. But Joanna had a spirit which I admired.

She said, with a heat quite understandable under the circumstances, "Chuza has spared no expense, but nothing has helped me yet. We are praying the Lord to send me a greater physician than those in Laodicea."

Herodias did not say much after this.

Later I got to talk to Joanna at some length. I learned that, like me, she had never been able to bear a child. Though in their younger days she and Chuza had tried to have children, God had willed otherwise; and so for many years now, she had traveled with her husband in his round of duties, visiting Herod's estates in Galilee and Perea. She could read and write well—an unusual accomplishment in a Jewish woman—and had previously helped Chuza with his accounts. But with her failing eyesight, she had been unable to do much lately. So she stayed behind in Tiberias while he made his rounds through the two provinces, and she waited on Herodias when the Herods held court in Tiberias.

I do not think Joanna was telling me these things to get my sympathy but to encourage me. Possibly she was also trying to direct me to the God of the Jews. She said, "But you are still young, and with God, there is nothing impossible." She told me about a relative of hers, a woman named Elizabeth, who had died some years before—how she was able to conceive and bear a child under miraculous circumstances.

Elizabeth and her husband Zechariah were well along in years when their son John was born. His birth was in accordance with the promise of an angel sent by God. When he was born, Zechariah had prophesied that he would be called the prophet of the Most High, for he would go before the Lord to prepare his ways. And Zechariah's prediction has been fulfilled, for Joanna told me their son has indeed grown up to point the way to salvation through forgiveness of sins. As John the Baptist, he has touched many hearts with his message of repentance—but not the hearts of Herod Antipas and his wife Herodias.

Joanna told me she and Chuza feared for John's safety when the Herods would move their court in a few weeks to the fortress of Machaerus in Perea on the other side of the Jordan. Up to now John had been able to escape arrest by distancing himself from the tetrarch and his men. Before we parted, Joanna promised to correspond with me. She said she would write me more about John. He was a great prophet, but he did not have the gift of healing, or he would have restored her sight. However, he had pointed the way to someone greater than himself, a man called Jesus of Nazareth.

I asked, "Where is Nazareth?" I learned it was one of the tiny villages we had passed through on the outskirts of Sepphoris. I asked, "How can you be sure of this? How can a great prophet come from a place like Nazareth?"

Joanna told me how Jesus came to John where he was baptizing in the Jordan, requesting baptism. John complied although under protest, saying to Jesus, "I need to be baptized by you, and do you come to me?" For the Holy Spirit, in the form of a dove, came and rested on him.

Joanna said, "Jesus has started to preach and heal in the villages around the lake. As soon as Herod and his court move across Jordan to Perea—" she pointed to the hills in the southeast—"I am going to see this man Jesus. If he really is who Chuza and I believe he is, he will be able to heal my eyes."

Joanna and I had just met and we did not know each other well. She hesitated to be more specific, and I hesitated to ask her what she meant. Now I know she and Chuza believe Jesus to be their Messiah. According to the Jews, when the Messiah comes, he will be able to heal the blind.

Several months later I received my first letter from Joanna. I assumed it had been written by a secretary since she was practically blind. The first thing she told me was how Herod's men had arrested John, who was now a prisoner in Perea at the fortress of Machaerus, where Herod was presently holding court. The second thing she told me was that her sight was now perfect—she had actually written the message with her own hand. She said this man Jesus had healed her.

She had made contact with him through a relative named Salome whose husband had a prosperous fishing business in Capernaum, a city on the north side of the lake. Salome's two sons, James and John, had become followers of Jesus, as had two of their fishing partners, Simon and Andrew. (I learned this Salome is the sister of Mary, the mother of Jesus.) Salome had suggested that Joanna join her and some other women whom Jesus had healed of various sicknesses. They wanted to follow Jesus and minister to him and his disciples.

Joanna said her husband Chuza was so delighted over her healing that he readily agreed for her to join the group and even contributed toward the expenses of the tour. As they traveled through the villages of Galilee, Jesus would stop and preach to the crowds. His disciples would baptize the people and Jesus would heal the sick. Joanna said she had seen him perform many amazing cures. She had talked to a mother whose child Jesus had raised up from a deathbed. Joanna said she believed there is nothing Jesus cannot do, the power of their God dwells so strongly in him. When I read about all these things, I wished I had been born Jewish. For from what she told me, it seemed Jesus' ministry was only to the Jews. Therefore I assumed I must seek elsewhere if I wanted a miracle.

In her next letter, Joanna told me the true story of what everyone was discussing excitedly—the death of John the Baptist at the hands of Herod. I was not surprised to learn Herodias was behind it all. Joanna said Jesus and his disciples, many of them John's former followers, were deeply distressed. Now John was dead, rumors were flying around, connecting him with Jesus.

Some were even saying Jesus was John who had risen from the dead. These stories were stirring up the superstitious Herod, who apparently suffered from a guilty conscience. According to Joanna, he had feared John, believing him to be a prophet, and he had agreed to John's death most reluctantly. It was all the fault of Herodias and her evil schemes. Joanna was trying to keep her own involvement with Jesus as quiet as possible, as much for his sake as for hers. She and Chuza did not wish to be responsible for anything the Herods might do to Jesus after their return from Perea.

In the following letter, Joanna described what had happened between her and Herodias after the Herods' return to Tiberias. Herodias had started to order Joanna around as usual, but to her great surprise, Joanna had performed the requested tasks deftly without stumbling over objects or breaking anything.

Herodias had commented, "Either our Joanna was feigning blindness before to get our sympathy, or during our absence she found some secret healing spring. Tell us about your secret spring, Joanna."

Joanna said she was wondering anxiously if Herodias had heard about what Jesus had done for her. But she merely smiled and said, "Yes, Mistress, I have found a secret healing spring. But if I should tell you about it, it would no longer be a secret." Some of the other women tittered. Herodias said no more. She liked it when the others laughed at Joanna's clumsiness and her own smart remarks, but not when they laughed at Joanna's cleverness and her own embarrassment.

Joanna had received her miracle, and I rejoiced for her. But there would be no miracle for me, a Gentile. I remained childless. This gnawing emptiness, I felt it now perhaps even more keenly. Moreover, I had never fully recovered from my shocking experience in Jerusalem when the angry mob rose up against Pilate. I could think of nothing else but going home to Rome and getting away from the scenes of madness. When I received word of my father's serious illness, I made up my mind to leave immediately. (This was two years ago in the late spring.) Before I left, I dispatched a brief message to Joanna, and I told her I would write her from Rome. I did not know that soon after my arrival, madness would break out in Rome also.

My mental and emotional condition grew worse. If I had known some Jews in Rome, I might have turned to them and their God for help. But I knew only my own people, and they could not help me. My father was old and sick, and his philosophy seemed completely useless. My mother's blind devotion to Juno, Patroness of Women, seemed equally inadequate. In Rome today it is easy to contact cultish groups. And as Pilate says, I am susceptible. I turned to strange gods, and they nearly destroyed me. In my folly, I thought they would be my salvation.

I did not realize the depth of the deception until after my return to Judea nearly a year ago. The priest of Isis had promised me I should bear a child in one year. He was playing it safe, for he knew I would not be trying to get pregnant until after a two months' voyage and a reunion with my husband in Caesarea. While I was arriving with high hopes, back in Rome he was spending the money I had given him. Pilate and I came together, but nothing happened. After several weeks, I was starting to worry. Pilate taunted me for my gullibility, which didn't help. I had fallen into a state of such deep dejection that it threatened to become a way of life.

Then I received a letter from Joanna. She was concerned about me. My letters from Rome had been short and few. I did not write much because I felt guilty about turning to strange gods—which she would not have understood—and I did not know what to say to her. In the last letter she received from me, I had told her when I would return to Judea. Now I was back, she wanted to tell me more about Jesus and the wonderful things she had seen him do.

She said she believed he would heal me, even though I am not Jewish. She said she had known him to heal people who were not Jews if they had the faith to be healed. She spoke about being in Capernaum when the local centurion came to Jesus and asked him to heal his sick servant. Jesus volunteered to go to him and heal him, but the centurion would not ask Jesus to defile himself by entering a Gentile house. He said he, too, was a man under authority with soldiers under him who could carry out his orders. So if Jesus would give the word, his servant would be healed. Jesus marveled at such faith in a Gentile. He said to the centurion, "Be it done to you as you have believed." And his servant was healed at that very minute.

All of this agrees with the reports about Jesus which Pilate has been reading to me lately. He thinks he is warning me against religious deceivers. He does not realize he is only fanning the flame. It is my new faith which gives me the courage to return to Jerusalem and to the Antonia Fortress, a place I dread. Hope is stronger than fear, and now I have real hope. My husband must not find out about my actual reason for accompanying him to Jerusalem—my desire to meet Jesus and be healed by him....

Pilate is speaking to me, but he still will not look me in the eye. He says, "Claudia, you embarrassed me today in front of my people." This is all he says. It will take him a little longer to work out of his peevishness. So I embarrassed *him*. I wonder if the man has any idea of how many times he has embarrassed *me*....

CHAPTER 4

A Lack of Sensitivity

He embarrassed me in front of Herod and Herodias several years ago when we were visiting them in Tiberias. One of the limitations of our life in Judea is having few social equals. Now Pilate and Antipas are neither political nor social equals: However, while Pilate governs more territory (if one counts the sparsely populated Idumea in addition to Judea and Samaria), Antipas is the son of a famous king, which ought to balance the scales between them.

I wanted so much for Pilate to make a good impression when we visited the Herods. When Antipas and Herodias had paid us short visits in Caesarea, Pilate had managed to behave like a proper host. So his conduct in Tiberias caught me by surprise. Why is the man so inept in some social situations? It seems I can trust him to behave in his own home; but when he is a guest of other people, I can count on him to act like a pompous bore—if he keeps his mouth shut—or an insensitive fool if he opens it. He must feel insecure when he is suddenly placed among foreign people in an alien environment. Yet he was not so bad when we were in Syria as he is here.

Perhaps it is his distaste for the Jews which increases his insecurity. Of course Antipas and Herodias are not like most Jews. They have been brought up in the Greco-Roman culture although they profess the Jewish religion—I suspect, for political reasons. They make Pilate nervous because he is unable to anticipate their reactions. When he gets uneasy in social situations, he drinks just enough to dull his inhibitions, so that he doesn't care what he says. And when he gets flustered, he has a natural tendency to say the wrong thing. I found this out when he and I had our very first conversation. He has never learned how to talk to women socially. Whatever the reasons may be, my poor husband made a fool of himself in front of Herodias, as I told him in private later. But I was never able to get him to face up to the fact.

Herodias was making conversation with us over the dinner table. We had been discussing Antipas's father, Herod the Great, and his genius for building. Herodias asked Pilate what he thought of the Jewish temple in Jerusalem. He replied that he didn't care much for the Temple because it was too ornate. If only he had stopped there, if only... When we were alone at last, I tried to explain to him what he had done.

"What was wrong with what I said?"

"Nothing at first. Your first comment about the Temple was an honest opinion, briefly expressed. But then you had to go on and on, in spite of my frowns and gestures!"

"I thought you had something in your eye."

"You had to say, 'If you want my opinion about Herod's Temple, all this oriental ornamentation spoils its classic lines. If something serves no useful purpose, to me it is not beautiful.'"

"That is exactly how I feel."

"You do not have to tell your hostess exactly how you feel when it is a criticism of her artistic taste. You should have had the sense to leave off there. But no, you went on and on, getting in deeper and deeper. You had to say there was only one part of the ornamentation which served a useful purpose—the golden spikes on the roof—because at least they kept the birds from alighting and fouling up the sanctuary. Pilate, this was in very bad taste."

"I thought I was saying something nice for a change."

"But then you reached the absolute depths. You knew how to the Jews, the Temple is Herod's masterpiece. But you said that to you,

Pontius Pilate, Herod's crowning achievement was *the sewage system of Caesarea*. Now, really!"

"What's so wrong with what I said?"

"Just listen to yourself. If I may quote you: 'The complicated network of vaults and channels under the city is a work of the highest genius, and because it is truly useful, it is truly beautiful.' Pilate, didn't you think about what you were saying?"

"I thought I was expressing myself rather well, to tell the truth."

"What you said was in the worst imaginable taste—at the table, to be discussing a sewer! And you had to continue describing in fulsome detail the workings of the system, 'like a giant latrine, receiving the filth of the citizens, flushed out twice a day by the tides of the Great Sea.' And you topped it off by saying, 'To me that is more beautiful than any temple.' Pilate, you were comparing their sanctuary with a sewer—and even worse, you were comparing it unfavorably. Now can you understand why Herodias looked so shocked?"

"I suppose so, but at the time I was too involved in my own opinions and in expressing them to notice the reactions of others."

"This is one of your faults. You speak first and think afterwards, if at all. You don't consider how what you say and do will affect other people until it is too late."

"You are probably right, but Herodias herself will win no prize for sensitivity. She has outraged the feelings of the Jewish people by leaving her own husband and marrying Antipas, his brother."

"I don't like her any better than you do, but we must be polite for the sake of your position. Do you consider Herodias attractive?"

"She is a fine-looking woman, but she overdoes the hair-do, the make-up, and the jewelry. You are much more beautiful to me because you look natural."

Pilate may seem like a boor to Herodias, but he is precious to me. He has been with many women in his soldiering days; but as far as I know, since our marriage, I have been the only woman in his life. Now in Roman society today, that is most unusual. He may embarrass me sometimes, but I love and appreciate this man. Though he is difficult to live with, he makes me feel special. And he has another good quality—he is generous to me. He always keeps close accounts in his financial administration of Judea and Samaria, but he has never complained about the way I spend money.

I did not tell Pilate how long it takes me to look natural for him every day. At least that remark of his was one thing I could remember pleasantly about our visit....

He has finally recovered. He turns toward me and touches my arm. He says, "Claudia, I am sorry I was so abrupt with you back in Caesarea. I know how much you love children. But I am concerned about what people will think of us, especially in Jerusalem, where the Jews are in the majority. Cities like Caesarea and Antipatris are different, new towns built by Herod the Great and settled by him with non-Jews he knew would be loyal to him. The majority of the people there—including the large Jewish minority—do not object to Roman rule, and we can be more relaxed among them. But you must not wave and smile in Jerusalem. They will despise us if we become too familiar with them. Remember, in Jerusalem the watchword is 'self-control and discretion.'"

"Yes, Pilate." Well, I could tell my husband something about exercising self-control and discretion, but if I did so right now, he might not talk to me again for another two hours. Most of the trouble he has stirred up back here in Judea has occurred because of his failures along this line. The embarrassing incident of the gilded shields would never have happened if he had first placed the shields where they are now—in the Temple of Augustus, where he wrote me he planned to put them.

I can imagine how it must have happened. He wanted to do something to flatter Tiberius. He ordered the shields to be made at his own expense, without any images and with only a simple inscription dedicating them to the emperor. He intended to put them in Caesarea, but he changed his mind suddenly. Perhaps he was drinking and his judgment was impaired. He probably heard about Herod making some move which threatened his authority in Jerusalem. So he countered by placing the shields there. Of course Herod and his brothers complained and asked Pilate to move the offensive shields. Of course Pilate refused. He even challenged them to carry their complaints to Rome. Pilate spoke out of his irritation, not out of his better judgment. He should have remembered

Tiberius's new policy of favoring the Jews. So now he has created a real rift between himself and Herod Antipas, and he has suffered the real humiliation of a reprimand by the emperor he was aiming to please.

CHAPTER 5

Defending a Friendship

"Claudia, I have been meaning to tell you for some time—you are entirely too free with the servants, our own and other people's. In our own household..."

"Pilate, are you referring to my Eunice? Eunice, who nursed me as a baby and took care of me as a young child? Who taught me to speak Greek and introduced me to my earliest letters before I was old enough to go to school?"

"No, of course not. For Eunice was then a slave of your family, and in those days, house slaves were treated like family members. Now that she is free, she stays with you as much for love as for pay or obligation. No, I did not mean Eunice. But these Jewish women who are your hired servants here—for instance, this girl Hannah who is riding behind us in the carriage with Eunice—you chatter with them as if they were your equals. I would not expect this laxity in a descendant of the Claudia gens. Have you no pride of station?"

"It has never occurred to me to doubt my own worth. I feel no need to belabor others with my station. Do you want me to be proud and haughty, despising the law, despising those who stand in my way? Do you want me to be like—*Herodias*?"

"No, of course not. I want you to continue to be your own sweet self. But I want you to put a little more distance between yourself and these Jewish maids. And now you have mentioned Herodias—why do you have to pick as your special friend a servant of hers, this Joanna? You are always writing letters to this woman or receiving letters from her. I can't imagine what you two have in common. Now if you were corresponding with friends back in Rome, women of your own rank..."

"Really, Pilate!" (Be careful, Claudia, not to say too much. Pilate must not learn about our secrets.) "Joanna is not a servant of Herodias. She is a lady, a member of her court. There is a difference between a servant and a lady-in-waiting. Haven't I told you about Joanna being a descendant of King David? If she has royal blood, it makes her as good as I, even by your standards."

"Wasn't David the father of Solomon, who had a thousand wives? And who knows how many other wives David had besides Solomon's mother. Can you imagine how many direct descendants the father and son would have by now, roughly a thousand years later? In a country whose people are as inbred as the Jews are, every other person could be a descendant of King David. So Joanna's claim carries no special distinction, even if it is true. And besides, she is not like you."

"What do you mean?"

"For one thing, she is old enough to be your mother."

"I miss my own mother, and Joanna is a motherly person."

"And she is a Jew."

"What is so wrong with that? What is wrong with making friends with a Jewish person?"

"Their ways are not our ways."

"Perhaps some of their ways are better than our ways."

"Name two, if you can."

"Well, Jewish couples are faithful to each other."

"You and I are Roman, not Jewish, and we are faithful."

"We are Roman, but we are not typical today. Divorce is nearly as common as marriage in Rome nowadays. And for another thing, Jewish parents consider their children their greatest treasure."

"Remember Cornelia, mother of the Gracchi? When someone asked to see her jewels, she displayed her two sons, whom she herself educated."

"That was two hundred years ago. Roman mothers today aren't

what they used to be, especially women of the upper classes. They are not like your mother and my mother. Either they choose to have no children or else they turn their children over to their slaves to bring up, while they spend their time in idleness."

"All right, you have made your two points. But aside from this, what do you have in common with Joanna?"

"She understands how I feel because like me, she is childless. She is a caring person. She does not look down on me because I am a Roman. And I do not look down on her because she is a Jew. I do not share your prejudices, perhaps because I am not a legitimate descendant of the noble Claudia clan. And Pilate, you ought to make some Jewish friends yourself. If you would stop considering how different they are from you and start looking for things you have in common with them, you would find something to talk about."

"Humph!"

"For example, take Joanna's husband Chuza, Herod's steward. He is in charge of all Herod's business—collecting rents, administering funds, keeping accounts. When you met him, you could have talked to him about such things, so similar to what you have to do much of the time. That would have built a common bond between you two. You could have made a friend of him as I did of Joanna. Think it over. It would help you to have a friend in Herod's palace to keep you informed of what is happening there."

"I have my informants."

"A friend inside the palace could give more timely and reliable information. For instance, in one of her letters Joanna told me what really occurred in the execution of John the Baptist."

"I remember how Herodias was involved in some way. Fill me in on the details."

"She was angry with John, as you know, and she got Herod to arrest him because he had preached against their marriage. But she could not persuade Herod to put the man to death—Herod is just Jewish enough to be afraid to kill a prophet. So she got her teen-aged daughter to trick him.... You do remember Salome, don't you?"

"That voluptuous thing? Of course I do."

"I thought you would. Well, she got Salome to dance at Herod's birthday party. It must have been quite a dance because Herod vowed before all his guests to give her anything she would ask, up to half his kingdom. And then when the girl asked him to give her the head of John the Baptist on a platter, because of the presence of his guests, he had to keep his word."

"Like mother, like daughter. Herodias, the perfect hostess, whose delicate sensibilities you accused me of offending."

"Now you know all this, do you really prefer that I write to my social equal, Herodias, rather than to Joanna, whom you call her servant?"

"You always twist my words around and use them against me. Go ahead and continue writing to your Joanna. I have noticed how it perks up your spirits when you get a letter from her. I don't want you looking thin and pale again as you did for so long after you returned from Rome. Forget everything I said. Whether you admit it or not, you are a true daughter of the Claudia clan, and by one means or another, you always get your way."

"No, *you* always get *your* way. But you are trying to make up with me because we're nearing Antipatris and tonight we will probably be sharing the same room...."

"And the same bed. Yes, I do believe giving you your way might make you act more friendly in close quarters. Now you know, tomorrow night we'll be sleeping in a tent. And after that we'll be sharing the quarters for visiting dignitaries at the Antonia—which are very compact, if you remember. So if I don't start giving you your way, I'm not being too smart."

CHAPTER 6

At the Post in Antipatris

Pilate and I and our company are spending the night at the military post in Antipatris. The accommodations are adequate if not luxurious; at least they are better than the tent we shall be sleeping in tomorrow night.

When my maid Hannah came in to remove my make-up and take down my hair, I know he regarded it as an intrusion. In the Promontory Palace back in Caesarea, he can take refuge in his own room while such things are going on. Of course after she left to rejoin Eunice in another room, he had to make some comment about servants and Jews in general.

As I lie awake beside my sleeping husband, I think about how differently we regard people of other races, religions, and cultures. My family have been "more illustrious equestrians" for hundreds of years, whereas Pilate's family—the Pontians—are relative newcomers to Rome and have had to fight their way upward inch by inch.

I suppose it is natural for him to be more class-conscious. Back in Samnium, his ancestors were of the highest rank, but they were demoted after the Roman conquest. What you have lost once, you fear to lose again, and you hold it to yourself all the more jealously. Old Romans, like the Proculus branch of the Claudians—who have never lost their social status—can be less self-conscious of their dignity. Perhaps this is Pilate's problem.

I am wondering if I told him too much about Joanna. I do not believe he knows she and Chuza are supporters of Jesus and she herself is an active follower. I am sure he does not know she is related to Jesus on his mother's side. Pilate may have learned through his sources that Jesus is of the house of David, though according to him, this is no great thing. I do not want Pilate to guess that through Joanna's letters I too have become a believer. Pilate thinks all I know about Jesus has come from the reports he has read to me. He thinks I accepted unquestioningly his far-fetched rationalizations of Jesus' miracles. He does not know I am pinning all my hopes on Jesus. If Jesus and his God can give me a child, I will serve them forever.

Before he dropped off to sleep, Pilate put his arms around me and hugged me close. That was his way of apologizing again for giving me a hard time today. Although he does not know it yet, the tables will be turned tomorrow. Little Claudia has her ways of slipping in a word of wifely advice and getting him to do what *she* wants.

CHAPTER 7

A Wild Ass and a Lost Ark

It is Saturday morning and we have made an early start, first heading south along the coastal plain of Samaria from Antipatris to Lydda, where we will pick up the road which goes through Beth Horon into the hill country of Judea. Pilate is in a better mood today than he was yesterday. Instead of becoming increasingly edgy as we approach the area of steep rocky hillsides and V-shaped valleys, where I know he periodically dreads surprise attacks, he appears unusually cheerful. He must have received a favorable report from his augur, a nervous little man whose face is always muffled in a hooded cloak whenever he travels abroad, lest he see something which could bring bad luck on our company. (I have never been able to understand what difference that would make.) Or perhaps my husband's good mood is due to something easier to explain: There is much to be said for the plebeian custom of husband and wife sharing the same room and the same bed at night.

Pilate turns to me and says, "Claudia, last year at Passover I was wretched without you. I had no one to talk to, no one I could relax with. But this year because you are with me, things will go better." He pats my hand.

"They will, if you will heed two words of advice."

"Start advising."

"Don't use wine to steady your nerves. And think before you speak."

"That's a lot to ask. You know how I react when I feel myself surrounded by no one but Jews. Remember the time in Egypt?"

"When we stopped off at Alexandria, on our way to Judea? How could I ever forget the garden party!"

"The governor wanted me to meet some prominent members of the Jewish colony. He said it would help me to build up self-confidence before meeting my own subjects. So he put on the reception in the palace gardens."

"I know, I know. I was there too, remember. Since Jewish men don't believe in taking wives to social affairs, the governor's wife and I stayed out of sight—but not out of earshot. From the sunken garden behind the shrubbery, we could hear what people were saying as they walked around. We heard you talking to the Jewish scholar.... What was his name?"

"Philo. I'll never forget the man."

"He'll never forget you, either. When you two stopped to talk a few feet away on the other side of the bushes, I recognized your voice immediately. I whispered to the governor's lady, 'Why, that's my husband speaking. Can you identify the other man?'

"She said, 'With the peculiar voice? Of course—it has to be Philo, the brother of the alabarch, the leader of our Jewish community here. When he becomes excited over something, his voice gets high and shrill.' Then we hushed so we could hear what you two were saying."

"Claudia, you know me—I'm a soldier, not a diplomat. I was never ill at ease among my troops or among the barbarian tribes of Germany. But when Galerius introduced me to those Jews and then walked off and left me to talk to them, I was in a sudden sweat. All those men with their beards and long robes, looking down their Semitic noses at me, converging on smooth-shaven me in my short dress uniform. I felt like a boy with my knees as bare as my chin. I had never been around Jews socially before, and after the first civilities I didn't know what to say. I would have been tempted to make my escape into the shrubbery if I hadn't fortified myself beforehand with a little wine, you know."

"Yes, I know. But tell me about Philo."

"Galerius had told me he was a Hellenized Jew, a teacher and a writer, an expert on Greek philosophy and Jewish religion. Quite an interesting combination. I started to talk to him about philosophy. We were getting along quite well. So I left the disconcerting crowd of Jews and walked off with just this one. Surely, I thought, I can handle one Jew at a time."

"What did you say to make him so excited?"

"As I told you, we were getting along quite well, until I asked him a question about the Jewish religion. I asked him if it was true about the Jews worshiping an image of a wild ass. You know, this is what we have always heard in Rome."

"Yes, but you were most indiscreet to mention it."

"I soon realized my blunder, for the man began to jump around and talk and gesture excitedly, as if he were trying to ward off a swarm of biting flies. It was unnerving yet comical at the same time."

"It sounded funny to us on the other side of the shrubbery. That thin, piping voice got higher and higher. I was wondering what a man with such a voice would look like."

"Believe me, not like what you would expect. When I first met him, it struck me how the man looked like an eagle. He was maybe ten years my senior, with a high forehead and a receding hairline. Piercing eyes, deep-set under bushy brows. A curved beak of a nose. And of course, a full beard, black shot with gray. When he got so excited, he reminded me even more of an eagle, an eagle disturbed on the nest, ready to defend its young. Yet instead of loud rasping cries, *those squeaks*! But let me get on with the story."

"I'm not stopping you."

"He called what I had said a blasphemous calumny against his God. He asked me where I had heard such an outrageous thing. I told him I had heard it all my life, for in Rome it is common knowledge."

"What did he say to that?"

"He called it common ignorance. He launched into a real tirade about how we Romans believe everything we hear and don't take the trouble to check it out. He said the Greeks are the real thinkers—they do the research and verify their sources before they quote them. He said we Romans would have no culture at all without the Greeks. I was starting to get angry, but I heard him out."

"Good for you."

"After he had calmed down a little, he asked me what else I had heard about the ass's image. So I told him the whole tale about how the Jews were supposedly dying of thirst in the desert and a herd of wild asses led them to a spring of fresh water.... About how, when they built the Temple, they put the statue of a wild ass or a wild ass's head in the Holy of Holies."

"Oh-oh!"

"Then he started to get excited all over again. He told me that the worship of idols is absolutely forbidden to Jews, and they are allowed to make no representations of men or animals which might be worshiped as gods because their God is the one and only God—a Spirit who is invisible, all-knowing, all-seeing, and all-powerful. He said the Holy of Holies has been empty since the first Temple was destroyed when the Jews were led into captivity in Babylon."

"What was in it before then?"

"He told me there used to be in it a sacred chest called the Ark of the Covenant which contained the sacred book of their law. Their God had given it to them through a man named Moses who had led them out of Egypt. He said that formerly the presence of the Lord had hovered over this chest, and anyone who touched it was struck dead instantly. He told me no one knows to this day whether the chest was destroyed by fire or was hidden somewhere."

"Hidden? But where could it be? Did he give you any clues?"

"He said there is a rabbinical tradition about the time when the Jews were deported from Jerusalem to Babylon, how to keep the Ark of the Covenant from falling into the hands of the Babylonians, the Prophet Jeremiah took it and hid it in a cave."

"Did Philo tell you where the cave was?"

"Apparently the traditions aren't so specific. It seems reasonable to me that to keep a cult object as precious as the Ark from falling into the hands of people who would desecrate it, somebody would hide it in a safe place."

"Then why didn't they go back and get it later, after the Temple was rebuilt?"

"I understand it was many years later when this happened, and probably Jeremiah and the few who knew his secret had died off by this time."

"Fascinating. So the sacred Ark may be somewhere in hiding today."

"Exactly. But, what with the thousands of caves with which Judea is honeycombed, chances of its being found are minimal.... Now, back to Philo. I asked him where the spirit power of his God would go without a material object to focus on. He said the Jewish God doesn't need material things; he is present in the Temple and the Holy City in a special way, yet his power extends throughout the world. I asked him why, then, if his God is so powerful, Rome is the master of the world and not Judea."

"What did he say to that?"

"He got really upset, and he became quite offensive. He ranted about a Jewish king named Solomon whose empire covered most of the Middle East. This was a thousand years ago, he said, in the golden age of Jewish culture when Rome would not be founded for several hundred years and the Italic tribes were running around in a state of barbarism."

"And how did you answer him?"

"I finally lost my temper. I told him, 'That was ten centuries ago, and you Jews haven't had another empire since. Meanwhile Italy's barbaric tribes, as you call them, have conquered the world. And your territory has shrunk into a minor dependency of Syria, one of Rome's most remote provinces. It looks to me as though your God has walked out on you. If not, I'd hate to have him on my side. Or if he hasn't left you, his power has been so weakened by the loss of this Ark that he can't do anything. Philo, let me give you a piece of advice: You Jews should either search for this missing Ark or get yourselves a god who is worth his salt.'"

"He must have been furious."

"I thought he had gone mad. He threw up his hands and began to jabber in a foreign language."

"It was probably Hebrew."

"I can't stand it when people do stuff like that. At least when they talk in the common Greek, you know what they are saying about you. So I asked him what on earth he was doing. He said he was praying in Hebrew for the peace of Jerusalem. He said they would need all the prayers they could get with me as their governor. Then he turned on his heel and left me with his own word of advice: 'Find yourself a counselor who understands the Jews, and for the love of heaven, listen to him.'"

"It might not have been bad advice."

"If he had not left in such a huff, I would have given him some more advice of my own."

"Well, what would you have told him?"

"I would have said, 'You Jews would be a lot better off if you were not so clannish, if you would mix socially with other peoples. But wherever you go, you withdraw into your own group. You are not the only nation to be conquered by Rome. If you would get to know others, you could use the situation to your advantage. For example, take me and my people. They came from Samnium in the south central part of Italy. About three hundred years ago, in their desire for expansion, they issued from their mountain fastnesses, entering into conflict with the Romans. One of my ancestors, a general named Pontius, defeated the Roman army in one of the mountain passes near Caudium and compelled them to pass under the yoke. It was not till thirty years later that he was defeated, taken prisoner, and put to death. Down through the centuries, we Samnites have given Rome more trouble than any other tribe. But in time we learned to cooperate, and we submitted to assimilation.

"At first our clan lost everything, but eventually we recovered our ancestral lands in Caudium. Though my family has not yet gained senatorial rank, at least we are now recognized as 'illustrious equestrians'. And under Rome we have advanced in wealth and power. I ask you, which is better? To be one of the principal men of the Samnites—a remote mountain tribe—or one of the lesser nobles of Rome, the mighty empire? No one thinks of the Pontians as Samnites any more. We are Romans and have been so for generations. Now why can't you Jews do likewise?"

"A convincing declamation, but I don't think Philo would have heard you out, even if he had stayed on. I have listened patiently to the end of your story. Now, I have something to add."

"Go ahead."

"While you were talking with Philo, Galerius's wife and I could catch only a word here and there, but we got enough to understand that you and Philo were having a big argument over religion. She said to me, 'This Jew Philo is a noted writer, a historian. You'd better hope he never writes anything about your husband, for once he makes up his mind about a person, they say he never changes it.'"

"Let him write. During the past seven years of my governorship, I'm sure he has gathered plenty of information which he can slant his way to influence his readers. But this does not concern me. Who cares about a book only Jews will read?"

(My husband! I ask myself privately, what if Jews are the only ones who write about you?)

I say to him, "You don't really mean that. You looked quite serious later when Galerius told you Philo had given you some good advice about getting a knowledgeable counselor."

(He also told Pilate in so many words how if he couldn't get along with the relatively cooperative Jews in Alexandria, he could expect big trouble with those in Jerusalem. But I won't mention that, not now.)

"In some ways we Romans are poorly prepared for public office. We have to learn on the job, for there are no books to tell us the things we need to know. For instance, until Galerius told me, I had never heard how a hundred years ago when Pompey the Great took Jerusalem, he entered the Holy of Holies in the Temple and found it completely empty. No Ark, no wild ass either."

"It is true about the lack of preparation. But you were forewarned in Alexandria. After this episode with Philo, you should have known better than to offend the Jews with those ensigns soon after we arrived." (I let that one slip, and I may regret it.)

"Claudia, you have just insulted my intelligence. Or perhaps you have forgotten how I explained my position, given the political climate which existed at that time. We will talk more about this later, but for now, let's change the subject. And let's stop for lunch—ho, driver!"

Claudia, this is definitely your day. You got off much lighter than you expected—and you made a few good points.

CHAPTER 8

A Priest Who Gets His Way by Doing Nothing

After lunch near Lydda, where we pick up the Beth Horon Road, we resume our journey and our previous conversation. Pilate tries to explain why he acted as he did in the matter of the ensigns.

He says, "I received conflicting signals from those who advised me. First Galerius tells me, 'You must be diplomatic with these Jews if you want a long term in office.' But I remember Sejanus' parting words when we left Rome, 'From the very first day, let them know who is the master.' Then the next day, here comes Valerius Gratus, my predecessor, on his way back to Rome from Caesarea, and he gives me this sage advice:

"You must be firm with these Jews if you want a long term in office.' That is two against one. Gratus went on to tell me the Jews of Judea are harder to control than the Jews in any other country.

"He told me how in his eleven years in office, he had to appoint and dismiss two High Priests before he found one he could work with—Joseph Caiaphas. He said, 'You could do worse than stick with Caiaphas, but he is highly intelligent and will take advantage of you if you give him half a chance.' It was on this last advice that I acted in the affair of the ensigns."

"Well, if you were aiming for Caiaphas with the ensigns, you seem to have missed the mark. It was the common people who became so upset they practically besieged us in Caesarea."

"Oh, Caiaphas got my point, all right. But he let the people react for him. He knew something which I was unaware of at the time, the religious fanaticism of the common people. He did not have to tell them to run to Caesarea and camp on our doorstep. He probably could not have prevented them from going if he had wanted to. So he let them deliver his message for him."

" 'Remove the abominations!' I shall never forget that chant, continuing for five days and nights. Half a mile away in the Promontory Palace, I could hear it. I knew you had your back to the wall, and I was dreadfully frightened."

"The crowd was non-violent, and as far as I could tell, they were unarmed. If I had given the order, my soldiers would have cut them down with minimal resistance."

"That last day you told them you would order the attack if they did not disperse immediately and return to their homes. Would you have actually done it?"

"I was bluffing. It was a trick which worked for Caesar and others, time and time again. But I found out quickly that it would not work with these Jews when they all threw themselves down and bared their necks before my soldiers. I could hardly believe that several thousand people would be willing to die over something as trivial as the effigies on the standards, but Rome does not slaughter unarmed civilians on their knees in submission. So I had to back down and agree to their request about the ensigns."

"Pilate, it looks to me as though you suffered a real defeat, while Caiaphas got his way without saying or doing anything."

"You are partly right, but I worked it to my advantage when I met with Caiaphas several weeks later. Our meeting was courteous and business-like, but each of us now knew the kind of man he was dealing with. I knew why Valerius Gratus had left Caiaphas in the office of High Priest, and he knew why the emperor had picked me to replace Gratus."

"It was still a defeat. How could it possibly be used to your advantage?"

"I was trying to enlist the High Priest's help in building the aqueduct. Since I had made the first concession, I hoped he would be disposed to cooperate now. I impressed him with my desire to be a good governor and improve the quality of life for the people of the province. Well, everything went smoothly for some time—until we discussed the funding of the project."

"How did you get Caiaphas to agree to pay for the aqueduct out of the temple treasury?"

"It wasn't easy. My experts discovered a little-known statute which permitted the use of the *Corban* for such a purpose. And as an added inducement, I let him know I would put off his reappointment as High Priest until after he had signed the agreement and had demonstrated his compliance with its provisions."

"What was the agreement?"

"He would turn over the money secretly with the understanding that if the truth should leak out, he would claim he had done so under pressure from me."

"Why couldn't you have taken the money out of taxes?"

"They are already allocated, and if there is any surplus, I have to return it to the emperor. We are not living in the days of the republic, when governors did not have to account for everything down to the last *sesterce*. And the people are already taxed so heavily by their religious establishment that I was unwilling to increase the Roman tribute. So I could see no other way to finance my aqueduct except by drawing on the vast surplus in the Temple treasury."

"When we attended the dedication ceremony, I was very proud of you and what you had done. Everyone was praising you. Those poor people who always had to do without a good water supply now had more than they could use for the first time in their lives. The children were splashing happily in the fountains, and even the sheep seemed to bleat less plaintively. You were a real hero and a Roman benefactor. How could the climate have changed so completely in less than two weeks?"

"I didn't think the secret would come out about the use of the *Corban*. A revelation of the truth was to no one's advantage. But again I made the mistake of expecting Jews to act like Romans, like rational people. Some disgruntled member of the Sanhedrin must have let it slip, probably one of those rabid younger Pharisees. It could not have been a Sadducee—they have more common sense."

"You should always consider unlikely possibilities. Didn't you anticipate the people's reaction if they should find out?"

"I underestimated them again. I expected them to respond like the Roman plebeians—to accept their good fortune gladly and not worry about the source of the funding. To us Romans, abundant water is a vital necessity. Apparently to these Jews it is less important than their precious traditions. Never in human memory had the *Corban* been used for such a purpose, and law or no law, they would not accept it without a fight. Not even Caiaphas could persuade them to break with tradition."

"Do you think Caiaphas himself stirred up trouble while we were on our tour to Tiberias?"

"Once the secret was out, the fat was in the fire, and he did not have to do anything. I was taking all the blame, and he was in the clear. Besides, unrest is as dangerous to him as it is to me. He had done nothing to start it, and there was nothing he could have done to stop it."

"So he did nothing. I see what you mean about his cleverness. He could plead his own helplessness in the matter of the *Corban*, and the people would not blame him. They would even sympathize with him as a victim of your high-handedness."

"The man is devilishly clever. He himself has the reputation for greed and high-handedness among his own people. They dislike him personally because he uses his office to enrich himself and his extended family at their expense; but he knows the majority of the people will support him as High Priest, especially if they see him forced to yield to Rome in what they consider a religious matter."

"Then you think he was not responsible for the riot which resulted?"

"Only in the most general sense. When he got my message after our return, he probably told a few people Pontius Pilate was back again and was in the Antonia. That was all he had to do. The news was sure to spread. If he had been involved in any way, there would have been some religious leaders in the crowd. There were none. At least none came forth when I called for their leaders. They were just the usual malcontents, rabble waiting for a cause. When one came along, they turned into an angry mob overnight. But I imagine Caiaphas was enjoying my discomfiture. He knew all that ill will directed against me would result in good will for him."

"After three years I still remember vividly how petrified I was when I looked out of the window and saw those people milling below. I could not see your tribunal close to the gate because of the wall between us. I knew you were out there, but I didn't know where. I didn't know about your plans to infiltrate the crowd and subdue them if they should become violent. When one doesn't know what to expect, one fears the worst."

"Caiaphas is not the only clever one; I can be tricky too. Planting my troops in the crowd, disguised as civilians, is what saved the day."

"But did you have to kill all those people?"

"It would never have happened except for an over-reaction on the part of my soldiers. Their orders were only to club the unruly, but when the people started to hurl insults against me, their leader, and against Rome in general, my soldiers drew their swords. And that was the signal for chaos."

"It was horrible to watch. I was glued to the window. I heard what the people were shouting—I understood the tone, if not the words. I knew you were down below somewhere, perhaps in the hands of that mob. It was an angry sea of humanity. When I saw swords flashing and clubs knocking people down, I felt sure the crowd was armed. But I was completely confused. Against whom were they fighting? I saw no Roman uniforms among them. All I knew was that you were down there, and I feared I would never see you alive again."

"I was shaken up a bit but in no real danger. The tide was moving the other way. When my soldiers forced back the crowd with their weapons, the people tried to escape. They trampled each other in their panic. The few narrow exits to the square became death traps. More were killed by the panic than by the sword thrusts."

"How tragic!"

"It was a tragic but unpreventable incident, and as things turned out, it forestalled a full-scale riot. The people of Jerusalem made no more trouble. The High Priest said nothing—he was probably secretly relieved. And Sejanus complimented me on my handling of the matter.

In fact he wrote me how if he had been there, he would have killed more of them intentionally as an object lesson to the others."

"So in spite of everything, it worked out all right."

"Amazing, isn't it. Fortune was with us, and I was glad of my unconscious timing; for if the dedication of the aqueduct had coincided with the Passover Feast, the riot could easily have become a general uprising. At such a time the most trifling episodes can get blown out of all proportion. Let me give you an example, something which happened while you were in Rome."

"Do you mean the thing about the gilded shields?"

"No. I'm not referring to that, although it certainly drew more attention than it deserved. You probably haven't even heard about this one. It occurred on one of their lesser festivals, the Feast of the Dedication, in the month of December."

"When they light all those candles?"

"Yes, in memory of the fresh consecration of their Temple after it had been profaned by Antiochus Epiphanes, a king of Greek descent whose memory they hate even more than they do us Romans. Well, I was back in Caesarea, minding my own business. And on the streets of Jerusalem, it seems some young bloods from Galilee started to egg on my soldiers, calling them names. Somebody threw a rock. Tempers flared and swords flashed. By the time the brief exchange of blows was over, a couple of the Galileans lay dead. My soldiers were only maintaining public order and defending themselves, but they were called butchers."

"It doesn't seem fair."

"No, it doesn't. But it gets even worse. Who draws the most criticism? Pontius Pilate, who wasn't even there, gets blamed for it all. And the dead troublemakers become popular heroes, referred to as 'those Galileans whose blood Pilate mingled with their sacrifices.' You'd think I had personally cut them down at the very altar of their Temple."

"Poor Pilate! I can see what you mean."

"All of their feasts, even the minor ones, arouse nationalistic fervor. But because of the weather and the difficulty in travel, the winter ones are not well-attended, but the Passover Feast is another matter. At such a time as this, when there are hundreds of thousands of visitors from all over Judea and all over the world, any little incident can become a real threat to Rome. This is the reason why I am so tense now, why you see me studying my reports—whenever you will leave off your chatter."

"Sorry, I was thoughtless. Do you want me to be quiet now?"

"No, I'm just trying to explain why I sometimes cut you short."

CHAPTER 9

Jesus Will Come

"You mean when you have your nose in those old papers?"

"These dossiers contain factual information about the cases I will have to conduct. I have gone over it again and again. But I must consider everything that could happen and determine what I would do if it should happen. This takes concentration. Now when you speak out, you break my train of thought."

"Which cases are you talking about? Barabbas and Jesus of Nazareth?"

"Exactly. But the only real case is the one of Barabbas. There is a lot of sentiment against him here in Jerusalem. Most citizens do not want to see a murderer and an insurrectionist go free. But there is much feeling for him elsewhere in the province and in Galilee. I have decided not to try him during Passover week because of all the hotheads in these crowds. Therefore I shall hold the trial the following week, and it ought to be a good show, a fitting epilogue for the Passover excitement. In the meantime Barabbas is safely locked up in the Antonia, so I am not too concerned about him at present.

"What I am mostly concerned with, Claudia, is this Nazarene affair. It is not yet a case or even an incident. It is more like a ground swell of popular support for this man Jesus of Nazareth. If he should come to Jerusalem for the feast, anything could happen."

"But Pilate, Jesus and his followers are non-violent. You have told me so yourself."

"True. The man Jesus appears to be nonviolent. But I happen to know there is at least one ex-Zealot among the twelve who are closest to him. And he is constantly surrounded by seventy or so others wherever he goes. I suspect that from time to time the crowd becomes much larger. Once earlier in his ministry a disorganized group of thousands wanted to make him their king because he gave them free bread. By the time the story reached me, it had expanded into a full-fledged miracle. But it seems Jesus would have none of their kingship; he managed to escape from the crowd as he has done on other occasions."

"Well, doesn't that prove Jesus presents no danger to Rome?"

"Claudia, I am not so concerned about him personally as I am about public reaction to him. And I am most concerned about the way he is perceived by the religious establishment, for Caiaphas and the chief priests and the Pharisees are out to get him. He may have escaped from the Herodians in Galilee, but the High Priest is determined to arrest him if he comes to Jerusalem for the feast. You remember, I told you the Sanhedrin had issued a warrant for his arrest over a month ago. I was just reviewing the documentation of the events leading up to this point."

"Didn't you tell me several months ago how Caiaphas had tried to seize him in the Temple during some festival, and Jesus slipped through the High Priest's fingers?"

"It was at the Feast of Dedication in December. My report gave no further details except that Jesus passed through the crowd and escaped with his followers to Perea across the Jordan."

"How do you suppose he did it?"

"The man must be a magician, to be able to walk right through a crowd of his enemies and escape so easily. He must count on his lucky stars or his God to protect him, since only a few weeks later, he returned to the vicinity of Jerusalem for long enough to perform the crowning feat of his career."

"You mean the raising of Lazarus?"

"Precisely. And the man did it in the presence of many reputable people, even some of the leading Pharisees. I would give a lot to find out how he did it. The priestly party saw this as a challenge to their authority among the people. How could they hope to compete with a popular leader who could not only heal the sick and feed the hungry but raise the dead? It wasn't long after this that they issued the warrant. And if Jesus does come to the feast, they are sure to arrest him this time. The man would be a fool to come—and yet..."

"Pilate, Jesus will come." (I must be careful not to reveal too much.) "He will come. Do you remember the letter I received from Joanna several weeks ago? Well, she told me she had it on good authority that Jesus was headed for Jerusalem."

"Why didn't you tell me then?"

"I volunteered to read you some of the letter, but after you heard the first few lines you said you weren't interested in that woman's chatter. So I read on to myself."

"Then this is the reason why you are so eager to accompany me to Jerusalem in spite of what happened there before: You want to see what will happen when Jesus arrives. Am I right?"

"Partly right. I also want to come because it is my wifely duty. You need me at your side in Jerusalem to advise and encourage you."

"Claudia, why is it that whenever you talk to me about doing your wifely duty I have this uncomfortable feeling of being used? It causes me to remember who you are—a descendant of the illustrious Claudia clan, who always get their way, by fair means or foul.... Enough of this. Since you are so concerned about your wifely duties, tell me what you will do to entertain your husband in Jerusalem."

CHAPTER 10

A Devious Daughter of the Claudians

"Well, for a starter, how about a nice little dinner party Monday night? We could invite Jesus to the Antonia, and you would have a chance to talk to him privately. Wouldn't that be interesting?"

"You don't give up, do you? It is a tempting possibility, but it won't work. Remember, your pious Jews won't eat with Gentiles or even enter their houses. I seriously doubt that Jesus would accept; besides, Caiaphas would be sure to hear of it. The secret would leak out. Moreover, at the present I am on good terms with the man. I don't need to turn him against me again for what he would interpret as meddling in his sphere—religious matters."

"If we can't invite Jesus to come to us, then could I go to him?"

"Remember your position as my wife. That is always of primary importance. Think about what could happen. In the first place, like your 'private' dinner, such a visit would be reported to Caiaphas. In the second place, at a time like this, you should be accompanied by an armed guard when you go abroad. And in the third place, I seriously doubt also that this Jesus and his disciples would stand their ground if approached by a body of soldiers. They would probably duck into some alley to avoid the confrontation."

"If I should meet him at the Temple, where he is sure to go, I would not need an armed escort because Roman guards are stationed throughout the area. And Jesus and his followers would not feel threatened."

"I positively forbid you to go into the Temple. If you have this in mind, forget it now. I know you, Claudia. And I would worry about you as you worried about me in that angry mob."

"Why should you worry about me? There are Temple guards inside. And I know it for a fact, Gentiles are admitted freely into the outer court of the Temple. I could wait for Jesus there."

"Claudia, I am well aware of all this. But did you know there is a point beyond which all non-Jews are forbidden to enter on pain of death? I can just picture you in your religious susceptibility, wandering past that point. You would not see the warning sign. Your eyes would be on that Holy of Holies rising above your head. You could be struck dead by their Temple police. Or if they merely seized you, it would create an ugly incident which would be sure to make trouble for me."

"Of course you would not let them kill me?"

"Not if I had the chance. But suppose they struck first and asked questions afterwards? I would have to destroy their Temple. And you know what that would cause."

"A general rebellion in Judea and uprisings among the Jews in every province. And punishment from Rome."

"Would you want that to happen?"

"Pilate, you're right. I promise not to go within the Temple precincts. As the governor's wife, I must not compromise your position. Naturally I am disappointed because I had looked forward to going inside the Temple. But I can watch what is going on below from the towers of the Antonia."

"You can see nearly everything from up there. And what about Jesus? Of course you will have to give up any thought of seeing him."

"I will not promise to do it, but I will promise not to try to meet him in such a way as to compromise either my safety or your official position."

Watch your words, Claudia. Pilate must not learn that Joanna also said I could meet Jesus on the south side of the Temple at the Huldah Gate, near what they call the Teacher's Steps. She said this is a place where the rabbis and their disciples often linger and where people can ask them questions. Although the area is too congested for such activities during Passover, if I can catch Jesus when he comes out of the door, surely he will step aside and talk with me. I can disguise myself like one of my women servants and mingle with the crowd. Even pious Jews must break at noon. If I wait on the steps long enough, I am sure to meet Jesus there.

"I shall hold you to your word."

(...These promises are all the concessions I can expect from the daughter of the Claudians. And the chances she could arrange to see Jesus under such restrictive conditions are too remote to trouble me. I shall put this out of my mind. I have enough real problems without entertaining imaginary ones.)

"You can still give me a party Monday night, even though Jesus will not be coming."

"It will be more intimate with just the two of us. But I'll need some furnishings from the Herodian Palace. As I remember those quarters reserved for visitors at the Antonia, they lack a woman's touch."

"Naturally. The Antonia is a fortress, not a palace, and the official visitors who come don't usually bring their wives. Of course there are private baths, but not much else. Now I suppose Tribune Manlius's wife has fixed up the commander's suite...."

"But as we know, not the visitors' quarters. Pilate, in addition to the things for our party, we are going to need a few luxuries to make our lives more pleasant in those rather stark surroundings."

"You were here once before; you know what you're up against. Naturally there are no frills in a barracks. And the visitor's suite consists of only one bedroom and a dressing room and a general living-and-dining area. Of course there are servant's quarters. There is also a room which can serve both as an office and a place to receive formal calls. I am a soldier and I can live like this for a couple of weeks, but can you?"

"I think it will be rather pleasant, just you and I, living together in a few rooms like common people, not like the governor and his wife."

"I think I'll enjoy it too. But while I'm busy, what will you do with yourself all day?"

"I'm sure Manlius's wife will at least offer to entertain me. The poor thing must get fortress fever here without any other women to socialize with."

"Now don't forget your expressed purpose for coming to Jerusalem was to entertain your husband, not the tribune's wife."

"I won't. I promise you I'll devote myself to your comfort and convenience—to making our quarters more attractive and livable. I will arrange for an evening meal which will suit your tastes. I will spend a lot of time in the baths and on personal grooming—my hair and my wardrobe. If I have any extra time, I will go shopping and sightseeing downtown—perhaps with Manlius's wife—and an armed escort, of course. If there are any idle moments, I shall go up into the towers of the Antonia and watch what is going on in the streets of the city and in the Temple courts. And all day long I shall be waiting for you. My main assignment will be to make your evening hours enjoyable."

"That sounds too good to be true. I love you, Claudia, but sometimes I don't quite trust you. Don't misunderstand me—I trust your faithfulness to me—but after what happened when you were in Rome, I distrust your religious susceptibility and the extremes to which it may lead you."

"I love you too, Pilate, and because I do, you can trust me to do nothing that is not for your best interest. I may be a daughter of the Claudians, as you like to call me when I seem to cross your will, but first of all, I am your wife. Is this enough for you?"

"I know it will have to be enough...."

CHAPTER 11

At the Way Station

We are camped with all our own company and many fellow travelers at the way station in the Judean hills just beyond Beth-Horon. It is a half-day's journey from Jerusalem; we should be arriving there by early afternoon tomorrow. Pilate and I are in a little tent. We are wrapped up in blankets, but I can feel the cold ground through them. How I miss my bed! High in these hills it gets quite chilly at night even in late March. It has been a lonely trip today through nearly empty country. The thin rocky soil must not be good for much except raising sheep and goats. Even now, at the end of the rainy season, things look quite bleak. No trees on the hillsides, just a few around the watercourses in the valleys. I would not want to live here.

I think Pilate likes camping out. He says it is nice to see the stars, to feel the night air. Let him keep his tents, but give me a house! I can open the window and see the stars and feel the night air whenever I want to—and then I can settle back in my comfortable bed.

We are snuggling close together. Pilate makes some remark about Germanicus and Agrippina—how they slept in a tent for most of their married life and why they had nine children. I do not bother to remind him he has told me before how they usually lived in a fixed camp like a walled city with permanent buildings and spacious quarters for the general and his family. Pilate will stretch the truth to make a point. This is not a good time to question my husband's truthfulness.

Pilate is holding forth on his pet theory about the decline in the population of Rome, saying separate bedrooms among the upper classes tend to keep it down and sleeping in a tent, wrapped up in blankets, makes a couple more passionate and procreative. I don't know about him—but all it does for me is make me cold.

I say to Pilate, "Before you get any ideas, let's make one thing clear: When I snuggle up close to you, it's not because I'm so passionate, it's because I'm freezing. And sometimes I get tired of hearing about Germanicus and Agrippina. Now I have my own theory about their large family. The reason they had nine children was not because she was so fond of making love—it was those long winter nights in Germany. Those long cold winter nights in a flimsy little tent. There was nothing else to do and she wanted to get warm.

"But I am no Agrippina. When I make love, I want more than a blanket under me and a blanket over me. I want a bed and a roof. I would like a little luxury, if you please, in order to make the act a special occasion. And therefore you will have to wait until I fix up the rooms at the Antonia to suit my taste."

He says, "How long?"

I say, "Can you wait till Monday night?"

He says, "I think I can."

I say, "It's a promise. And now will you warm my feet?"

Poor Pilate, asleep beside me. I know I'm no Agrippina, and I have said so. I could not tell him he's no Germanicus either. He does not have the personality to make him a popular leader like his idol. He is too self-centered in his interests, too pompous in his bearing. He lacks the common touch. But he is a good man as men go. He is a good husband, and I believe he would make a good father. If only I could bear him one child—not nine, only one! He would be so proud, so happy....

On Monday before I prepare for our private dinner party, I am going to the south steps of the Temple to wait for Jesus. I am sure a touch from Jesus will change both our lives.

CHAPTER 12

A Complaining Camel and a Wild Ride

It is morning. I am standing outside our tent beside my husband. He is watching his orderlies oversee the break-up of our camp. Our party is not alone here at the way station. There are many people around us, all packing their gear and getting ready to leave. Pilate and I are the only two with the leisure to be observers.

"Oh, Pilate—look over there—if that isn't the funniest sight!"

"What are you talking about?"

"The camel over there—the man is making it kneel."

"What's so unusual? One sees it all the time."

"I've never really watched them do that before. First its front legs go down one at a time and then its hind legs. But it seems to have two joints in the upper part, and when it kneels, the legs bend first backward and then forward. Look, they are folding up, just like a campstool."

"Claudia, don't act like a child. And stay where you are—don't get any closer."

"I'm not afraid; you know, I get along well with animals."

"Horses are the only animals you are familiar with. And this is not a horse but a camel, an ugly beast with a most foul-smelling breath."

"I think it's so homely, it's cute. And a horse's breath isn't exactly attar of roses. Look, Pilate, how sweet! See how the thing is kneeling before its master."

"Sweet, my eye! Don't be deceived by that attitude of meekness. A camel has a nasty disposition, dangerous and unpredictable. A horse is intelligent and loyal to its master, but you can never trust a camel. It is likely to kick or bite at any time, with or without a cause."

"See, they're strapping those big bundles on the poor creature's back. They must be hurting it. Listen to it whine!"

"Camels often complain while they are being loaded. From listening to them, you would think someone was beating them. But once they get started, they bear their loads patiently."

"How can the animal get up with such a heavy burden?"

"I don't know, but camels are able to carry loads which weigh up to a thousand pounds."

"Don't they store food and water in those humps?"

"Yes, that's why they're called 'ships of the desert.' I must admit camels are useful beasts. But I don't like them and I don't trust them.... Look at the one they haven't loaded, moving in our direction. Get out of here, you! I don't want you nibbling on my tent ropes!"

"It was just eating grass."

"It was getting too close to our tent. You don't know these animals. They'll eat almost anything, and nothing seems to bother their digestion."

"But surely not *our tent*! Aren't you overreacting?"

"I've heard some kinds of camels will eat even leather and blankets, and I'm taking no chances. Get out of here, I say!"

"Pilate, don't get too close or the thing might bite you."

"Don't worry—I've learned my lesson. I want nothing to do with the beasts. Give me a horse every time...."

My husband pauses. I think he must be a little embarrassed because I have surprised him in such a violent reaction to a simple beast of burden.

"Claudia, I don't want you to think I'm afraid of the stupid thing. It's just that I try to stay clear of camels because I know they have a very unpleasant habit: They will spit on you. In fact, it once happened to me."

"You never told me about it."

"I was too embarrassed. It happened soon after our marriage, when you still thought I was perfect, and I didn't want to destroy your illusions."

"Well, go on. Now I know you aren't perfect, but I still love you."

"You remember how pleased I was when I got promoted to tribune soon after they transferred me to Syria?"

"You were prouder than when they made you governor of Judea."

"I was sure of myself and I wanted to impress my fellow officers. So I decided to learn to ride a camel; I thought it might prove useful if I should ever see duty in the Arabian Desert, and having such a skill would look good on my record. So I asked my fellows to set me up with some nomad who had a good steady camel. They set me up, all right!"

"Oh-oh!"

"I was expecting some beast who would plod along at a couple of miles per hour. How was I to know they had fixed me up with a racing camel capable of traveling a hundred miles in a single day? They had me completely fooled. They stood around with straight faces as I mounted. I was scarcely on my perch on the saddle on top of the hump, with the reins in my hand, when the camel's master whistled and the beast started off at a breakneck speed like an arrow shot from a bow."

"That must have been one exciting ride."

"Exciting is not the word for it. You have no conception of how a camel moves. It does not trot or gallop. It lumbers along like a pacing horse. The two legs on the same side of its body move forward at the same time—a most uncomfortable gait to a rider even when it is moving slowly. But this camel was running headlong, and I was lurching from side to side on the saddle on top of its hump."

"Doesn't sound like much fun."

"It wasn't. I felt like a sailor riding out a storm on the deck of a ship, with nothing secure to hold on to, afraid of being washed overboard at any minute. A really wild ride. At the outset, I had dropped the reins in surprise. I was clinging to the horn of the saddle, the only thing I could reach, and even that did not seem very secure. I was about to become violently ill."

"Poor dear!"

"Fortunately the nomad recognized my problem. He gave another shrill whistle. The beast slowed down and turned and shuffled back to him. It then knelt at his command, and I slipped out of the saddle."

"Be honest, Pilate—you fell out!"

"And I tried to reassume my dignity-until I saw the broad grins on the faces of my fellow tribunes."

"How embarrassing!"

"They were thoroughly enjoying my embarrassment. Well, I don't need to tell you how furious, how frustrated I was. I turned my back on the scoundrels and I walked around to the front of that wretched camel. At least I could glare at him and curse him to his face. He was rising slowly, bringing his head up to a level with mine. The beast gave me a supercilious stare, and would you believe it—he spat full in my face!"

"Ugh, how disgusting!"

"And dangerous. Camel saliva can blind a person. At least he missed my eyes, or I would have been in big trouble. I backed away fast, nearly knocking over one of the tribunes. They were practically doubled up with laughter by the time I had wiped my face clean of the foul-smelling stuff. Get the picture?"

"I can imagine how you must have felt, you with your precious dignity. But I can also imagine how funny you must have looked and how they must have relished the outcome of their little plot."

"Bet they're talking about it to this day."

"They probably do something similar with all the new tribunes—have to bring them down to earth, or they couldn't stand to live with them. But how did you handle the situation?"

"I tried to pass it off lightly. I swallowed my anger and my injured pride, and I never mentioned the incident again; but I never felt so friendly toward the other tribunes from that day onward, for they had made me a laughing stock. Now since then I have never liked camels."

"Do you know what your problem is, Pilate? You have no sense of humor."

"You're wrong. I like a good joke as much as anyone."

"But not when the joke is *on you*. If you could only take yourself less seriously, if you could only laugh at yourself when you are shown up in a ridiculous light! If you could have laughed along with your fellow tribunes, they would have slapped you on the back and called you a good fellow. You could have got rid of the pain of the embarrassment immediately, but here you have kept it bottled up inside yourself all these years...."

My poor Pilate! He definitely lacks the common touch.

CHAPTER 13

A Most Uneasy Seat

I have been thinking. Perhaps Claudia is right. Perhaps I do take myself too seriously. Perhaps I take everything too seriously. It makes me nervous to be surrounded by all these Jews even when I am in the midst of my cavalry unit. At this holiday time there are incidents all around us just waiting to happen, and any one of them could topple me from my uneasy seat.

The complaining camels are lumbering along far behind us. But I am still remembering that wild ride of mine and comparing that experience with what I am going through now. I am surrounded by Jews, people as unpredictable as any camel. I cannot understand their enthusiasms and their antipathies. I am unable to anticipate their behavior even after seven years. In a sense I am still riding a camel, holding on to the saddle for dear life. A treacherous camel who will throw you off and kick you or turn around and bite you if he can. At the very least, he will fix on you that idiotic stare of smug satisfaction—and spit in your eye. Just like these Jews, always complaining over minor matters, always superior to those who are trying to govern them, always unforeseeable in their moods and their reactions. To be governor of Judea is to be perched on a most uneasy seat.

What is the use of them anyway—Judea and the Jews? What is

good about them? I suppose Judea is useful as a buffer between Syria and Egypt. Yet neither of them has ever given Rome as much trouble as Judea has in the last hundred years. But they are survivors—both the Jews and the camels are survivors. They have been able to survive under conditions which would have destroyed other breeds. They have even prospered, Jews and camels. Rulers and riders will come and go, but they will both outlast us. Who knows? Perhaps they will even outlast Rome.

But I must try to hold my place in the saddle just a little longer. This time in Jerusalem I must keep control—I must not drop the reins. In a year or two Tiberius is sure to die. When Caius becomes our next emperor, perhaps I shall be recalled and given a better assignment.

CHAPTER 14

A Singing Serpent

I am running over in my mind the things I shall have to do this week before the Passover Feast starts at sundown Friday night. I must firm up security in the Antonia and throughout the city. I must double the guards in the precincts of the Temple. I must contact Caiaphas and remind him that Rome has authority in capital cases lest he take it upon himself in the matter of Jesus. At the same time I must reassure him that I will not intervene in purely religious affairs. I must try the court cases which have accumulated since my last visit here. I must meet with my tax collectors for Judea, the greedy lot, and make sure Rome gets its legitimate share out of what they exact from the people. If they were not protected by law in what they do, I would make these publicans change their grasping ways.

And somehow I must think of a way to placate Herod. How shortsighted I was to turn him against me in the business of the gilded shields! I did not think he would run to Tiberius and tell him how I do not understand the Jews or respect their ancient customs. And through all of this I must get my food and rest, for I must keep alert. Trouble could break out at any time, not just during working hours. I must stay ready.

The closer we get to the city, the tenser I become. I am unable to carry on a conversation with Claudia. She seems to sense this and she says nothing to distract me. Unlike me, she enjoys crowds. She likes to look at everything around her, the landscape, the buildings, the people and their animals and their vehicles. She is almost like a child. The roadway never gets too congested or the going too slow for her. But as for me, I am impatient to get to our destination. I want to arrive and do what I have to do and return to Caesarea. Time will go faster with Claudia at my side. She will brighten up the Antonia and enliven my off-duty hours. She will be safe enough inside the fortress. If only I could be sure she will keep her promise....

Pilate and I are pausing on a ridge to the north of Jerusalem, looking down at the city. It is like standing on the rim of a big bowl full of lesser hills and valleys. Jerusalem clings to their slopes. Compared with Rome, this city is small, and its public buildings, though impressive, are but few. There is only one Temple—but then, the Jews have only one God. The Temple and the Antonia Fortress are clearly visible on an eminence in the northeast, on the far side of the bowl.

"Look, Pilate, they're praying!"

"As if I couldn't hear them! Just the sight of their Temple throws these Jews into a religious frenzy. But let me enjoy this view in my own way."

Beyond the Temple and the fortress, the Kidron Valley and the Mount of Olives. On the near side, I look down at the stately Herodian Palace and the Western Gate through which we shall enter the city. Where the hills surrounding the city are bare of trees, they are dotted with the tents and makeshift shelters of thousands of pilgrims. How many of them are fanatical enough to start an uprising? How many are armed? Impossible to tell....

Claudia grabs my arm, startling me.

"What is it, Claudia?"

"Pilate! Across the city, on the Mount of Olives—what is that thing coming down the hillside? It looks like a long green snake."

"Must be a procession of some sort. The undulating green effect is probably created by people waving branches of trees."

"I think I can hear them miles away. They seem to be chanting something. How strange—a singing serpent. A swaying, singing serpent. What do you think it all means?"

"It means my wife has a very active imagination. How could you hear such a thing, as far away as the Mount is and as much noise as these pilgrims are making?"

"Pilate, I don't know how I can hear them, yet I know they are singing."

"You may just be right. I don't know what it means, but I intend to find out. It could be a harmless band of pilgrims singing holiday songs. Or it could be an organized demonstration of a political sort—something I need to become aware of."

"Do you think it might possibly be Jesus and his disciples arriving on the other side of the city?"

"If he has been hiding out in the Judean wilderness, that might well be. We will find out soon enough."

"I promise to be quiet and not bother you again...."

Jerusalem, the Holy City! At last I am going to be really near the glorious Temple although I may not enter it. Bless the Antonia Fortress, as many times as I have cursed it for its ugliness. I know it is useful, but unlike Pilate, I cannot bring myself to call it beautiful. For once I am glad to see those foursquare towers. From their height, I know I shall be able to see everything which goes on in the courts of the Temple below me. And I hope that tomorrow, on the south steps beside the Huldah Gates, I shall see Jesus....

So many people lining the streets, watching us pass. What must they think of us? They show no open reaction except curiosity. So many children clinging to their mothers' skirts, their dark eyes big with wonder at the sight of our company. I would give all I have for one such child of my own. Yet according to Joanna, Jesus never asks for a reward when he performs his healing miracles. He is not like those lying priests of Isis....

When we passed the governor's palace, I felt no twinges of regret at leaving behind us those spacious halls with their lavish decorations, those gardens with their deep canals and bronze statues spouting water into the pools. They no longer entice me, for my heart is set on reaching the Antonia Fortress. I will cheerfully endure the cramped conditions, the sight and the sound and the smell of the barracks and the stables, in order to meet Jesus.

Jerusalem—Joanna says the name means the City of Peace. For me this year it shall be the City of Hope.

Part III

Promise and Compromise

Table of Contents

Chapter	1	Two Views and a Sudden Stampede	165
Chapter	2	The Promise Given	171
Chapter	3	Last Minute Preparations	181
Chapter	4	A Busy Day	185
Chapter	5	A Private Dinner Party	187
Chapter	6	A Reformed Tax Collector and Some Unanswered Questions	195
Chapter	7	A Night of Interrogation	199
Chapter	8	The Glorious Vision	205
Chapter	9	The Gloomy Prediction	207
Chapter	10	Table Talk	211
Chapter	11	Stones and Blood	215
Chapter	12	Up from the Baths	217
Chapter	13	A Late Visitor	219
Chapter	14	The Interrupted Proceedings	223
Chapter	15	A Most Unlikely King	227
Chapter	16	A Man Who Wants to Die and My Attempts to Save Him	229
Chapter	17	The Unfinished Dream	233
Chapter	18	A Scheme that Fails	235
Chapter	19	The Whipping Post	237
Chapter	20	The Sight of Blood	239
Chapter	21	A God With Knobby Knees	241
Chapter	22	I Wash My Hands	245

CHAPTER 1

Two Views and a Sudden Stampede

It is just before sunset on Sunday, the day of our arrival. Pilate and are going up into the southeast tower of the Antonia Fortress. We are accompanied by its commander, Tribune Manlius, and his wife Aemilia. They have just served us a very nice supper in their apartment.

They will be leaving for Caesarea tomorrow with half of the old Jerusalem Cohort. After six bleak months in Jerusalem, they'll be eager to see the coast again. My husband will literally hold down the fort until Tribune Florus comes from Caesarea to replace him with the other half of the summer Jerusalem Cohort. Because nearly three hundred soldiers will be en route most of the time, our forces in both cities will be somewhat depleted for a few days.

Pilate says it doesn't matter so much about Caesarea because all the troublemakers (he means the Jews) will be in Jerusalem for Passover. But even when half the Caesarean Cohort is gone, there is always half of the Italian Band, as we call the regiment of crack troops from the peninsula which the emperor has put at Pilate's disposal. The other half is deployed at Sebaste.

Although the tribune must remember our brief and disastrous visit here two years ago as well as I do, he is taking us around the Antonia as if we were seeing it for the first time. (For any practical purpose, it is the first time for me; all I can remember from that other occasion is bad stuff which I'm trying to forget.)

Manlius is showing us the view from this high point in the Holy City. Pilate insists on calling my attention to the fortress which will be my home for several weeks, but I am much more interested in the Temple at my back than I am in the fortress all around me.

I listen politely for the sake of our host and hostess, and I make suitable comments. The Antonia is a square fortress, more functional than ornamental, which is probably why Pilate considers it beautiful. A central wing bisects it, thus forming two courtyards. In the lower floor of this wing are administrative offices, the guardroom, and a long hall where Pilate will try his cases. In the second story are the visitors' quarters, where we will be staying. The commander's private rooms, where we ate, are built on the side of the fortress which is adjacent to the Temple. Unfortunately his apartment has no windows on that side—a lost opportunity for a wonderful view. The Jerusalem Cohort is quartered in rooms built into the surrounding walls.

I am looking down at the two cloistered courtyards, which are teeming with activity. The front one opens westward on the city through gates approached by a broad staircase. Manlius is telling me how the pavement of this courtyard is called the *Lithostratos* because it is paved with stone; under it there is a huge cistern which provides ample water for the fortress. Much water is needed to supply a cohort and a cavalry unit. The rear courtyard contains the stables, workshops, and storage areas.

I am more interested in people than I am in places, particularly such military arrangements. Tribune Manlius is a middle-aged man with a square jaw. The lines in his lower face make him look rather like a walnut. He tries to conceal his receding hairline by combing his side hair across his forehead and plastering it down with oil. In my opinion, because such a hairstyle isn't in fashion, this makes his hair loss more noticeable. (My husband has the barber comb his back hair fashionably forward so as to cover the thin spot on his crown—but I can see through the strands.) The vanity of these men! They are fooling only themselves.

Manlius is apologizing for the aspects of castle life which may be offensive to a lady. I assume he means the sounds and smells of several hundred horses nearby. I'm looking at his wife, wondering how she has been able to stand it here for six months. Aemilia is a dainty little woman past her prime, but she must have been pretty when she was young. She has a lot of loose skin hanging under her chin and a lot of tight curls piled on top of her head. Her nostrils seem to be drawn up in a permanent sniff of distaste—no wonder!

Manlius expresses regret for the limited guest accommodations. He offers to move out of his apartment so we can use it during our stay. I tell him and Aemilia that after camping out, this will seem like a palace to me. I wouldn't think of putting them out of their own quarters on their last night here. Moreover, Tribune Florus will soon be moving into the commander's suite. I do ask Manlius for a few things to fix up the guestrooms. He tells me he will put a detail of men at my disposal before he leaves in the morning. They will go to the Herodian Palace and bring back anything I need to make the quarters more comfortable. I compliment the pair on the huge baked fish which they served us at dinner.

"Aemilia, it was simply delicious. Where did it come from?"

"From the Sea of Galilee. Such fish are very popular in Jerusalem, especially for the Sabbath meal."

Her husband adds, "The cook in charge of the officer's mess will be at your disposal, Lady Claudia. He will work with you and your household staff."

"Thank you for your thoughtfulness, Tribune. I shall contact him early tomorrow morning."

We look eastward. On our right we see the northern wall of the Temple Mount. Manlius says the gate in this wall is called the Tadi Gate. It has over it two stones leaning one against the other. The massive eastern wall of the Temple Mount forms part of the city wall. In the area just outside the wall are a sheep market and a pool where they wash the sheep. I comment on how the setting sun makes it look like a pool of blood. The tribune remarks that this week the market will be full of sheep for the sacrifices, but the pools of blood will be in the Temple.

We turn around, facing the Temple, as I have been wanting to do ever since we climbed the tower. The scene is breath-taking, gorgeous.

The Temple rises like an earthly extension of the sunset clouds, its summits all afire with red and gold. Though words fail me, I cannot help exclaiming at the beauty of the sight. I remark prosaically that the Antonia Fortress, as compared with the adjoining Temple Mount, stands up like a little thumb on a huge extended hand. Pilate reminds me that as small as it seems, the thumb controls the hand. And he also reminds me of my promise not to try to enter the Temple.

Manlius says, "Your Excellency, Lady Claudia would be perfectly safe in the outer court, which they call the Court of the Gentiles."

Pilate answers, "Not if there are disturbances like the one this afternoon."

This is the first I have heard of such a disturbance in the Temple. I ask for particulars. The tribune tells me how in mid-afternoon, not long after our arrival, one of his watchmen on the wall of the Antonia detected a commotion in the Court of the Gentiles. He promptly dispatched a detail to investigate the incident. The officer in charge reported back to him within the hour. Apparently the disturbance was over almost as soon as it started. I ask him what happened.

Tribune Manlius says, "It was this prophet, Jesus of Nazareth. He and his followers had just arrived in the city, and they were making a tour of the Temple. Apparently he was disgusted by the commercialism in the outer court, and he decided to clean it up all by himself. So he got rid of the merchants and the money-changers."

"All by himself? How did he ever do it?"

"He made a whip out of rope and drove out the lot of them with their sheep and their oxen. He spilled the coins of the money-changers on the ground and overturned their tables. And he stopped everyone from bringing loads of merchandise into the Temple. He told those who sold the pigeons to take their things away and to stop making God's house a house of trade. By the time our detail got there, the Temple courtyard was peaceful, quiet, and very clean."

Pilate says, "You made no arrest?"

Manlius explains, "There was no need to. Besides, Caiaphas is in charge, and he has his Temple police. Apparently he chose to let the incident pass unchallenged."

My husband chuckles, "I wish I could have seen it. I wish I could have seen those coins rolling and those money-grubbers ducking and scrambling to get out of the way of Jesus' whip. I wish I could have seen the faces of the chief priests when they realized their profitable business had been broken up. Claudia, I think we should give your Jesus a medal instead of arresting him."

I ask, "Why do you think Caiaphas didn't arrest Jesus? You say he has just been waiting for an opportunity."

Pilate answers, "Probably he was afraid to because of the people, who consider Jesus to be a prophet. The sudden stampede could have turned into a full-scale riot which Rome would have had to put down. That is the last thing Caiaphas wants. So he will bide his time and wait for a less public occasion to arrest Jesus. What do you think, Manlius?"

The tribune agrees. Then I ask him if he considers the Temple precincts safe for me to visit. He says any time I want to go there, the officer in charge will furnish me with an armed guard. I thank him. I reassure Pilate that I will not compromise him, and he need not worry about me. I will not try to enter the Temple itself.

CHAPTER 2

The Promise Given

It is now Monday, late morning. I have been up for hours making arrangements and giving orders so that everything will be ready for tonight's private party. At last I can slip away with my favorite maids, Hannah and Eunice. We are going to meet Jesus on the south steps of the Temple. Joanna told me in her latest letter how to recognize him:

"He is a man in his mid-thirties, taller than the average Jew. Erect bearing, slender build, commanding presence. Medium complexion. Shoulder-length hair, dark brown and parted in the middle. Short beard, the same."

She went on to say my Hannah will be able to pick out Jesus and his disciples by the way they dress and talk. And Hannah can translate if they speak their native Aramaic. However, they all know Greek because of the presence of so many Gentiles in Galilee.

I have promised my husband not to compromise him, so I disguise myself as a Jewish woman. First I take off all my facial make-up. I borrow a robe and a mantle from Hannah. She helps me put on the costume, complete with head veil and sandals. She reminds me to remove my jewelry.

We wait in the front courtyard of the Antonia Fortress until it is nearly noon, the time for the changing of the Roman guard in the Temple precincts. A whole century of soldiers is about to leave in smaller groups of eight. Eunice speaks to the centurion in charge. She tells him we three are Lady Claudia's women, and she wants them to escort us to the Huldah Gates.

He tells her he will order his men to look after us. We set off between two groups of soldiers, walking briskly to keep pace with them.

I'm sure they are giving us a quick look askance. But how much can they see? Just a female figure veiled to the eyes, accompanied by a little old woman and a pretty young one—the last, the only one worthy of a second glance. Certainly nothing which would expose my identity.

In less than ten minutes we reach the south steps of the Temple. Again Eunice speaks briefly with the soldiers. Then the troops disperse and leave us.

When Eunice comes back, she tells us if we want to return to the Antonia within the hour, we can accompany the unit which they are now relieving. The men who will be going off duty will be congregating in the square below us near the tomb of the Prophetess Huldah. She points out this monument. She explains how since the members of the old century are deployed throughout the whole area, it will take time for them to be relieved and then congregate and regroup in the square. Therefore if we watch carefully, we can fall in with the troops returning to the Antonia. Now we have made the necessary arrangements, all we have to do is wait for Jesus.

We three climb the broad stairway leading up to the Huldah Gate in the massive south wall of the Temple. There are actually two doors and two huge staircases separated by a cliff-like continuation of what I visualize as the plateau at the top. We go up the staircase by which people enter, and we walk across this platform toward the door by which people are exiting. We are standing in the relatively open area between the entrance and the exit doors.

I am too excited to focus my attention on anything else but the people who are issuing from the doorway. I suppose most of them are Jewish, but I never realized before that Jews could look so different—in the color of the skin, the cut of the hair and beard, in their clothing—or that they could sound so different. I hear a dozen languages I do not know and only one familiar tongue, the common Greek.

Suddenly I am not so sure I shall recognize Jesus when he comes out, if he does come out. He may have left early before our arrival. And even if he does come out, how will I get to him in this crowd? How will I be able to detain him for long enough to tell him of my need, or for him to meet my need? The steady stream of people issuing forth is like a tide which pushes everything before it. And for that matter, in all the noise of the multitude, how will he be able to hear me—or I, him? I feel over-heated, half-stifled with the mantle and the veil wrapped around my face and neck. In addition to the brisk walk and the climb up the stairway, my nervousness is making me hot and faint.

I tell Eunice, "I must sit down."

She says, "Keep up your courage and lean on me."

A band of countrymen attract my attention as they burst out of the gate. They are clustering protectively around a tall silent man in their midst. I hear a babble of excited voices.

Hannah touches my sleeve. She says, "These men are Galileans—I recognize their accent."

I say, "The tall one in the middle could be Jesus. If he says anything, please translate."

She answers, "I will, but so far, he has said nothing; and if he did, I would not be able to understand him because of all the commotion around him."

She is right about the commotion. I remember Joanna telling me that wherever Jesus goes, he stirs up a controversy. There is a difference in those closest to the tall man and those on the fringes of the group who are trying to get closer to him. From their dress and bearing, they seem to be city dwellers, perhaps religious leaders. They are either arguing loudly or muttering in muffled tones and making threatening gestures. The tall man does not seem to notice them any more than he would the honkings of a gaggle of angry geese, but his followers do, and they try to shield him from them. Realizing that they are being ignored and left behind, the angry huddle breaks up harmlessly with a shrug of the shoulders and a lifting up of hands and eyebrows.

When the tall man's followers see he is no longer being pursued, they slow down and change their direction. Instead of going down the staircase, they move with their leader out onto the projection like a promontory, the extension of my plateau. Apparently they too want to talk to him apart in a quieter place. Those closest to the man who we think is Jesus start to ask him questions.

My women and I have moved out with the men onto what I call the cliff. The farther out we go, the more the noise decreases as we distance ourselves from the descending and ascending streams of humanity on either side. We do not move so close as to be obtrusive, only close enough to overhear what is being said. I pull Hannah's sleeve; she knows what I want.

"Mistress, they are saying they don't understand the story he just told inside the Temple. Evidently the chief priests and the Pharisees understood because they got so furious that they acted as though they wanted to seize him."

The tall man is standing by the low wall at the edge of the platform. By this time he has turned around and is facing his disciples. He motions to them to sit down. He must see this as an opportunity for an expanded teaching session. He is bound to be aware of us three women, especially when we move in close so Hannah can hear better, but he gives no sign of such an awareness.

Hannah is translating now.

"You don't understand the parable of the vineyard?" The tall man shakes his head and sighs. "How is it that the chief priests, the scribes, and the Pharisees all understand perfectly well, but you do not? The Lord is the landowner who planted the vineyard, and Israel is the vineyard."

It helps Hannah translate because he pauses frequently as if waiting for his disciples to ask questions.

"The tenant farmers to whom he leases the vineyard are the chief priests and the rulers. When the landowner goes away, he sends his servants at the time of the harvest to collect his share of the grapes. The landowner's servants are the Lord's prophets. The tenants beat, kill, and stone them. When he sends a larger group, they do the same. Finally the owner (that is, the Lord) sends his son to them, thinking they will surely respect him...."

The man pauses and looks around at his followers. They say nothing. He asks them, "Who is the owner's son?"

One ventures hesitantly, "Is it you, Master?"

He answers, "Yes, mark my words: It is I, Jesus of Nazareth, the Son of man."

I clutch Hannah's sleeve compulsively. Eunice gives my other hand a squeeze.

The man who calls himself Jesus the Son of man keeps talking. He says, "But when the tenants—that is, the chief priests and rulers—see the son arriving, they say among themselves, 'Here comes the heir to this estate; come on, let's kill him and get it for ourselves.' So they drag him out of the vineyard and kill him."

Jesus looks around at his men, inviting some response, but they seem reluctant to question him.

Jesus resumes. He says to them, "Do you understand what I am saying? This is what they are going to do to me, the Son of man. You remember, at this point I broke off my story and turned to the chief priests and the Pharisees. You saw their sullen looks when I asked them what the owner of the vineyard would do. And what did they answer?"

One of the disciples says, "They replied that he will put the wicked men to a horrible death and lease the vineyard to others who will pay him promptly."

Jesus says, "They convicted themselves out of their own mouths. They understood well enough that I was speaking about them; why can't you understand? Didn't you see how enraged they became when I quoted from the Holy Scriptures: 'The very stone which the builders rejected has become the head of the corner; this was the Lord's doing, and it is marvelous in our eyes?'"

All of a sudden I can recognize the words Jesus is saying. It is because he is now using the common Greek. I remember Hannah telling me how since Hebrew is nowadays the language of the learned and not easily understood by the common people (in particular, those who live among Gentiles) many Jews read their Scriptures in a Greek translation.

Jesus continues in the Greek. "Everyone who falls on that stone will be broken to pieces; but when it falls on anyone, it will crush him."

I understand Jesus is applying the sacred writings to himself. He is the stone of which he is speaking. The men who were chasing after him angrily are some of those on whom the stone will fall. Jesus lapses again into Aramaic. Again I have to rely on Hannah's translation.

He says, "Now do you understand why they wanted to seize me?"

A burly man blurts out, "Master, we would have fought for you if they had tried to touch you."

Jesus replies, "They knew it, and they knew many people would have joined you. That is the only reason they did not seize me when I said to them, 'Therefore I tell you, the kingdom of God will be taken away from you and given to a nation producing the fruits of it.' But they will not give up so easily. You saw how they pursued us as far as the gate. Here in this public place they will make no trouble. But tomorrow, or the next day or the next, they will seize the shepherd on the hillside and carry him away while his flock is sleeping...."

Jesus stops talking. He seems sad and abstracted. He stands looking off across the Kidron Valley at the green slopes of the Mount of Olives. His followers grow silent and reflective. They seem afraid to question him. Jesus starts to move as though he is about to leave. His followers rise to their feet, facing us women. I realize that if I do not act now, I may never again have the chance to speak to him. I push myself forward.

I say in Greek to one of his men, "Sir, I must talk to Jesus."

He leads me through the semicircle, which parts to receive me. I am standing between the men and Jesus, looking up into his face. I can see all of his features, but he can see only my eyes. It is as though we are on a promontory rising above the sea, high and apart from the restless multitude below us. Jesus and I are standing on a cliff of quietness in the midst of a sea of murmuring sound. It is as though I am alone with Jesus, out of all the world. And even before he speaks, I know I have nothing to fear. His eyes reassure me.

I hear the voice of his disciple saying, as if from a long way off, "Master, here is a woman who wants to talk to you."

For a moment we study each other. I wonder if this man who can foresee the future sees more of me than my eyes. I see a long serious face, strong yet sensitive. Although there are lines of frowning in his brow, I think I can detect the signs of smiling around his eyes and mouth. Whatever his lips may say, I will trust his eyes. They seem wonderfully kind and understanding.

Jesus addresses me in Greek. He says, "Woman, what do you want me to do for you?"

Suddenly I feel at perfect ease. I have rehearsed this scene in my mind so many times. I say to him, "Sir, I am unable to bear children. Can you heal my barrenness?"

Jesus answers sharply, "*If* I can! Do you believe I can?"

With an imploring gesture, I lift my eyes to his. I say, "Sir, I believe you can do anything."

He pauses, fingering his beard. Why this hesitation? My heart is beating so hard I am sure he can hear it.

"Woman, I must tell you that I was sent to the lost sheep of Israel and not to the barren ewes of Rome."

He has seen through my disguise—he must know who I am. I drop to my knees before him. "Please, sir! The gods of my people can do nothing for me. You are my only hope."

His eyes are glistening. He covers his face with his hand as if trying to shut out what is going on around him. I wonder what he is thinking. Perhaps he is praying silently. Perhaps he is receiving a message from his God. The tension I feel is almost unbearable. Now his hand drops to his side.

Jesus says to me, "Woman, I have asked my Father, and though the time of the Gentiles has not yet come, you shall have your request."

I am speechless with joy. I embrace his legs.

He goes on, "I promise you—a year from this day, you shall bear a son...." He pauses and searches my eyes as if he expects a strong reaction. He gets it.

Can what happened before in Rome be happening again here in Jerusalem? A year from this day! Why could he not say nine months or fourteen months from today? This "year from today" sounds like the all-too-familiar pattern of deception. First came the awful doubt. Now the heat of indignation starts to rise within me. What right does this man have to play such games with *me*, a daughter of the noble Claudians, the wife of the governor of Judea?

Jesus says, "Do you really believe? You cannot receive from God unless you believe. Everything depends on your faith in me and my words."

Jesus knows what I have done. Can he read my heart? If so, he knows my present doubt, my injured pride and my indignation. He must know about Rome and the priest of Isis, and he is testing me to see if my faith will stand. I flush to the roots of my hair as I answer meekly, "I believe in the God of Israel, the God of power. He is the only real God. The gods of the nations are only idols. They cannot answer prayer, and I repent of seeking after them."

The sternness of Jesus' brow melts away, and I think I can see the beginning of a twinkle in his eyes. A smile starts to curl the corners of his mouth. He says, "Be it done to you according to your faith. And let your son be called 'a gift from God.'"

My gratitude is too deep for mere words. I kiss his feet more ardently than I have ever kissed an idol's feet. (His feet—they smell like perfume. Am I imagining this in my deep emotion?) Jesus reaches down to me. He takes me by the hand and he lifts me up. My veil has fallen loosely around my neck, and he can see my whole face. What does it matter now? For he has seen my heart. Jesus understands the deepest needs of a woman, so he is truly the Son of man. And I believe he can fulfill his promise, which means he is truly the Son of God. I grip his hand tightly.

I exclaim with tears of joy, "What can I do to thank you?"

"Do not thank me—thank the God of Israel and worship him only. And now, go in peace." He withdraws his hand from mine.

Jesus motions to his disciples, and the band moves past us women, back toward the main platform and the staircase for descent. They move down the steps. I go to my servants, who are bubbling with excitement. They want to know what has happened. I make them swear an oath of secrecy before I will tell them anything, for Pilate must not learn what went on here. I shudder to think of what he might do if he should hear what Jesus promised me. He would be sure to associate Jesus' words with the lying words of that priest of Isis. And if Jesus should have to stand before Pilate, he would deal with him very harshly.

My maids have remembered what I have completely forgotten— the return of the off-duty unit to the Antonia. They point out the glint of spears and helmets in the square below. We go down the broad staircase and then continue toward a smaller one directly in front of us. We descend to the pavement around the Huldah Monument. Eunice speaks to the officer in charge, and soon we are walking back to the fortress under military escort.

It is now a little past noon. I find it hard to believe my life has changed so much in such a short time. I now have hope. Yes, Jesus has given me his promise, and I now have hope.

CHAPTER 3

Last Minute Preparations

Once back in the Antonia, I find my staff hard at work in the apartment. I dispatch Eunice to the kitchen to check with the cook about tonight's special meal. I send Hannah to my dressing room to lay out my party clothing, my make-up and my ornaments. Then I look around me.

The large living room is starting to appear much more livable. The once-bare walls are now decorated with rich hangings and there are costly lamp stands that will furnish beauty as well as light. There are bright-colored cushions and lavish drapes on the couches which surround the table on three sides. It is laid with the finest tableware, brought from the Herodian Palace. In the four corners of the room are huge ornamental vases. I decide they need a touch of living beauty. So I send out servants to cut some branches from the almond trees, now white with blossoms.

Eunice returns to tell me the meal will be ready to serve any time after three o'clock. I do not expect my husband before that time. When he stops work, he will go to the baths before he comes up for supper. As soon as I arrange these flowering branches, I must bathe myself. Fortunately there is a private facility here which the commander's lady shares with any female guests.

Eunice may be shriveling up and getting a bit deaf, but she is as curious and as outspoken as ever. (Pilate calls it "nosy and meddlesome.") Of course, as my old nurse, teacher, and companion since my childhood days, she stands—or thinks she stands—in the place of my mother. So I ask her advice (which she is sure to give me even without my asking) on a most important matter: What I should tell Pilate about today's proceedings.

She says dryly, "Why tell him anything at all?"

I answer, "But when he sees me so excited, he is bound to suspect something."

Moving closer, she says in a confidential tone, "You have promised him a private party. Men are so conceited that he'll think your excitement is aroused by his masculine attractiveness."

Hannah is standing by with the boxes which contain my toilet articles and my make-up. I will need her services after the bath as much as I did this morning on arising. Out of consideration for her modesty as an unmarried Jewish girl, I lower my voice.

I say to Eunice, "But sooner or later, I am going to have to tell him about the promise, if I can do so without involving Jesus. I must not involve Jesus. You know how Pilate feels about the Jews and the Jewish God. If he should learn Jesus has made me the very same promise as that lying priest of Isis, there is no telling what my husband might do to Jesus."

Eunice suggests, "Just tell him you want to get pregnant. Men like to think there is nothing they can't accomplish sexually. Think of how it will flatter his male ego to think he has done it at his age."

I reply, "After ten years of marriage? Pilate is not so easily duped. If he hasn't been able to make me pregnant in that time, it will not just happen now. It will take a miracle. I shall have to tell him, and the longer I wait, the harder it will be. I must tell him tonight."

She asks, "How will you do it?"

I answer, "I will play it by ear. After all, Pilate is a man, and I am a woman and a daughter of the Claudians. I will find a way."

Eunice says nothing further; in her place, she knows how far she can go and where her limits are. Making disapproving noises, she bustles off toward the inner room.

A little later, on the way to the baths, I discuss with Hannah the clothing she has laid out for me to change into when I return to the apartment: My gown of the finest muslin with the gold border on the hem. (I know better than to talk about the reason for this gala occasion; I confine my remarks to what I want her to do.)

"For jewelry, what do you think about the gold bracelets and the collar and earrings Pilate gave me on my last birthday?"

"That will be perfect, Mistress."

"And to complete my outfit with a royal flourish, I'll throw over my shoulders the shawl I bought in Rome...You did lay that out for me?"

"Yes, Mistress Claudia."

"You know it is pure silk, imported from far-away China?"

"Yes, Mistress, I believe you've already told me about that."

"Silks are all the rage in Rome because they look and feel so good and they drape so well."

"I love to look at your new shawl, to feel of it—the red silk embroidered in gold. I think it's just the most beautiful thing I have ever seen."

"It is as spectacular in its way as last night's sunset. I have been saving it for a special occasion like this...."

"Yes, Mistress?"

I decide against saying any more, although I feel sure that our innocent Hannah knows more than she lets on about what happens in the bedroom.

"Oh, I want you to fix my hair the way Pilate likes it best—you know, the natural look. You have the knack of making your art look artless."

"Why, thank you, Mistress Claudia."

"Nothing fancy which will require your services at bedtime. You do understand?"

"Yes, Mistress, *I understand.*" She giggles.

We enter the women's bathhouse.

Whether or not Hannah strained her ears to catch the previous conversation, she knows what's going on. I remember how I was ten years ago, when *I* was her age. Unmarried Roman girls, at least those of good family, aren't supposed to know these things either. Now I may not have known much, but I daydreamed a lot.

CHAPTER 4

A Busy Day

Monday I get up shortly after dawn without disturbing Claudia. Dressing for informal occasions here in the provinces is just a matter of putting on my shoes; today it is less quickly accomplished because as the presiding magistrate over the Jerusalem tribunal, I must wear the obligatory toga in place of a lighter and more manageable cloak. It is the adjustment of this garment which takes the most time. My barber combs my hair carefully over the thin spot on my crown and pomades it with olive oil. My shave will wait until the afternoon when I go to the baths....

Breakfast as usual, a glass of water and a piece of bread. By eight o'clock I am busy down below in the hall of justice, installed in my magistrate's chair. The cases here in Jerusalem are mostly petty stuff which the Jews themselves can handle. But according to our law, only Rome can carry out a sentence of death, and so whenever I come to the city for the great feasts, for the first few days I have a full docket of capital cases. They usually consist of highway robbers and occasionally some disgruntled Jew who has staged a riot and killed someone. To my knowledge, the only big case coming up is one of Jesus Barabbas, which I have scheduled for next week after the Passover.

Of course there is the matter of Jesus of Nazareth. After what happened yesterday in the Temple, it may well become a case. Poor Caiaphas, poor Annas! (As his father-in-law and the former High Priest, that man controls him—and through him, the entire religious establishment.) Ha! It must have hurt them in their most tender part—their purses—when the shekels rolled, the pigeons flew away, and the sheep were scattered. They must get immensely wealthy from the profit of this one Temple concession. If I know them, they will get their man, by fair means or foul. Their activities will bear watching....

So there goes my morning. Lunch is just a light snack which I pick up while going over the briefs for the cases that will come up in the afternoon session. At forty-four a man must watch his waistline. I must look like the soldier I used to be if I wish to impress these provincials. After all, I represent Rome. Supper will be my one big meal. A pleasant supper with Claudia, a little wine for the digestion, a good night's sleep—all this to look forward to....

Now that the session is over and I'm in the baths, I find myself thinking of my wife and the diversion she has promised me tonight. What will she do this time before we end up in bed together? The minx always keeps me guessing; it is one of her charms....

CHAPTER 5

A Private Dinner Party

When I come out of the baths, I notice it is nearly five by the water clock in the outer courtyard of the Antonia. I waste no time in going upstairs to the guest quarters. I feel like a different man after I have been duly bathed, anointed, massaged, and shaved. When I step through the door of the largest room, I stop short in my tracks. Enticing sounds, smells, and sights assail my senses. Is this a military barracks or some eastern monarch's harem? When I hesitate, Claudia takes me by the arm and leads me inside. She is looking wonderful and she knows it, for she simpers like a schoolgirl when I ask her if tonight we are playing Caesar and Cleopatra or Ulysses and Circe.

She says, "Wait and see. Do you like what I've done with the room?"

I say, "You've made a palace out of a plain fortress in just a few hours. It must be magic, and you must be a sorceress. What kind of beast are you going to turn me into?"

She says, "Wait and see."

She seats me at the table, on the couch which faces the longest side. I prepare to recline on the middle one of the three sections. She insists on helping me take off my cloak and she removes my sandals. When I protest, she says she is my slave girl tonight and will meet all my needs. She helps me to get comfortable on the couch, lying on my left side, propped up with my left elbow on the cushion of the fulcrum—the head—which rises a few inches above the level of the table. The only civilized way for a man to eat is to recline on the graceful upward curve of the Roman *triclinium*, shaped like a wave which is about to break.

I ask her, "Where are the musicians and the Gaditanas?"

She laughs, "Oh, you mean those seductive Spanish dancing girls. I'll see what I can do. But I have already planned for music."

She rings for the servants. They bring in various courses, hot and cold, and leave them on the table. She dismisses them for the evening, telling them that she herself will serve me. They disappear and I do not see them again. She takes her place on the serving side of the table, and she reaches across to pour wine in my cup. The light from the lamp stand sets afire her jewels; it makes a shimmering wonder of the red-and-gold shawl she is wearing. I ask her what it is made of. She tells me it is silk, that exotic fabric from the orient.

I say, "Does it come from a plant or an animal?"

She says, "In Rome it's common knowledge that silk comes from a certain tree which grows only in China."

I remind her of what Philo said about how common knowledge frequently turns out to have been common ignorance where we Romans are concerned. I ask her with mock seriousness, "Would you be so proud of your new shawl if you found out it was made of strands spun from the gut of spiders?"

"Ugh! Of course not." She shudders. After a brief pause, she laughs and says, "You made it all up, didn't you? I know you're teasing because if you were serious, you wouldn't be feeling of my shawl like this."

I ask her, "What did you have to pay for it?"

She says, "Too much—I suppose that's why they call silk "the cloth of kings."

I stroke and admire the rich folds falling from her extended arm. I say, "Well, it makes you look like a queen, and so I suppose this silk is worth whatever you had to pay for it."

She says, "I just love the way it feels."

I say, "So do I. It's almost as soft as your skin. Don't let any man except me touch it while you are wearing it, or you will get yourself into a lot of trouble." I sip my wine, watching her. I say, "You look stunning, but you are not dressed properly for a serving girl. Why don't you take off the shawl before you soil it?"

She removes the shawl and wraps it around her hips, tucking in the ends at her waist. She says, "There! You have your Gaditana, and my arms are now free to serve you. Too bad I don't dance."

I say, "You don't need to. Just walk across the room, and I'll pretend I hear the castanets."

When she crosses the room, the lamplight dramatizes the silken movement of her hips. She picks up an instrument, comes back, and perches opposite me on a stool. She starts to play and sing. I recognize and admire the bracelets I gave her recently. They set off admirably the roundness of those beautiful bare arms. She frequently pauses to wait on me. It is pleasant to be treated like an oriental monarch, but as a Roman husband, I am starting to feel rather guilty.

I ask her, "When will you eat?"

She tells me she has already eaten. I will not accept this for an answer. I insist that she leave off her serving and entertaining and take her place on the couch at my left side, where my wife ought to be. She reclines next to me, leaning on her left elbow. With her right arm she refills my cup. I pinch the inside of her forearm. A woman is soft where a man is hard. She has to caution me about cleaning my fingers on my napkin before I touch this expensive shawl around her hips. I find the shawl so fascinating that I forget about eating.

I don't know how it happens, on the sloping couch with the bolster between us, but somehow we wind up like this: I with my head in her lap and she half-sitting, leaning over me. Nature will have its way, but it isn't easy, and it isn't comfortable. A *triclinium* was not designed for love-play. She starts to run her fingers through my hair. I protest feebly about her disarranging it. She reminds me there was a time when I wanted her to do this.

She says, "You are still my sea-god."

I give in. I realize I am being wooed by Venus tonight, and I might as well enjoy it. What with the smell of her perfume, the feel of her silken shawl against my skin, the fullness of her bosom hanging over me and this devil of a loose curl which is teasing my cheek, I am rapidly being reduced to a state of happy imbecility. I know when I am beaten. If it were not for the blasted bolster....

"What do you want of me?" I ask. "Name it—it's yours."

"I want to get pregnant."

I laugh outright. "This is a good way to start, but the worst possible place. The wretched bolster is killing me. But what makes you think I can get you pregnant now after ten years of trying?"

Claudia says nothing, but she starts to massage my shoulders. I think back rapidly to what she told me about her experiences in Rome. If I had been there with her, I would not have put up with the outrageous things she did to herself, encouraged by her Eunice. That woman is addicted to strange religions. She is always adding to her god-shelf new images, charms, medallions and amulets. She must have infected Claudia with her passion. My wife spoke of trying every new divinity for long enough to find out it could do nothing for her. She went from Cybele, the Great Mother Goddess of ancient Anatolia, to Isis of Egypt and the dead Osiris. She threw herself into cultish practices like bathing in the Tiber in January, seeking purification and immortal life. She ruined her health with fasting.

I have seen those linen-clad priests with their shaven heads and tattooed foreheads who go around trying to impress foolish women. One of their kind took her money and told her she was healed of her infertility. And she believed him. Of course when she returned to Caesarea, she found out she still could not conceive. It has been nearly a year now since her return, and I thought she had at last resigned herself to childlessness.

I say to her gently, "Claudia, you must accept the facts: There are some things which even the gods are powerless to do. Perhaps it is your fate to have no children."

She says, "I believe I'm healed, and I'm going to get pregnant."

I make derisive sounds, and I ask, "Why now?"

She says, "Promise not to laugh—this is serious to me."

I say, "No more serious than this back rub is to *me*. Go on-I'll restrain myself."

"Today I met a man who promised me that his God would heal my barrenness... You're laughing! And you promised...."

"I can't help it—you're so gullible! But speaking of promises, I should have known you would break yours."

"What promise?"

"You swore you would not leave the Antonia without an armed escort."

"Oh, *that promise*. Well, I kept it. Eunice and Hannah and I were under the protection of a whole century of soldiers going and coming."

"Going and coming where?"

"To the square of the Huldah Monument, south of the Temple. We walked down with the fresh group and returned within the hour with the group they were sent to relieve."

"I don't believe you. The centurion in charge would have given me a report. Claudia, you don't realize the danger...."

"Please let me speak. The centurion didn't know I was one of the three because I was veiled to the eyes. Eunice told him the three of us were Lady Claudia's attendants and asked him to let us walk between the groups...Pilate, you doubted me. You've hurt my feelings."

"I'm sorry about your feelings, but what about my back? Don't stop rubbing. Toward the middle, please. Now, when and where did you meet this man?"

"South of the Temple, during the changing of the guard, around mid-day."

"Claudia, it hurts me to see you hurting yourself this way. It's like a repeat of Rome and the priest of Isis. Sometimes I think you are losing your mind...A little lower down, please, lower...How do you know you're healed?"

"When he made me the promise, I had a burning sensation in my loins."

"That's not unusual. When you rub me like this, so do I. But what exactly did he say?"

"He promised me I shall bear a son a year from today—and I am *so happy, so happy...!*"

"A year from today? The same rubbish and trickery! I didn't know Isis had priests here in Jerusalem."

"This man is not a priest of Isis."

"I suppose they all talk the same talk. If not Isis, what god is it this time?"

"The man called God his Father, but he didn't mention his name."

"He was probably afraid to, at the very gates of the Temple. But then, look at what Jesus got away with doing just inside the gates. At least do you know the priest's name?"

"I do, but I won't tell you."

"I demand that you tell me his name."

"If I do, it will just make you angrier and you will cause trouble for him."

"I swear I will! Just let me get my hands on him!"

She is sobbing now. "Pilate, this is *my* secret. Don't you have some things you would rather not tell *me*?"

I say nothing for the moment, but privately I have to agree.

She is blubbering all over me. "Don't you want me to be happy?"

I say, "All right, you can keep your secret. Just one thing: How much did you pay this priest?"

"I asked the man how I could ever thank him. He said I should give thanks to his God and worship him only. There was no mention of money. When I get back to Caesarea, I'll get rid of all my other gods...."

"And Eunice's god-shelf?"

"That, too."

"I'll believe it when I see it."

"I shall set up an altar to my unknown God and worship him daily."

"What if I forbid it?"

"I shall do it whether you forbid me to or not."

She is no longer crying and she rises. She tosses her head imperiously. The lamplight catches the wine-red glint in her hair.

"Where are you going?"

"It depends on you."

This is a different Claudia. Her little chin has a defiant tilt that is most attractive, maddeningly attractive. Has the goddess who was wooing me decided to cast me away? I think to myself, this is insane. I'm becoming upset about something which will never happen, and worst of all, I am upsetting her. Like a fool, I am throwing away my chances for a really good night...Let her be happy. Soon enough she will find out that this too was just a hoax.

"For pity's sake, Claudia, have a heart!" I stand up. I take my wife in my arms. I caress her hair and her shoulders. Surprisingly she melts. She buries her head in my chest and cries just a little more. I melt. I think how soft and weak a woman is—soft where a man is hard, weak where a man is strong. But something deep inside me says, "Pilate, you are a fool. She is hard where you are soft, strong where you are weak. She has made a tame beast of you and she is leading you around by a ring in your nose." It is true. I could break away, but it would be too painful. So I will let her lead me around by a ring in my nose.

I say to Claudia, "I'll make a deal with you. If you'll stop crying and come on to bed, I'll promise you anything you want. I won't ask you any more questions about your priest. I'll do my very best to get you pregnant. And when I see you starting to swell, I'll let you put away all your images, the Roman gods and the foreign ones too. You can worship your nameless God. In fact, if he can cause you to conceive, I will worship him, too."

"Will you agree to name the baby Theodorus, the gift of God, as the man said?"

"Whatever. We can talk about it later. For the gods' sake, woman, have mercy on me and come to bed...."

Later on, just before we fall asleep in each other's arms, she gets me to agree to one more thing. It is like an afterthought. She asks my permission to go to the south steps of the Temple tomorrow, so she can wait there for Jesus. I tell her I cannot spare a whole century to place at her disposal; ten or fifteen men should be enough. I will assign them to her, but this time they must be informed about whom they are guarding, since she will be disguised. She says she will act like a spy, listening in on Jesus and reporting to me first hand what he says and does.

I like the idea. But I think of how the people will react if they see a detail of soldiers surrounding three women standing on the south steps; surely no teacher and his disciples will stop to talk there. Claudia makes a good suggestion. She reminds me of the clever scheme I used in the aqueduct affair, how I disguised my armed soldiers like civilians. She says if her guards will conceal their uniforms and their weapons under Jewish robes, no one will know the difference. I approve the plan. Furthermore, I am pleased because she has asked my permission. I tell her so and she snuggles closer. Now perhaps she will be quiet and let me go to sleep.

   Did I win or did I lose? I have had such a good night that I don't really care....

CHAPTER 6

A Reformed Tax Collector and Some Unanswered Questions

It is Tuesday, half way through the afternoon. My official day is over and I am in the baths. As the attendants work on me, I am thinking about my day. The morning was uneventful but so busy that I did not break for lunch. It was petty stuff—clear-cut cases where the guilt was obvious. I must cram all judicial proceedings into tomorrow and Thursday because Friday will be the Jewish Day of Preparation, and Saturday will be the Passover. I must close down at noon on Friday so the Jews can go to the Temple and present their lambs for the annual sacrifice. Then every house in the city will smell of the roasting meat. Their feast will begin at sundown on Friday. Until sundown on Saturday, all civic life will come to a standstill.

A slave is oiling my body and scraping me down. I am thinking about the recently concluded meeting with my head customs officers. I am reminded of Zacchaeus, the unctuous little tax farmer from Jericho who gives me such a hard time. I usually have to scrape him down to get the annual tribute out of him. He'll bow and smile and ask me about my health and offer me a hundred oriental civilities, but money? I have to scrape to get it out of him. He'll say business is slow, which of course will affect the collecting of the customs. Everybody knows Zacchaeus has grown quite wealthy since he began to oversee all the city's lesser publicans, those who collect the *publicum* for Rome. And yet every year I have to haggle to get it out of him, like some hawker with his customers at an oriental street bazaar. It is demeaning to Rome that I should have to do this, but it is the only way I can get him to pay up.

Well, today Zacchaeus was a changed man. I was completely dumbfounded when after the usual salaams, he came up and laid a big bag of money in front of me before I could even request it. His round face was wreathed in smiles as he told me how last week he entertained a visitor who changed his life. I listened with interest as he described this encounter, especially when I learned the man was Jesus of Nazareth. Apparently Jesus was able to persuade him to give up his grasping ways, to pay back four-fold any people whom he had defrauded. According to him, he had actually given away half of his fortune to the poor.

I marveled, "Man, have you lost your mind?"

He smiled broadly. "No, Excellency, *I've found it*. I'm happier now, giving money away, than I ever was while holding onto it."

Is this Jesus a sorcerer, to be able to effect such changes on the human personality? For Zacchaeus was not mad. The things he said made some sort of sense, but he was completely different from the man I knew before.

I am looking forward to supper and a chance to quiz my wife about her spying activities. I wonder if she was able to find Jesus and listen in on his discussions and observe any of his so-called miracles. The devious little minx should be good at it. I would not have agreed to her going unless I had been satisfied with our precautions to insure her safety. Perhaps if she has seen Jesus, it will take her mind off the promise of the lying priest.

I would ask her more questions about yesterday morning if I hadn't given her my word in a moment of weakness. She made me pay in advance for my pleasure. I would question her servants, but they are loyal to her and would surely lie for her. So I chose another approach. This morning I called in Paronius, the centurion who escorted my wife and her attendants to the south Temple area at noon yesterday. He was surprised to learn that Claudia was the veiled woman. I asked him if he had seen any cultish types in the area, possibly priests of one of the eastern mystery religions. He said he saw several who might possibly fit the description. Since people from all over the world come to Jerusalem for the Passover, you are bound to see some outlandish types this week.

I asked Paronius if he saw the veiled woman go up to one of them. He said his orders were to escort the three serving women to the south Temple area. Not knowing Lady Claudia was one of them, he felt free to dismiss them from his mind and go about his duties after they arrived. He said he would question the members of the squad who were assigned to the area and would report back to me later. He returned within the hour with a negative report. The men on duty there had seen nothing suspicious. I feared as much. It was a long chance to start with, and I doubt I shall hear anything more of this.

Perhaps I shall never find out what really went on yesterday in the square south of the Temple. But I intend to find out what has gone on there today. Tonight I shall put Claudia through an interrogation about her day's activities. With seven years of experience in handling Roman law here in Judea, I should be able to worm the truth out of one relatively unlearned woman. Of course I must be casual about it, so as not to put her on her defensive.

I wonder what kind of welcome I shall receive tonight. Will everything be back to normal? With a wife like mine, one never knows.

CHAPTER 7

A Night of Interrogation

When I open the door of our quarters, all is nearly back to normal. The added luxuries are still in place, but the atmosphere has changed noticeably. Supper is being served by the household staff. It is adequate but not exceptional. Claudia is not playing the part of the exotic temptress. Tonight she is acting like the model wife with her solicitude about my needs, her interest in my day's activities. Perhaps she is a bit too perfect. I think I detect a certain tenseness as though she is wondering when I will start the interrogation, as though with her chatter she hopes to put off the dreaded moment. Or am I imagining all this?

I feel slightly guilty about studying my wife as if she were a prisoner at my bench, especially after our intimacy last night. Yet, when I think about it, I realize she has been studying me for the past ten years, my strengths and my weaknesses. Last night she got me where she wanted me. She was in control. Tonight will be my turn.

I am enjoying my dessert, a slice of melon from Jericho. Trying to sound casual, I turn to Claudia and say, "Well, what did you do today?" I am leading the witness.

"Stuff which wouldn't interest you." Is she being evasive?

She goes through a lot of *minutiae*—women's stuff, things I could care less about. But I feign interest. I want to break in and ask her, "Did you go to see Jesus?" but I restrain myself and wait patiently. At last it comes out.

She remarks, "I saw Jesus this morning. He was very impressive."

I ask, "How were you able to identify him?"

She says, "I kept looking until I saw a man who fitted Joanna's description of him." She gives me a detailed account of Jesus' appearance.

I say, "There must be a hundred men who look like that. How can you be so sure the man was Jesus?"

She says, "Hannah heard him refer to himself as Jesus of Nazareth."

I interject, "Since you were so eager to see him, I'm surprised you didn't hunt for him yesterday."

She gives me a reproachful look and reminds me of my promise. I apologize to her. It was worth a try. I ask her for the details of her story. She says she was about to tell all until I interrupted her. I apologize again, and she resumes the tale. Now I am listening with an interest I do not have to feign. She tells me how she and her maids carried out the plan we had agreed on. What with her disguise and the disguises of the armed escort, we hoped they would all escape attention.

I ask, "Are you sure no one recognized the auxiliaries?"

She says, "How could they? Your soldiers blended right in with the crowd, just as they did several years ago when you narrowly avoided the riot. Remember, the original scheme was your own."

My original assumption was that since my auxiliaries are mostly Semitic types recruited from the adjoining provinces, they look like everyone else when they dress like the citizens of Judea.

I ask her another question, "Are you sure no one recognized *you*?"

She comes back a little too quickly, "How could they? Remember, I was dressed like the Jewish women and heavily veiled."

I rephrase my question: "Did Jesus himself know who you were?"

She is still on the defensive. Why won't she answer me directly? Instead she says, "If he did, what difference would it make?"

I explain myself. "If he knew you to be the wife of Pontius Pilate, governor of Judea, he might choose his words more carefully or even stage some prearranged scene so that you would give me a favorable report." I think but do not say, especially if you and he had talked the day before.

After a slight pause, she says, "He did not seem to notice us women. He was otherwise occupied." At least she did not ask me another question.

I ask her, "What was he doing?"

She says, "I'll tell you if you'll stop questioning me like one of your prisoners. Please, be nice." She reaches over and gives me an affectionate tap on the shoulder.

I decide to be nice—perhaps I'll get more information out of her this way. I cut off a bit of my melon and I pop it into her mouth.

She sputters good-naturedly, "That is male logic for you! You ask me to tell you my news and then you stop up my mouth so I can't talk. Well, this is what happened..." She seems to relax a bit, enjoying the telling of her story.

"When Jesus and his disciples came out the Huldah Gate, a man who appeared to be following him got him over to the side. The man asked Jesus in a voice that seemed unnecessarily loud, *'Master, is it lawful to pay tribute to Caesar?'*"

"People started to gather in a crowd around them to hear what Jesus would answer. Jesus asked for a coin and the man gave him a denarius. Jesus looked it over carefully on both sides. Then he asked the man, 'Whose likeness and inscription does it bear?'"

"The man replied, 'Caesar's!'"

"Jesus handed him back his coin, with this remark: 'Then render to Caesar the things that are Caesar's and to God the things that are God's.'

"He did not give the man a fixed look. He did not so much as raise his voice to him. But the man was so taken aback that his mouth flew open and his fingers also. Of course he dropped the coin. It was really funny. Some around us who heard what Jesus had said began to laugh, and there was a general murmur of approval."

"They should have applauded. Your prophet answered well. No lawyer could pick a flaw in his response. Are you sure it was spontaneous and unrehearsed?"

"If you had seen the expression on the man's face, you wouldn't have asked me such a question. He was simply thunderstruck."

"Did Jesus say anything else?"

"After this, nobody dared to ask him anything. So he left with his men."

"Did you see him perform any of his famous miracles?"

"I have not actually seen him do anything, but...."

"But what?"

"But I believe he can do anything God wants him to do."

"Aha!"

"What is wrong with that? Is it a crime to believe?"

"Not in Roman law. A Roman court will not condemn a person for what he says he believes—only for what he does. Now a Jewish court is different. For them the most serious crime is blasphemy—using the sacred name of their God or offering some indignity to him. And the penalty is death by stoning. You remember when they tried to stone Jesus a few weeks ago?"

"Yes, but isn't stoning against our laws?"

"Of course it is. That's why they are trying to trick him into some word or deed which is a capital offense in Roman law. They think they can get me to do their dirty work for them."

"Pilate, you must protect Jesus. If he should come before you, you must give him justice."

"I intend to, if it happens. But perhaps I will not have to—at least, not now."

"What do you mean?"

"I mean the Jews are in a quandary. The leaders hate Jesus because he attacks their record here right under their noses. But they fear his popularity with the people. So unless they can pick him up quietly within the next day or so, they will once again have to let him slip through their fingers. There's no way they will risk an uprising by seizing him publicly during the Passover."

"Oh, Pilate, do you think he will get away this time?"

"The man has been lucky before. But it will be as the Fates decide."

I congratulate my little spy on what she has found out. Se she must have thoroughly enjoyed herself while exercising her talent for intrigue. I wish her good fortune tomorrow, since it goes without saying that she will return to the south Temple area. She is able to deliver to me information which may prove valuable if I ever have to try the man. Yet in the back of my mind there lurks an uneasy thought: I already know about Jesus' uncanny power over people's minds. What if my wife should become a follower of his? Well, at least it would make her forget the lying priest....

It is time to retire. Did I win or lose tonight? I dropped my interrogation of the witness and I let her question me. She was clever enough to ask my opinion and get me talking. It took my attention off her and it made me feel good. How do women pick up such tricks? They are not taught how to manipulate men in grammar school. They do not go on to higher learning as men do. They do not study law or logic. Perhaps they learn to manage men by watching their mothers with their fathers.

As I am preparing for bed, there is a knock on the door. I open it and see an orderly who has a message for me. I read it hurriedly, and because it requires no answer, I dismiss him. Then I dispose of the note. It would not do for Claudia to find it—she might try to interfere. She might make things worse for Jesus, in spite of her good intentions.

The message is from the High Priest. He apologizes for the interruption at this late hour. He has just had a late visitor himself—a disgruntled follower of the Nazarene, who has agreed to turn his master over at a convenient time and place when he is not surrounded by crowds. Caiaphas says it will probably occur within the next forty-eight hours. He says that whenever it happens, day or night, he will notify me promptly.

No, I will say nothing about this to Claudia. The affair must come to a head eventually, and it might as well be now, before the Passover, when perhaps it may be accomplished without public disorder. Let them seize him and try him. Let them throw him into prison. They cannot put him to death. In a capital case, Rome and I will have the last word.

From the bed Claudia asks me sleepily, "What was *that all* about?"

I answer, "Just a message which should have been delivered earlier."

"Was it anything so important?

"Just routine. Now let's go to sleep."

As I am dropping off, I am thinking that tonight was neither good nor bad. I was neither a winner nor a loser. I got no prize but I made no promises. It has been an almost normal night.

CHAPTER 8

The Glorious Vision

It is early Wednesday morning, a beautiful clear day. Pilate has just gone below to the judgment hall. Instead of lying in bed for an hour longer, I have decided to climb this tower on the southeast corner of the Antonia and look down at the Temple touched by the rising sun.

Pilate speaks about having seen the Alps when he was serving with Germanicus. He describes snowy peaks in the early morning light, all ice and fire. The Holy of Holies is like a snowy marble peak rising amid lesser summits. It faces the east, and the golden spikes on the roof sparkle in the sunlight. I think I have never seen a more glorious vision.

Yet I do not look at the Temple today with the anticipation I felt before I met Jesus on Monday. I realize I shall never be any closer to the Sanctuary than I am right now. There is a barrier between me as a Gentile and the house of the Jewish God—an impassable barrier. And even among the Jews, only the High Priest may ever enter that Holy of Holies on one day out of all the year. This is according to Joanna. She has told me he will enter on Friday of this week, and he will offer to his invisible God some of the blood of the sacrifice. The Sanctuary is glorious on the outside, but inside it is said to be a place of fear and awesome darkness because of the presence of God.

Something just dawned on me: I have been closer to God than the Jews in the Temple, and I have not felt afraid. I have felt unworthy but not afraid. I do not know how to explain it, but I know I met God on the south steps of the Temple when I met Jesus, the Son of the Jewish God. Jesus is all the God I need. He looks on the outside like an ordinary man, but he is glorious within. I will never kneel and kiss the feet of an idol again. I have kissed the warm living feet of a man who talks with God and calls him Father. He prayed to his Father for me, and he told me I am healed. When he raised me to my feet, I felt something like a spark which passed from him to me, coursing through my body. I am healed and I shall bear a child. I could not be surer if I already felt life stirring within me.

I must go again to Jesus. I do not need to touch him or talk to him again. I wish only to see him and listen while he talks to others. I wish I could go away with him, like Joanna, and minister to his needs.

But Pilate would never understand—he is not Chuza. He is the Roman governor of Judea and I am the governor's wife. So I must continue to be careful about what I say to him, for Jesus' sake as well as for my own. I told my husband only half the truth. I said I had never *seen* Jesus heal anyone; I didn't tell him I have felt his healing within my body. Pilate must never make the connection between Jesus and the priest I allowed him to imagine. He must never make the connection between the Jewish God and the unknown God to whom I referred. I do not feel as if I was lying to him because I do not know the real name of the Jewish God—it is too holy for anyone to say. I didn't tell my husband anything actually untrue— I just let him make some false assumptions which I did not correct....

It is now broad daylight. The Temple is very beautiful, but it has lost that first breath-taking glow. Tomorrow morning its glory will be renewed. I need to go down now. I need to go down again to the south steps of the Temple. I need to see Jesus again. I must have another glimpse of *his* glory....

CHAPTER 9

The Gloomy Prediction

Later in the morning I walk with my two women to the south steps of the Temple, accompanied by the disguised auxiliaries. As we draw closer to the Passover, the crowds grow daily larger. We take our places on the steps and wait for Jesus to come out of the Temple. When I spot him, I realize he looked different today. Monday I made personal contact with a compassionate healer. Tuesday I observed a wise teacher. Today he looks more like a wrathful prophet—black-browed and frowning, his mouth set in a hard firm line.

He and his disciples do not linger today in the area of the steps. They move through the congestion around the Huldah Gates, down the crowded stairway and across the paved terrace to the edge of the retaining wall. They stand along the rim of this revetment, looking down at the square thirty feet below. We follow them with difficulty, pushing and shoving our way until we are standing behind them in the relatively clear space next to the low wall on the edge of the scarp. I am close enough to hear them, but I cannot see their faces. They seem to be waiting for Jesus to say something. He is shaking his head. Finally he says, "Truly, I say to you, all this will come upon this generation."

The burly disciple who is standing beside him says, "Master, you really told them today, those pious pretenders with their holier-than-thou attitude! You warned them of the wrath that will come upon them for persecuting the godly."

Jesus is silent for a moment. Then he points to his left, where the Temple Mount and the lower city fall off steeply into the Kidron Valley. His shoulders heave slightly; do I detect a sigh? He says, "Do you see the tombs in the valley? These hypocrites will lay flowers on the graves of the prophets whom their fathers killed, but all the righteous blood ever shed on earth shall come upon them. Truly, I say to you, all this will come on this generation."

He seems more sad than angry at this moment. Then he turns to his right and looks out over Jerusalem, across the central valley to the lower city and the small white houses of the poor which seem to climb the slopes of the western hill. On its summit rises the upper city with the mansions of the wealthy.

I see Jesus' face in profile as he reaches out his arms toward the Holy City. I realize with a slight shock that he is weeping. Roman men do not weep—at least, not in public. But Jewish men are different. I have heard that weeping to them is a mark of piety.

Jesus mourns over the city. "O Jerusalem, Jerusalem, killing the prophets and stoning those who are sent to you! How often would I have gathered your children together as a hen gathers her brood under her wings, and you would not!"

His emotion is such that he must pause before he can go on. How different he seems from a Roman man—imagine comparing himself to a hen with her chickens! One minute he seems so hard, the next, so tender. He cares about the poor people who live in those small white houses. He wants to protect them from the wealthy who would make them their prey. Some of them will come to him and find shelter and safety, but so many will run the other way and be consumed. It is breaking his mighty heart.

My eyes fill with tears of sympathy. This man who cares is the Son of a God who must care. He must care about hens and chickens, about mothers and their children. He must care about women like me who long for children of their own. He must care about the Gentiles as well as the Jews.

Jesus continues, "Behold, your house is forsaken and desolate. For I tell you, you will not see me again until you say, 'Blessed is he who comes in the name of the Lord.'"

I realize Jesus is deeply grieved because as a prophet he can see what lies ahead—the gloom of desolation. His disciples seem distressed and abashed. They understand his wrath and they sympathize with his grief, but they cannot relate to his prophetic vision. One of them tries to change the subject by drawing his attention to something else. He takes Jesus by the arm and gestures toward the monumental grandeur rising behind us.

"Master, just look at all these tremendous stones—aren't they beautiful?"

And Jesus, looking backward, says to his men, "You see all of these, do you not? I say to you, truly, there will not be left here one stone upon another which will not be thrown down." His voice is strained and sad. For the first time today, I see his face fully, the face of a prophet more sorrowful than wrathful.

This time Jesus himself is the one to change the subject. He says to the other, "But let us be going. It is lunchtime and I have much to tell you privately."

They walk down one of the small staircases to the square below and disappear into the throng. My women and I give a prearranged signal and our escort leads off, with us safely in their midst. We head back toward the Antonia Fortress. It has been a depressing encounter, and I cannot shake off this mood of sad foreboding.

CHAPTER 10

Table Talk

I am sitting with my wife at dinner. Last night's disturbing message is on my mind. I am wondering if perhaps I should tell Claudia about it. It may be easier for her to accept the fact of Jesus' coming arrest if I prepare her for it now. Tonight she seems sad and subdued. I wonder if she has already found out. Who could have told her? I decide to try the direct approach.

"Well, what happened today to make you look so glum?"

"I went to see Jesus again. Pilate, I am worried about what may happen to him. I think he is worried, too, though not about himself. Maybe worried is not the right word. He was more like a soothsayer prophesying doom. He seemed preoccupied with the woes he had been pronouncing on the scribes and Pharisees."

"What did he accuse them of?"

"He said they were hypocrites, claiming to be so religious while persecuting the righteous. He said the curse of innocent blood would come on this generation."

"Did he tell them so to their faces?"

"I gathered as much from listening to the conversation between him and his disciples. Today instead of lingering on the steps, they walked to the edge of the terrace which looks down on the lower city.

Jesus observed the crowds of people below him and the houses on the slope of the western hill. He shook his head and grieved over Jerusalem because the people will not respond to his message, and therefore their doom is sealed."

"Either the man is insane or else he is a faker. How could he know about future events?"

"I tell you, he is a prophet; his God reveals to him what is going to happen."

"Nonsense!"

"How can you say that? You yourself are so superstitious you won't do anything without consulting your augur."

"Humph! Augury is a decent Roman practice which fosters civil religion and holds our empire together. Did your Jesus make any more predictions?"

"He predicted the destruction of the Temple."

"And how was he going to accomplish *that*?"

"One of his disciples tried to change the subject by drawing his attention to the massive stones of the Temple behind us. Jesus answered him grimly, 'Do you see all these things? I tell you the truth, not one stone will be left upon another which shall not be thrown down.'"

"Did he say any word or make any gesture that would lead you to believe he himself was plotting to destroy the Temple, either by force or by magic?"

"Absolutely not. He was simply grieving because of what he foresaw would happen."

"Did he say when or how all this would come to pass? Did he mention Rome?"

"He gave no details and he did not implicate Rome in any way. I concluded that God himself would be the agent of destruction."

"On his own people?"

"Yes."

"This seems highly unlikely. If what you have told me is all you heard, it seems to me that you are jumping at conclusions."

"It isn't all. I have been mulling over some things I heard Jesus say the first day I saw him. I was too excited then to worry about them. I was too busy trying to keep up with Hannah's running translation of

Jesus' words to think about what they meant. But I have discussed them with her since, and they tie in with what he said today."

"What did you—or Hannah—hear the other day?"

"Jesus had just aroused the opposition of the Jews by a story he told against them. His disciples couldn't understand the story or the Jews' violent reaction to it. So Jesus explained to his men the deeper meaning."

"What was the story about?"

"The owner of a vineyard—God—and some tenant farmers—the Jewish leaders."

"What happened?"

"The owner sent his servants—the prophets—to collect from the tenants at harvest time. But they refused to pay the servants and they beat them up. So the owner sent his son to them, thinking they would respect him...."

"And who was the owner's son?"

"Jesus himself."

"That would amount to a claim of divinity. If the Jews understood Jesus to mean it in such a way, naturally they would be angry." I think to myself, this is deeply disturbing, but all I say aloud is "What happened next?"

"The tenants killed the owner's son and cast him out of the vineyard. Then Jesus asked the Jewish leaders to finish the story for him: 'What would the owner of the vineyard do?' They answered that he would come and destroy the tenants and give the vineyard to someone else. Jesus told them they had just convicted themselves."

"No wonder they were furious."

"They wanted to arrest him, but they couldn't without causing a riot...."

"Which Rome would have to put down. No, they can't arrest him publicly...You say you learned this indirectly through Hannah's translation. Did you observe anything directly? In other words, did you ever hear him say anything in Greek?"

"Yes, I did. I think Jesus was quoting the Greek versions of the Jewish Scriptures. He said, 'The very stone which the builders rejected has become the head of the corner; this was the Lord's doing, and it is marvelous in our eyes. Everyone who falls on that stone will be broken to pieces; but when it falls on anyone it will crush him.' Later I double-checked with Eunice, and I wrote the words down. They have made a strong impression on my mind."

"Did he interpret to the Jews?"

"He didn't need to—they got the point. Now do you see why I say Jesus was prophesying divine judgment? When you put together what I heard him say or others say in his presence, I can draw no other conclusion."

"Yes, and I also see why the Jewish leaders are out to get him. Claudia, my little spy, you have done an excellent job. Because of what you have told me yesterday and today, I will be able to test the truth of the charges against Jesus."

"You speak as though he were already on trial."

"He will be, very soon. I don't know exactly when, but we will hear before long."

"The message last night?"

"Yes, but don't ask me for details. It's better for you not to know. But I tell you this in all seriousness: Do not go looking for Jesus any more. Do not go near the temple tomorrow or into the lower city. Stay here in the fortress tomorrow and Friday. You can see more anyway from the tower of the Antonia than you could in the streets below."

"But Pilate...."

"Claudia, do as I say. I am thinking of your welfare."

CHAPTER 11

Stones and Blood

It is Thursday morning. Pilate had a good idea—for me to watch the day's proceedings in the Temple from the top of the southeast tower of the Antonia. I love this spot. I am in the center of everything—in the heart of the white city, in the heart of the gray-green mountains. As I look down at the Temple, for the moment I am as contented as a bee, buzzing over the golden heart of a flower.

It is so peaceful up here that it soothes my worries. Look at all the activity in the sheep market just north of the Temple—lambs by the thousands. They are running them through the pools so they will be spotless for the sacrifice. Poor lambs! By tomorrow evening, they will be turning on spits in hundreds of courtyards and thousands of camps on the hillsides. Pilate says the Jews from Galilee often celebrate their Passover on Thursday night, but the majority of Jews will observe it on Friday. This means they will soon be starting to kill those lambs. I do not want to look down and see an endless procession of little white lambs on that great white altar. I do not want to see their blood on the stones. It will be the same tomorrow, so Pilate says, and much more.

I wonder where Jesus is now. I hope he is safe. I wonder if he will keep the Passover tonight or tomorrow night. I suppose he and his disciples will eat at someone's house, or perhaps at some camp on the hillside. They will have the priest kill their lamb and then they will take it home and roast it and eat it with bitter herbs. They will do these things unless Jesus' enemies capture him first.

I like the taste of roast lamb, but I could not enjoy it after watching so many of them die. They have such soft brown eyes. The little things are so gentle and trusting. I could not eat one after seeing the rivers of blood on the stones.

Stones and blood—Jesus spoke about them. I remember what he said on Monday about the stone that the builders rejected, how it would fall on the people and crush them. I remember yesterday how he prophesied about the destruction of the Temple and the blood which will come upon this generation. Stones and blood. And my faith in Jesus' promise. My fears that the promise may fail if something happens to Jesus, especially if my husband should become involved. Pilate's hints about danger today and tomorrow....

As much as I love this place, I will stand here no longer. I will go below to the visitors' quarters. I will take my women and head for the baths. I will soak and relax and prepare myself for Pilate's return. Perhaps I will be able to forget the stones and the blood. I will not even mention the sight of all those lambs. Perhaps we can get through the evening meal without talking about Jesus. But I shall still think about him. I shall think of little else.

CHAPTER 12

Up from the Baths

I am on my way upstairs. It was nearly five when I left the baths. The daily bath failed to relax me as it usually does. I suppose I have too much on my mind.

When and where will the High Priest's men capture Jesus? Since I still have received no word, it will have to be this evening, unless they plan to hold him in custody till after the holiday.

I do not think they can try him tomorrow, according to Jewish law. It is illegal for them to conduct a trial for a capital offense on a Friday. The reason is that the sentence cannot be pronounced till the day after the trial. And on the next day, their Sabbath, sentence and execution are equally impossible. It is somewhat like the case of the two highwaymen I tried this afternoon. There wasn't enough time for sentencing and execution; therefore I suspended the judgment and sentence till the first thing Friday morning.

It takes all day for a proper crucifixion. Even so, the soldiers may have to break the criminals' legs to hasten death, for it also goes against Jewish law to let a body hang on a cross overnight, especially on a high Sabbath like this one, when one of the great feasts happens to fall on the same day as their weekly holy day. If I should leave the men on the crosses overnight, someone would be bound to report it to the emperor as a gross infraction of their law.

I suppose this matter is of little consequence, but I get tired of making these small concessions to their religious traditions. Why can't the Jews themselves make a few concessions to Rome? They could have been broad-minded in the matter of those gilded shields. After all, the things were in the Herodian Palace, where good Jews never go and would never see them. But Herod had to tattle to Tiberius, and the tetrarch and I are still not on speaking terms.

I shall have to watch what I say at supper tonight. No need to talk about troubles before they happen, so at least Claudia will be able to enjoy the meal.

CHAPTER 13

A Late Visitor

Supper tonight was tense for both of us. Claudia had practically nothing to say. I told her about the cases I conducted this morning. I thought the last one I tried would interest her most because of the scene of the crime—the Jericho Road. She would remember our hasty trip by night over that lonely and dangerous terrain. I told her about the two men accused of committing robbery and murder on this road several weeks ago. Although the outcome was assured in advance, I had to hear lengthy testimony from all the witnesses, and I did not have time to conclude my case. Since Roman law decrees that the death sentence must be carried out immediately, and since by midmorning it was too late for a crucifixion, I decided to postpone the sentencing until early tomorrow. Then the crucified men could hang on the cross a whole day, and if they were not dead by sunset....

As I went on, I noticed Claudia had stopped eating. Apparently my shoptalk wasn't helping the situation. I asked her about her day. She told me she had been following my orders, hanging around the fortress and doing nothing except for worrying. She said she did climb up in the tower as I suggested, but after a while the sight of the preparations for the Passover in the Temple area depressed her. Then she came down and took a bath. There was nothing else to do.

I decided then to tell her all I knew, which wasn't much. But knowing nothing and fearing everything is worse than knowing a little with certainty. I revealed to her the contents of the message I received the night before last....

The servants have just cleared the table and left us with our dessert. Without much appetite, Claudia and I are dallying over the ripe fruit. She is asking me questions which I cannot really answer except with conjectures.

"Pilate, what will happen if they don't catch Jesus tonight?"

"He may very likely get away altogether because during the Passover, no one would dare to arrest him."

"But you don't think he will get away this time?"

"Not if one of his associates has contracted to betray him. It is in this defector's interest to deliver the goods within the specified time, or he will not get his money. So my guess is that we will hear of the arrest sometime tonight."

"What do you think they will do to Jesus after they arrest him?"

"They hate him enough to kill him outright, but they do not have the authority to do so themselves. Therefore they will try to prove him guilty of a crime we Romans recognize as deserving of death, like sedition or high treason. And they will try to get me to execute their sentence."

"Will you, Pilate?"

"Only if I am convinced the man is guilty. On the basis of what you've told me, he doesn't sound like the type to commit a capital crime. And as the governor, I do have the power of life and death. So stop worrying and trust your husband...."

Having heard nothing, we go to bed around ten. It must be nearly midnight when we are roused by a knock on the door. Sleepily, I answer. It is a messenger from the High Priest. I read his note, which does not require any answer. I go back to my bedroom. By the lamplight I see Claudia sitting upright in the bed.

"Have they captured Jesus?"

"Yes, less than an hour ago. Practically without resistance. Caiaphas assures me that Jesus will receive a fair trial by the Great Sanhedrin. He says if their court condemns Jesus to death, they will bring him to me in the morning for the sentencing and crucifixion.

He asks me to keep the Antonia forces on full alert until the case is concluded because of the danger of rioting."

"Pilate, do you think they will try Jesus tonight?"

"I seriously doubt it because in the Jewish law, such a trial would be illegal. But I'll hazard a guess: They will marshal their witnesses tonight and firm up their case against him. They will try him the first thing in the morning. Then they will bring him to me, say around nine o'clock. Any earlier would not allow time for them to give him a proper trial. Yes, the more I think of it, the more I believe that is what they will do."

"Even though the Friday trial is illegal?"

"They are so eager to dispose of your prophet that they won't be too scrupulous."

"Pilate, you can't let them get away with it."

"I don't intend to. Remember, Rome and I will have the last word. So trust me and try to get back to sleep."

CHAPTER 14

The Interrupted Proceedings

It is just after dawn Friday morning, and I am up and dressed, ready to go below and pick up the cases where I left off yesterday. Claudia has been restless most of the night, but now she is lying quietly. When I got up, she murmured, "Is it morning already?"

I answered, "Yes, but it is very early and you have not slept well. Try to go back to sleep and get some rest."

I go downstairs to the judgment hall. The two highwaymen do not take long to dispose of. I am starting another case when a messenger from Caiaphas interrupts me. He tells me the High Priest and the members of the Great Sanhedrin have brought Jesus to me. I am justifiably angry. What kind of Jewish trickery is this? But I table my cases and I ask the courier to bring them in. He informs me that the Jews will not come in, for it would defile them to enter a Gentile palace, and they would not be able to eat their Passover meal tonight. I will have to go out to them. I reluctantly agree, but I am seething within.

While we are crossing the courtyard, the messenger briefs me on what has already happened. It seems they held a meeting of scribes and elders last night at the High Priest's house. After hearing testimony against the Nazarene, they pronounced him guilty and worthy of death. Then at dawn this morning, the Great Sanhedrin met on the Temple Mount to confirm the verdict officially. So now they are bringing Jesus to me for sentencing and execution. I am highly incensed, but I try to appear calm.

I have my magistrate's chair removed from the raised dais in the hall and placed outside the gates, at the top of the stairs. My official judgment seat, moved unceremoniously like any common campstool. I feel this indignity keenly. Am I the lackey of these Jews? Must I follow after them at their convenience, at any hour? Last night they interrupted my sleep. This morning they have interrupted my court proceedings. I am not in a mood to be cooperative. I sit in the magistrate's chair and I confront the crowd assembled below me. The condemned man stands directly in front of me on a lower step.

He does not seem like the criminal type or the Zealot type or the Messiah type. And if John the Baptist was a typical prophet, this Jesus of Nazareth does not look like the prophet type either. He certainly does not appear to be a man who knows he is guilty and is going to die. I feel a sudden surge of interest in this man. I am resolved not to let the Jewish authorities force my hand into making a hasty sentence. I will hear this case. I am indignant that they should deny this Jesus justice in the mockery of a trial they seem to have conducted.

The Jewish leaders are assembled in a wide fan, to the right and to the left of Jesus. The whole Sanhedrin is here, High Priest and all. Behind them, a number of scribes and Pharisees. At the entrance to the square, a crowd of the curious is starting to gather. Claudia's prophet shall have justice. I raise my voice and turn to those on the right where Caiaphas and the chief priests are standing. I am familiar with the names of many and the appearance of all.

"What charges do you bring against this man?"

I enjoy the look on their faces, one of complete consternation, for they recognize the opening statement of a Roman trial, my *interrogatio*.

One of them says sullenly, "If he were not a criminal, we would not be handing him over to you."

That is no way to talk to the governor of Judea. I snap back at them, "Take him yourselves and judge him by your own law."

One who seems to be their spokesman says to me, "It is not lawful for us to put any man to death."

I secretly enjoy their obvious humiliation. I repeat, "What are your charges?"

They huddle and confer. The rabbi who is their spokesman says, "We found this man perverting our nation and forbidding us to give tribute to Caesar and saying that he himself is Messiah, a king."

Purely political charges—a smokescreen, I suspect, for their real motives. I know the first two charges are false because of my own informants and Claudia's spying. The third charge is definitely the most serious. It is high treason to proclaim yourself a king if you mean it in a literal sense. I decide to conduct a short private hearing to get the facts from Jesus. He is not likely to tell me much in front of his accusers. We pass through the line of soldiers who are guarding the gate. Once within the courtyard, I back him up against the wall and prepare to question him.

CHAPTER 15

A Most Unlikely King

He seems a most unlikely candidate for a king, but I'll let him speak for himself. So I ask him, "Are *you* the king of the Jews?"

That secures his attention. He gives me a searching look and asks me, "Do you say this of your own accord, or did others say it to you about me?"

I refrain from telling him my opinion of his qualifications for kingship, but I answer, with some vexation, "Am I a Jew? Your own nation and the chief priests have handed you over to me; what have you done?"

He ignores my second question, returning to the first. "My kingdom is not of this world; if my kingdom were of this world, my servants would fight, so that I might not be handed over to the Jews; but my kingdom is not of this world."

If this man is a king, he must be a miserable specimen, since not even his own servants will defend him; why then this angry crowd of councilmen, united in seeking his death? I decide to humor this dreamer.

"So you are a king, then?"

Jesus answers, "As you say, I am a King. For this I was born, and for this I have come into the world, to bear witness to the truth."

The truth! I cannot believe what I am hearing. Such a statement might be discussed and analyzed by philosophers under the colonnaded porticos, but it can hardly be considered as grounds for the death sentence in a Roman court.

He goes on, "Everyone who is of the truth hears my voice."

Is this truth of which he speaks some secret knowledge unattainable except by the initiates of some eastern sect? He says no more. He looks down at the pavement and I look him over. I have sized up this man and this situation. This Jesus is no threat to Rome or anyone else, so far as I can see. He has incurred the wrath of the chief priests by overturning a few tables of moneychangers and releasing some animals and birds intended for the sacrifice, and now they are all out to get him. The scribes and Pharisees hate him because he has told the truth about them, exposing their hypocrisy, and they cannot bear it.

For a moment I meditate on the truth myself. Loyalty, honor, courage, decency, respect—I thought I knew the truth before my patron Sejanus fell and I lost my illusions. But now I am not sure.

I ask him half-seriously, "What is truth?" I do not expect an answer and he does not give one.

A king of truth would not be an earthly king. Would anyone take seriously such a claim to kingship? If I were a Galilean peasant instead of a Roman governor, I might feel differently about him. For the fellow has a certain dignity and a quiet sincerity which are strangely convincing. But the thought of him committing high treason is almost laughable.

CHAPTER 16

A Man Who Wants to Die and My Attempts to Save Him

I lead the prisoner back to the outdoor tribunal, and again I take my seat. I announce to those below, "I find no guilt in him."

That should have made an end if this were any place other than Judea, where the chief magistrate himself is constantly on trial.

I say, "What evidence do you have to substantiate your charges?"

The Jews huddle together and whisper, but not for long. Though at first I caught them by surprise, while I was talking to Jesus inside, they had a few minutes to plan their next strategy. They come forward in groups of two or three. In Roman as in Jewish law, it takes more than one witness to substantiate a charge. They back up their three-fold charges, they mention specific instances they have personally observed: Jesus' violence at the Temple, the affair of the coin for the tribute. I have heard about these things from my own witnesses, and I am not impressed. A councilman reports that Jesus claimed to be the Messiah in front of the entire Sanhedrin. After my private interview with Jesus, I know he is not the kind of king the Jews are expecting, and he is no threat to Rome, whatever the Sanhedrin may have trapped him into saying. I am surprised they got him to say anything, for he has been completely silent throughout these proceedings. They rest their case and I turn to the prisoner.

I ask him, "Don't you have anything to say in your own defense? Don't you hear this evidence against you?"

After our private conversation, I felt sure he would speak up when I called on him in public. But he says nothing. For the moment, it dumbfounds me. Such a thing has never happened in my court before. Defendants are always eager to speak up for themselves, even when their guilt is obvious. It is as though this man wants to die.

Then I raise my voice to the crowd. "Can anyone offer evidence favoring the defendant Jesus?"

I see a few waving their hands, trying to come forward. But in this jam-packed square, they can make no headway. I am beginning to realize that the Jewish crowd, as well as the Jewish leaders, are hostile to Jesus. This is both surprising and disturbing. One of those closest to me makes a comment about this deceiver who has been making trouble ever since he started his ministry in Galilee. This gives me a good idea.

Of course, the man is a Galilean. That puts him under the jurisdiction of the tetrarch of Galilee. Herod Antipas is in the city for the holidays. Why not turn the case over to him? I am amazed I did not think of this earlier. My deference to Herod in this matter will flatter him, and it will get this Jesus off my hands. Who knows? It may even patch up the breach in our relationship.

In a moment I announce my decision. I inform the accusers that because the defendant has committed the alleged crimes in Galilee, I am binding him over to his own tetrarch. They are disgruntled, objecting that Jesus also committed some of his crimes in Judea. I seek to convince them of how Herod is more qualified than I to deal with a case involving their religion. And finally they agree to accept adjudication by the tetrarch.

I adjourn the tribunal. Heralds instruct the crowds to proceed immediately to the nearby Hasmonean Palace, where Herod is lodging. Many of them leave along with the accusers.

I reenter the judgment hall and resume my scheduled cases. I am elated. I have relieved myself of an embarrassing situation. I have won out over the Jews and I have out-maneuvered Herod. I am still in control, the man on top....

My elation is short-lived. Less than an hour later, I get disappointing news when a courier brings me a note from Herod. He says he appreciates my thoughtfulness and my deference to his authority; yet due to the action of the Great Sanhedrin and the nature of the charges they have brought against Jesus, he is waiving his jurisdiction in the case. Apparently Herod is glad to have the chance to see and question the Prophet Jesus, but he is wary of any involvement with him which could lead to a death sentence. He has killed one prophet already; one is more than enough. I am not too surprised though naturally I am disappointed. But at least I have scored one point: It seems I have removed the hostility between us, for he has invited Claudia and me to dinner Tuesday night.

By the time I have read the note and go outside, the principals in the case have resumed their positions and the square is filling up. At my order heralds hush the crowd. I announce to the accusers, loud enough so that all assembled below me can hear it:

"You brought this man before me on a charge of subversion. I have examined him in your presence and have found him not guilty of any of your accusations; and neither has the Tetrarch Herod, for he has sent him back to me. Observe that he has done nothing worthy of death, whatever his violations against your religious law."

I pause, awaiting their reaction. I am amazed at the vehemence of their response. They are shouting, "Away with him! The man is guilty!" I have misjudged the mettle of this crowd. They are out for this man's blood, for whatever reason. I shall try another tack.

In a lower tone I attempt conciliation with the accusers. I tell Caiaphas and the others that perhaps they can gather better evidence and re-try him later. I raise my voice and announce to the assembly, "Therefore I will have him flogged for disturbing the peace and then release him."

They show no sign of readiness to compromise, so I have no choice but to reopen the case. But what can be done? All the evidence has already been presented. And I have heard Jesus' defense, "My kingdom is not of this world."

When a servant hands me a note, I am glad for a momentary

distraction which gives me a chance to think. I know it is from my wife, for I recognize her hand. At any other time, I would have cast it aside as something which could wait till later, but reading it will give me an opportunity to think about my next move. I read it slowly. This disturbing message helps me make up my mind about what I shall do next.

CHAPTER 17

The Unfinished Dream

It must be morning. I am lying in bed, all a-tremble. For a moment I wonder which is reality, the bedroom or the awful vision. Some noise must have waked me from my dream—a frightening dream whose end I shall never know. Monstrous fears rise up from the present and from the past. I relive my previous terror when I heard the mob roar outside this very window and thought they were about to kill my husband. Dimly I remember when Pilate left my side earlier this morning. After my restless night, I must have gone back to sleep. I summon Eunice and she hurries in.

"You've slept late," she says.

"What time is it?" I ask.

She answers me, "It must be around eight, and Pilate is already below conducting cases."

I ask her if she has heard any unusual sounds. She says she heard something strange a few minutes ago. It sounded like a thousand voices raised in an angry tumult. This must have been what awakened me.

"Oh, Eunice, I have just had the most terrifying dream about Jesus—at least, I think it was about Jesus. I must write a note to Pilate immediately. He must not condemn an innocent man to death, a man on whose life everything depends!"

Sobbing, as though I were still a child, I fall into the arms of my old nurse. She tries to comfort me. She makes me sit down and she brings me writing materials. Soon I am scribbling this note:

"Have nothing to do with Jesus, that righteous man, for today I have suffered much in a dream because of him. It was a dream of blood, an awful omen. I will tell you more later. Hastily, Claudia."

I summon an orderly who takes the note to Pilate. A little later, over a bit of bread and a warm soothing drink, I am able to tell Eunice of my dream.

"I saw Jesus standing on the steps outside the Temple. Then I looked up and saw some Jews about to kill him. They were trying to push a big stone off the wall, right over his head. I cried out to warn him, but he paid no attention to me. The stone remained poised for a moment, just long enough for me to read the name inscribed on it—'Pontius Pilate, Prefect of Judea.' Then the stone fell on Jesus, and I saw him no more.

"But a great stone from heaven fell on the Temple, reducing it to dust, causing an earthquake so severe that it parted the mountains and opened a new pathway to the Great Sea. Out of the side of the rock, there issued a fountain of blood and water. It filled the valleys and flowed down to the sea and moved in a great red wave across the flood. When last I saw it, it was moving up the Tiber, a wall of blood rising above the surface of the river. The muffled roar of the tidal wave waked me before the dream was finished."

Eunice says, "The noise I heard must have blended with your dream."

"Oh, Eunice, this dream was a warning sent from God. If only Pilate will heed it! Pray he will receive my message before it is too late."

Eunice calls in Hannah, who leads us in prayer. We pray fervently to the God of the Jews, the only God of power.

CHAPTER 18

A Scheme that Fails

An ingenious scheme comes into my mind as I read Claudia's note. I think of what she said to me last night: "It is all up to you now." She will be proud of me for thinking of this if it works. I have just remembered my practice of releasing to the Jews a prisoner at Passover time. I will give them a choice between Jesus of Nazareth and the more notorious Jesus, the one called Barabbas. Two obvious extremes, a harmless visionary and a murderer and insurrectionist. Will it work? I announce to the crowd that as a gesture of good will, I shall honor the established custom of releasing a prisoner accused of a capital offense.

As casually as I can, I say to them, "Whom do you want me to release? Jesus Barabbas or Jesus of Nazareth?"

"BARABBAS, BARABBAS!"

They are taking up the angry chant as though they have rehearsed it.

I cannot believe it. Can the Jews have anticipated this move of mine? In the minutes while I was studying Claudia's note, could Caiaphas have sent out his men to coach the people? I am beginning to suspect that this crowd is not a chance gathering; they must have been handpicked by Caiaphas.

"GIVE US BARABBAS!"

I am no longer dealing with Jesus' accusers—some two hundred men consisting of the scribes, the Pharisees and the chief priests; I am dealing with the crowd which is milling behind them.

I rise and wave my arms for silence. I cry out, "And what am I to do with Jesus?" It is a cry of complete exasperation.

"LET HIM BE CRUCIFIED!"

"Why, what evil has he done?"

"AWAY WITH HIM! GIVE US BARABBAS!"

"I have not found him guilty of any capital offense. I will therefore flog him and free him."

When the crowd hears Jesus is to be flogged, they shout their approval. They are eager for blood. They are so eager to see his blood that they ignore what I said about freeing him after the flogging. I take Jesus inside through the line of soldiers with their swords and shields. I hand him over to the captain of the guard, who barks out orders to his auxiliaries. They strip the prisoner and administer the warning beating. I stand and watch.

I have seen blood many times. To a soldier, the sight of blood is an everyday occurrence. Why is this man's blood so disturbing? Is it because I know he is innocent? Is it because of Claudia's dream of blood? I turn my back. I cannot stand and watch the mockery which follows the flogging. It is something typical of this barbaric East, a sickening game which my Syrian auxiliaries play periodically with men condemned to death. I do not like it, but I overlook it. In this case the mockery can actually help me carry out my next scheme—to secure the sympathy of the crowd. Although my "King of Truth" does not deserve such humiliating treatment, perhaps I can use it to help him....

CHAPTER 19

The Whipping Post

I am sitting on my bed, propped up with pillows. I was feeling better until the shouting started a little while ago. We women have been doing a lot of praying; there is nothing else we can do. It is frightening not to know what is going on outside, to get only bits and pieces of information which merely add to our common uneasiness.

The orderly returned to tell me he had delivered the note to Pilate. I questioned him anxiously about what was happening. He said he did not linger to find out, for the crowd which had assembled in the square was in an angry mood. The auxiliaries were standing by in the background, and so far there seemed to have been no violence.

I asked him with concern if he thought Pilate was in any personal danger. He replied that the rest of the troops were ranged in the courtyard, out of sight of the people. They were ready to issue forth at a signal from Pilate to subdue the crowd. Somewhat encouraged, I dismissed the man to resume his duties.

And then the shouting started. It has been like an awful storm, rising in surges and then subsiding, only to rise again with mounting intensity. I am torn between fear and curiosity. You do not open your casement during a storm, but it is the only way to find out how bad things are outside....

Things have been relatively quiet now for several minutes. Can the storm have passed? My women are as eager as I to find out what has happened. Closed off in this dark room, I feel stifled. I send Hannah to the window and she opens the casement. Light and air come flooding in. And sound, in short intervals—men's voices, raised in cheers, as though inciting some favorite athlete in a contest. What can the auxiliaries be doing in the courtyard under this window?

Hannah stands there, voiceless and motionless for the moment. Then she gives a muffled gasp, but she says nothing. She does not leave the window, but she beckons to us to join her. We three women stand at the open window, frozen in an attitude of amazement, pain, and unbelief.

Fearful for Pilate's safety, I scan the courtyard. It is full of the auxiliary troops. I pick him out easily. He is at the head of a group of soldiers about fifteen feet away. He is standing with his legs apart and his arms folded. He and the soldiers behind him are looking at something or someone right under this very window. It is a smaller group. They are gathered around a half-naked man tied to a post directly below us. He is facing us, his arms pulled above his head by the cords which bind his wrists. They are scourging him.

Every time the soldier with the ship draws blood, the other soldiers give a low cheer. They are keeping count—sixteen, seventeen, eighteen. The leather thongs wrap themselves around the man, writing scarlet lines on his back and sides. He throws his head backward in silent agony; no sounds come from his parted lips. His eyes, which are rolling upward, fix on the three of us, framed in the second-story window. He doesn't seem surprised to see us there. Can it be...? Does he recognize us? That face, contorted by pain...I have seen those eyes before... *This man is Jesus!* Dear God! My head reels with the shock of the revelation.

My maids carry me fainting to the bed. Hastily they close the casement, shutting out the awful sight. Everything is growing dim.

CHAPTER 20

The Sight of Blood

The mockery has gone on for long enough. I call a halt to it and I lead the prisoner out to face the crowd. I hail them and suddenly they get quiet, as much at the sight of the prisoner as at my words.

I say, "I bring him out to you to let you know I find no crime in him. You charged him with claiming to be your king. You obviously did not believe him, and neither did my soldiers. In spite of the purple cloak and the crown of thorns, he doesn't look much like a king, does he!"

My soldiers start laughing. They push him around a little with encouragement from me. The man Jesus staggers. A few voices rise in protest. Will there be more of them?

I throw out my hand in a theatrical gesture and I say, "Behold the man!"

Somebody yells, "Crucify, crucify!" Others take up the chant, drowning out the few friendly voices.

I have tried all my tricks and none have worked. Even the sight of Jesus' blood has failed to arouse their pity. My magistrate's seat is becoming most uneasy. I shout at the crowd, "*You* crucify him! I find no case against him!"

I am at the end of my wits and my patience, and I am about to set the man free. This time I do not need to glance behind me. I visualize the might of Rome. I remember that as chief magistrate of this land, I am sworn to uphold Roman justice.

My sarcasm has stung the Jewish leaders into revealing their real motive. Caiaphas walks up to me with thinly disguised anger. He says, "We have a law, Honorable Prefect, and according to our law, this man ought to die because he has claimed to be the Son of God."

I am disturbed, irritated, outraged in my position as chief magistrate. To come up with such a charge, at the end of the trial! It should have been stated at the very beginning; but then I would have thrown the case out, and they knew it—for a charge of divinity is not legal grounds for the death penalty. It is one we Romans tend to shy away from, and though I am not a religious man, I feel a certain dread. I tell this is most irregular; I shall now have to conduct a private hearing. I lead the prisoner back inside the courtyard.

CHAPTER 21

A God With Knobby Knees

So this man has actually claimed to be a god, if what they say is true. I feel slightly shaky, for I have never come up against such a charge before, and I am not quite sure how to handle it. At this moment my philosophic doubts seem rather irrelevant. There may be gods walking this earth today, and it will never do to condemn a god to death by crucifixion. Such a sacrilege would never be forgiven. No, I must be wary.

So I ask him a leading question, "Where are you from?"

He gives me no more of an answer than he gave Herod—he says nothing.

I stand there for a moment, waiting for the answer which never comes, my eyes fixed on his knees. Somehow at this moment I cannot face him eye to eye. His shanks are long, his knees, knobby. A god with knobby knees? That can never be. This man is no Hercules with legs like pillars. My eyes travel up his lanky frame. No barrel chest, muscled like a wrestler's. This man has a lean and sinewy build. True, he is no weakling, but he is certainly no god.

And still I await his answer. He stands with his hands tied behind him, head lowered, shoulders hunched forward. He looks no taller than I in this posture. I feel a trace of pity—or is it guilt—at the sight of what we have done to him. It was my intention to awaken the sympathy of the crowd. I failed to arouse their pity—they wanted to see more of his blood—but I myself am moved. I observe the crown of thorns, the purple cloak—these evidences of the mockery I permitted. For the first time, I think about what a modest Jew must feel—his shame and humiliation as he stands before me, his governor, wearing only a loincloth. I am alone with him and he, with me. I am the governor and he is the prisoner. Why should I feel guilty? But I fear my men have overdone the usual warning flogging when I see him at close hand. The cloak hanging over one shoulder does not conceal his back with its deep and angry wounds. Can this man be a god? Although he has said no word, I have my silent answer: His blood, the sight of his blood. Gods do not faint, gods do not bleed. You cannot kill the gods; they are immortal. This man Jesus bleeds; therefore, if he is crucified, he will die. That is logical.

If then he is innocent of the claim of divinity, why does he not answer me? This has gone on long enough. It is like defiance to me.

I move closer, and as I do, it hits me—from his head, from his hair—an aroma, which I can only describe as like that of the perfume used in anointing a king or a priest—snuminous, awe-inspiring. This is crazy and I don't believe it, so I shall dismiss it from my mind.

In my anger, I snap at him, "You will not speak to me? Do you not know I have power to release you and power to crucify you?"

Jesus is leaning against the wall to steady himself. At last he lifts his head and his eyes meet mine. And now I know why he did not deny the charge—this man really believes he is a god! He speaks with seeming reluctance.

"You would have no power over me if it were not given you from above."

What does he mean? (No, I've already rejected the possibility.) Then at face value, his statement must mean that the authority I wield over him comes from the emperor. This is self-evident. I am fully robed and I bear the hooked staff of the chief magistrate, while he stands before me in his underwear, with the badges of mockery and shame. Yet this man who has to lean against the wall to keep from falling thinks he is a god. I can see it in his eyes—a core of inner peace and resignation, a little sadness and weariness in suffering—above all, a curious submission to his fate, however he may conceive it.

With a sudden flash of insight, I realize the truth: The man believes it is his fate to die, my fate to condemn him. Then why does he continue thus, "Therefore he who delivered me to you has the greater sin"? Here I am, trying my best to save the man, and yet he accuses me of sin, although of a lesser degree!

For some reason I have to drop my eyes again. At the moment he has become the accuser and I, the man on trial...This has to stop immediately. The whole thing is preposterous.

Leaving him standing there, I go out to face the crowd. I fully intend to release this self-deluded man who most unaccountably wants to die. The crowd is waiting to see what I will do.

I talk to his accusers. They will not listen to me. They remind me I am sworn to uphold their law, for the emperor's proclamation to provincial governors has enjoined on me the protection of their religious traditions. I am sitting in a most uneasy seat. I grip the arms of my magistrate's chair. Everything under me seems to be rocking. I hold on for dear life.

I do not know who started the cry—one of the inner circle must have noticed the ring on my finger—this ring which I prize so highly because it marks me as an *amicus caesaris*.

Perhaps prompted by the High Priest, they cry out, "IF YOU RELEASE THIS MAN, YOU ARE NOT CAESAR'S FRIEND!"

CHAPTER 22

I Wash My Hands

I am defeated and I know it. But even in the moment of defeat, I taunt the victors. "Shall I crucify *your king*?"

Furious cries, "WE HAVE NO KING BUT CAESAR!"

I have lost, but in a sense, I have won.

I do as Roman law requires: I call on the accused to speak in his own defense. Legally I must call three times. And each time he says nothing. I am completely exhausted by my efforts on his behalf, completely frustrated by his lack of cooperation. All right, to the cross with him! Let him get what he wants, this man who is so eager to die. I appreciate the irony of the situation; who would ever have thought that these Jews, so difficult to govern, would be so anxious to yield to the lordship of Caesar?

Still I hesitate, weighing what it may cost me if I surrender to their wishes. The pros and cons are not clearly defined. If I hold out, I could face the loss of my governorship—the loss of my status as *amicus caesaris*, symbolized by the precious ring I am fingering now. Given my record of the past seven years and the present political climate, holding out could result, at the very least, in a forced retirement from public office; at the most, in exile and the loss of my fortune—possibly even in my death. This man is indeed innocent, but is he worth the risk to me? This Jew, this nobody?

A man might risk his life, even lay it down, for his country or for some lofty principle of honor, especially if this principle is embodied in something tangible. For example, take Horatius at the bridge—Horatius, that hero of the schoolboys' declamations: Horatius the One-Eyed, blocking the way to Rome almost single-handedly, holding off Lars Porsena and the whole Etruscan army at the banks of the Tiber until his Roman comrades have torn down the bridge behind him. Horatius plunging into the stream when the bridge falls. He does not know whether he will reach Rome and safety, to receive a hero's welcome, or whether he will sink in the Tiber, pierced by Etruscan arrows. Nor do we today, for the poet and the historian are divided on this issue. But at least our Horatius had a glorious cause to live or die for.

How long should I continue to hold the bridge, defending this King of Truth, this God with the Knobby Knees? If he were a real god or a king of somewhere in this world, I would defy the Jewish leaders. And if I fell in his defense, historians would recount my sacrifice, poets would praise me. But should I jeopardize my whole career—even risk my life—for an enigmatic Jew with a death wish, an obscure Galilean peasant who is important only to his personal friends and several hundred humble followers? No, it is not worth the risk. I will do the expedient thing, not the noble thing. Rather than take my chances, I will wash my hands. If I cannot save someone important and thus become a byword of heroism for the ages, let me at least become a model of expediency for my own times. It will not be the first occasion when I have had to back down to these people.

"Orderly, bring me a basin of water."

This crowd is becoming loud and unruly, increasingly dangerous. They will not listen to anything I say, but the symbolic act of the washing of hands will speak louder than my words to their Semitic minds. I have learned at least that much about the Jews. See, they are getting quiet. They know they have won when I stand and raise my dripping hands to them.

I lift my voice, "I am innocent of this man's blood; see to it yourselves!" Try as I may, I am unable to steady my voice, for as I am drying my hands, I am thinking about Claudia's letter and her dream of blood.

I feel a little sick when all the people shout, "HIS BLOOD BE ON US AND ON OUR CHILDREN!"

What if this man should turn out to have been who he believes he is? It is a fearful thing to shed innocent blood, but it is unthinkable to bear the guilt for condemning and killing the son of a god! Pilate, put these thoughts behind you—it is too late now. Remember this, it is impossible for a god to die. There is no blood in their veins, only ichor, the fluid of immortality. This Nazarene bleeds real blood, and so he will die. *Ergo*, he is no god.

Reluctantly I sit down again on the judgment seat and pronounce the final sentence: "Let him be crucified!" And I order the release of the man Barabbas.

The men of the execution squad take Jesus and dress him again in his own clothes. They bring him out along with the two men condemned for highway robbery. The usual jeers and cries as they load the crossbeams on the men's shoulders and lead them off to the Place of the Skull. A fitting name for the site of crucifixion.

I hope I have seen and heard the last of this Jesus. One more detail before I have done with him—I must prepare the *titulus*, the inscription of the official charge against him: "Jesus of Nazareth, the King of the Jews." I write it in three languages—in Hebrew (with the help of a learned aide), in my native Latin, and in the common Greek, which presents me with no problem. After all, I want to make sure everyone gets my message.

I am writing this in prudent consideration of the end-of-the-year report in which I will have to justify my judicial acts, but I also feel a certain secret pleasure in what I am doing. I am thinking about how my words will be carried before this man in the procession and will be seen by many citizens. I am thinking about how they will be nailed to the upright of the cross above his head, proclaiming to these Jews, in a not-so-subtle way, what we Romans think of them: "You deserve such a king!"

I send the placard by a courier to catch up with the death squad. My job is finished, for others will execute the sentence. No, not quite finished. When the chief priests see my insulting *titulus*, their spokesmen return to me within the half hour.

They say, "Do not write, 'The King of the Jews,' but 'This man said, I am the King of the Jews.;"

I enjoy their discomfiture. Now it is their turn to sweat. I answer them, "What I have written, I have written." Today I will have the last word in at least this one thing.

I have had enough for one day. I close my court and postpone my other cases until next week. I go upstairs to my quarters. I must calm down...Must check on Claudia. After her restless night, the dream, and all that has happened this morning, she may be indisposed. And to tell the truth, I feel rather sick myself.

Part IV

The Cost of Compromise

Table of Contents

❦

Chapter 1	An Awful Omen and an Accusation	253
Chapter 2	Gods Do Not Bleed	259
Chapter 3	The Darkness and the Earthquake	265
Chapter 4	A Torrent of Blood and Earthquake Damage	269
Chapter 5	A Most Un-Roman Weakness	273
Chapter 6	My Husband Has Blood on His Hands	277
Chapter 7	Don't Touch Me	281
Chapter 8	A Detailed Report	283
Chapter 9	A Request Denied	287
Chapter 10	I Did the Best I Could	289
Chapter 11	A Puzzling Prediction	293
Chapter 12	Another Tremor and an Empty Tomb	295
Chapter 13	Two Impossible Explanations	299
Chapter 14	Rumors of a Resurrection	305
Chapter 15	After Herod's Banquet	309
Chapter 16	Joanna Takes Her Stand	313
Chapter 17	The Promise Renewed	317
Chapter 18	Going Home Tomorrow	321

CHAPTER 1

An Awful Omen and an Accusation

My fears about Claudia were justified. When I enter our quarters, she is lying on a couch, pale and languid. Her eyelids are half open, and so I know she can see me. But she does not speak. I take Eunice aside and I ask her how long Claudia has been like this.

She says, "About three hours. She slept till nearly eight and was awakened by a bad dream. She insisted on writing a note to you immediately...."

"The note which was delivered to me on the judgment seat."

Eunice resumes, "We got her calmed down, and then the shouting began. That didn't help."

I conjecture, "Must have been when the crowd started to shout for Barabbas."

She continues, "When the shouting stopped, she asked us for fresh air, and we opened the bedroom window. And then—and then...."

"Ye gods, woman, you didn't...*She must have seen*...!"

"And then she saw you standing there watching the soldiers flog Jesus. And she fell down in a faint. We had a hard time bringing her out of it. She has been like this ever since."

"Woman, I blame *you*! You should never have opened that window. You should have carried her back here in the living room, where the windows open on the inner courtyard, away from the sound and the sight of action."

"Excellency, how were we to know there was a whipping post under that very window, or that you would be punishing the prisoner at the moment when we opened it?"

"True, true, and I didn't think to warn you earlier. This is a barracks and a prison, not a palace. It is no place for women. Leave us now. I want to be alone with her."

"But...."

"I'll tend to her."

Eunice and Hannah go out. I kiss Claudia on the forehead. For the first time I realize she hasn't put on her make-up today, and this is part of the reason she looks so pale. I have never seen her like this in the daytime before. A woman has to feel really bad to dispense with her daily beauty treatment.

She props up her head on one elbow and points a shaky finger at me. It seems she is trying to talk, but nothing comes out at first.

I query her anxiously, "Are you ill? Was it the dream? I got your note. And I did all I could for Jesus, but...."

Claudia sits bolt upright, her hair streaming over her shoulders, her eyes flashing with a passion I have never seen in them before. She finds her voice.

"You did what you could, did you? *You went back on your promise*! You had him stripped and flogged, right under our window! You stood there, gloating over him, while he suffered and bled. And you have the gall to say you did what you could for him!"

"Claudia—Claudia...."

"Don't you touch me, Pilate—your hands are red with Jesus' blood!"

Involuntarily I look down at my hands, the hands I washed hardly more than an hour ago in a despairing gesture.

"Claudia, you must let me explain. It was a ghastly blunder, a fearful oversight on my part. I didn't even think about the whipping post being under our bedroom window. I didn't know you would be sleeping so late. I didn't realize...."

"You still don't realize! The worst thing you did is not flogging Jesus right under my nose! The worst thing is flogging a man who is innocent, a man who—a man who...."

She falls into another fit of sobbing. "Pilate, if you loved me, you would have saved Jesus—you would have set him free! Even without my note! But with the note...Could I have said it any clearer? It was *a dream of blood*, I tell you—an awful omen!"

"Don't exert yourself, or you'll make yourself worse. You need to rest now. You can tell me about it tonight when you are feeling better."

She says she needs to talk now and get it out of her system. I try to make her comfortable with the pillows. I insist that she first eat something to restore her strength. The little she does eat, I must practically feed her. I begin to realize how much my wife is hurting. On top of everything else, she thinks I have betrayed her trust.

I recline on the couch beside her, sipping my cup of wine. She starts to tell me about her dream. Before she finishes, I have to pour myself another cup. Claudia does not try to stay my hand. She is right; the dream was an awful omen. My voice and my hand are steady, but my heart is trembling.

She says, "Remember Caesar's wife's dream. It, too, was a dream of blood. Her husband didn't heed her warning either, and look what happened to *him*!"

I say, "Don't compare yourself to Calpurnia or me to Julius Caesar. Don't compare your dream to her dream. Think about this rationally. Your dream was no warning from the gods. It was the result of things you have seen and heard about lately, things you had on your mind when you went to sleep. Things like the prophecies you heard Jesus make about stones and blood and the destruction of the Temple. And remember, you yourself said Jesus leveled these prophecies against the Jews, not against Rome."

I do not need my augur to tell me this is no ordinary dream but a prophecy of things to come. And I am more afraid than I will let her know. I say to her, "Of course you can't expect a dream to make sense, any more than a prophet's words. You can interpret both any way you wish."

"Caesar ignored his wife's warning and listened to a flattering interpretation of her dream. Look what it got him!"

"Claudia, let's talk no more of this for the time being. You've told me about your problems; now let me tell you about mine."

"But I'm not through yet. I want to get back to Jesus and that awful scene in the courtyard. Pilate, you broke a solemn promise—you, whom I have always looked up to as a man of your word...."

"Be patient and listen to me. Then perhaps you will understand why I did what I did."

I proceed to tell her about the events of the morning, how I tried to save Jesus, but to no avail. I say, "The only reason I had him flogged at all was in order to enlist the sympathy of the crowd. I thought the sight of his blood would arouse their pity. It only incited their lust for more blood."

"You are as bad as they are. You ordered the flogging and you stood by and watched it. You looked as though you were enjoying it."

"Claudia, this is not a palace. It is a military installation and a penal institution. I am sorry you saw what you saw, but I told you back in Caesarea that you must expect to see and hear things which might offend a sensitive woman. I have to administer these warning floggings as a deterrent to further crime. And after all, you knew what happened the last time we were here, but you insisted on coming."

"Are you blaming me for going here and seeing the shameful thing you authorized? You know Jesus is completely innocent, yet you had him punished like a common criminal. How could you be *so unjust, so unfeeling?*"

"Claudia, I hoped this lighter punishment would keep me from having to give him the death penalty. If you think scourging is so brutal, I hope you never see a crucifixion."

"Why didn't you simply turn him loose without any punishment?"

"Believe me, I thought of it. The whole trial was based on charges which I knew to be false, from talking to the man himself, from your spying activities, and from my informants. That is, until they brought up a completely new charge—blasphemy. The High Priest says Jesus claimed to be the Son of God."

Her eyes open very wide and she draws in her breath. She leans toward me, so close that when she exhales, I feel it against my face.

She says slowly, as if to let her words sink in, "Pilate, it was no blasphemy—*Jesus of Nazareth really is the Son of God.*"

I say, "If you can believe that, then the man has bewitched you—or else something happened between you two which you haven't told me about."

She flushes and she sips some water slowly until she regains her composure. I wonder if I have stumbled over something significant. But I made a promise to ask no questions about Monday. At any rate, I am thankful she did not also see the mockery of Jesus by my men. At least I had the good sense not to mention that. If she could not understand the rationale behind the flogging, she would surely fail to understand why I allowed the mockery.

CHAPTER 2

Gods Do Not Bleed

Claudia resumes, "Joanna has traveled with Jesus on some of his tours. She has told me so much about his teachings and his miracles that I feel as though I know him personally although I have only seen him several times."

I consider this a rather lame explanation for such a violent reaction on her part, but I make no further comment. I go on with my account.

"After I heard this new accusation, I took Jesus apart and questioned him. He did not actually claim divinity, but neither did he deny it. And he said some weird things which suggest that he thinks he really is the Son of God."

She asks with interest, "What things?"

I answer, "I can't make you understand unless I go back to the beginning of the interview. I started by asking him where he came from, and he knew I didn't mean Nazareth. But he wouldn't answer me. To get him to open up, I had to remind him that I'm the one with the power to set him free and the power to crucify him. Even after this, he seemed reluctant to speak. But he said some things I'll never forget as long as I live. He said, 'You would have no power over me *if it were not given to you from above.*'"

"*From above*? What does that mean?"

"Well, to a Roman it would mean the emperor or the gods or maybe the Fates. But to a Jew, I suppose it would mean the Jewish God. I can tell you, I was really baffled and humiliated."

"Explain yourself."

"I'll try. There I stood, the governor of Judea, with all the might and authority of Rome behind me, and that man I had just had stripped and beaten told me I couldn't do anything to him, if you please, except by the permission of his God! I couldn't understand it. He made me feel distinctly uncomfortable."

"Why in the world would Jesus' God allow you to harm him?"

"I have no idea. It's a mystery. What are gods for if not to take care of their own people? And you would think any god would defend his own son. But this wasn't all—the next thing he said really cut me down to size. He said, 'Therefore he who delivered me to you has the greater sin.' Now that made me feel as if he were the judge and I, the accused."

"Turn-about."

"Exactly. And he was pronouncing me guilty of sin, though in a lesser degree."

"I don't understand. I thought he had just said you had God's permission to do what you did."

"He was talking in riddles, and the more he said, the more confused I got. He must have realized I wouldn't understand him from the beginning, and this was why he didn't want to talk. You can't communicate with someone who speaks a different language. So I gave up on trying, and so did he."

"Is this all?"

"It is and it isn't. It's all he said, all I said. But there is more. At the beginning of the private hearing, when Jesus wasn't talking, he was looking down at the pavement, studying it. This gave me an opportunity to *study him*. It convinced me he is no Messiah, no God-King of the Jews."

"Why not?"

"Well, for one thing, his body type. As I understand it, the Messiah is supposed to be a warrior. Now Jesus doesn't have the muscular build you would expect in a warrior king—certainly not what you would expect in a god."

"How can you be so sure what a god looks like? Artists and

sculptors use people for their models, the best-looking ones they can get. But perhaps the Jewish God chose to make his Son look like an ordinary person."

"Possibly. At any rate, I wasn't impressed by his physique. But he did a sign for me which proved he is no god."

"What sign? What did he do?"

"He bled."

"Why is that a sign?"

"Gods do not bleed, gods do not die. He bleeds and so he will die; therefore he is no god."

"Maybe Roman gods don't die, but gods of other nations do die and then return to life. For instance, Isis and her dead Osiris...."

"I have heard enough of those two. Let me continue. On the basis of my observations, I had made up my mind that this Jesus was no god. And then he lifted up his head and spoke."

"Those puzzling words?"

"Those puzzling, humbling words. But it wasn't just his words, it was the look he gave me. It made me feel...But you wouldn't understand. You would have to have been alone with him, eye to eye, before you could understand."

"I think I can imagine how you felt; try me."

"He had a peace about him which I can't explain except by comparing it with the serenity we assume about the gods on Mt. Olympus. The gods are said to have no human feelings—nothing can disturb their Olympian calm. Well, you know a magistrate has to be a judge of character. I have to read men's faces. I read in this man's face, and especially in his eyes, something I have never seen in anyone before...."

"That peace?"

"That Olympian calm. Yet it did not take away from his human feelings. He obviously felt everything a man in his situation would feel, a man facing death."

"He was suffering because of the flogging you ordered and you supervised."

"Yes, and I must admit it pricked my conscience. But there is more. I can understand a man resigning himself to death; our Stoic philosophers teach such things. But this went far beyond Stoicism. The man Jesus is determined to die—I could read it in his face. I realized that there would be nothing I could do to save him. All my efforts would be in vain. Call it fate, what you will."

"Jesus would not call it fate."

"Probably not. As I said before, he and I speak a different language when it comes to such things."

"Is this all?"

"No, there is still a little more. I mean, about the way he made me feel. I was embarrassed by the way he looked at me."

"What do you mean?"

"He saw through me—I am sure he did. He looked into my eyes and he saw through me. He wasn't looking up at me in fear, as a man would do. He wasn't looking down at me in wrath, as I imagine his God would do. We were eye to eye, and he saw me as I am inside. He pronounced me guilty of sin, but he failed to sentence me. Or perhaps I should say he forbore to sentence me."

"Perhaps he was giving you a chance to say you were sorry."

"There is no way Pontius Pilate, governor of Judea, will ever apologize to a prisoner."

"That was the end of your interview?"

"I couldn't take any more of it, if you understand what I mean. I had to get out of there. So I returned to the judgment seat. I already knew what I needed to know."

"And what was that?"

"I knew Jesus believes he is the Son of God. I read it in his eyes and in his words."

"Does that make Jesus guilty or not guilty of the charges against him?"

"In a Jewish court, guilty. But mine is not a Jewish court. I could not condemn a man for believing he is a god. Now if he were some trickster, claiming to be a god, deceiving people and taking their money, it would be a different matter. But no one except Caiaphas and his crowd have ever come forth with such an accusation. Yet I know Jesus himself believes it."

"Then why didn't you believe? You have made a very good case for his divinity."

"Jesus believes equally firmly that he must die. Everything he said and did, everything he stubbornly refused to say and do—it all leads me to this conclusion. And I can't believe both of these things."

"That he is the Son of God and that he must die?"

"That he is the Son of God and that if crucified, he will die. If a man bleeds real blood, he is human, and he will die. The gods don't have red blood, they have ichor, the fluid of immortality, and they cannot die. I've heard this all my life and I believe it. What everybody says has got to be true."

"That's not necessarily so."

"Let me make an end of this. But even when I knew he was no god, I believed him innocent of any charge which would draw the death penalty in a Roman court. So I attempted to turn him loose. And then one shrewd counselor noticed the ring on my finger, which marks me as a friend of Caesar. He said, 'If you turn this man loose, you are not Caesar's friend!' After that, I knew I was beaten. I called for water and I washed my hands of the matter. Then I condemned Jesus to be crucified. I felt bad about it, but apparently it was what he wanted. I have washed my hands of the matter, and now I am through with it."

"How can you say you're through with it when a man you know is innocent is suffering on the cross because of your orders? Pilate, no matter how many times you wash your hands, *you are still responsible*. You cannot wash away responsibility for an act of injustice. It was just a gesture. And you are still responsible."

CHAPTER 3

The Darkness and the Earthquake

"Claudia, I've had a hard day, and I'm under a lot of stress. I just can't take any more of this right now. No more talk of dreams of blood or prophecies of doom. Let's talk about something else, the weather, anything...."

We both look out the window in surprise and alarm.

"Pilate, what time is it?"

"It must be around noon."

"Then why is it starting to get dark?"

I have no answer. This is not like the darkness of an approaching storm. It is like the darkness of approaching night. We are about to call for the servants, but they rush in unbidden. Claudia asks them to light the lamps. It is getting darker every minute. *O ye gods, what has happened to the sun?* A dream of blood is a bad omen, but *darkness at noon!* Eunice is wailing about the end of the world, and Hannah is on her knees, praying in Aramaic. Claudia and I say nothing. We are glued to the window.

We look out toward the Mount of Olives and see a flight of birds returning to their nests. I wonder what my augur would say about this. He reported nothing unusual about this morning's sightings.

He's probably hiding in his bed, as frightened as these women. When I get back to Caesarea, I shall certainly replace him.

For some reason, Claudia is not wailing or praying with the others—but I wish she were. She looks me in the eye, with the calm but tragic air of a prophetess whom no one will listen to. She says, "Pilate, I told you so. Now will you believe me? Jesus *really is* the Son of God...."

It's around two o'clock. I just checked the hour by the water clock in the courtyard. I have been putting up with a lot for a long time now, and my nerves cannot take much more of these wailing, praying women. And worst of all, the one who just stares at me. I have to get away. So I tell the maids to give Claudia a sleep-inducing potion, and I leave them to soothe her. Actually they need the potion more than she does.

First I look for my augur. I have to take a lantern to find my way around in the fortress. My guess was right—he is cowering in his bed. Fear has made him physically ill, and I have no wish for his company at present. I resolve to have it out with him as soon as he is well. And I head for the tower.

Ordinarily you get the best view in the city from the southeast tower; on a clear day they say you can glimpse the Great Sea on one side, the Salt Sea and the Mountains of Moab on the other. But today I can barely see the outlines of the huge Temple complex right below me. And I am looking down on a city which is cloaked in darkness, where pinpoints of light break the shadows. Bats, creatures of the night, streak across the sky in a zigzag course, issuing from their caves in the wilderness of Judea. I shudder. Now I am no augur, but everyone knows bats are ominous. The darkness is bad enough. But is something even worse about to happen?

A not-so-distant rumble startles me. It is a wave of sound, traveling through the sky. It is a tremor, traveling through the earth. *Earthquake!* Even in semi-darkness I can see it. It is coming toward us from the northwest quarter—cutting a diagonal path across the city—leaving destruction in its wake. Will it hit the fortress?

I fall to the pavement, covering my head. I hear a dull tearing sound and I feel a shaking. But no stones fall around me. Cautiously I rise. First I look down at the fortress. Fortune has favored us—we have been spared visible damage. Then I look down at the Temple on the other side. It is hard to tell what has happened in this twilight, but the people in the Temple must have felt the quake, which seems to have stopped on the other side of it in the Kidron Valley.

As I hurry below to check on everything, I recall the awful earthquake in Claudia's dream, which leveled the Temple. I think about more recent frightening omens like the darkness at noonday. And I wonder if this tremor was just the beginning—if perhaps there is more to follow. And I think about the judgment of an angry God.

I have had just enough wine to lose my discretion, to say the first thing which comes into my head. First I make sure Claudia is all right. Even the quake failed to wake her from her drugged sleep. The sun is now coming out and things are rapidly returning to normal. From all I can see, the city has sustained no extensive damage.

I make a joke out of it. I say, "Either the Jewish God has a very poor aim, or else he is angrier with his own people than he is with the Romans."

It was a very poor joke, and it fails to impress my hearers. To laugh at it, a person would have to be drunker than I....

CHAPTER 4

A Torrent of Blood and Earthquake Damage

It is between the hours of four and five. I am back in my office, expecting a visitor. Now the natural world has returned to normal, I have somewhat recovered from my superstitious fears.

An orderly announces Joseph of Arimathea, a councilman well respected by the Jews. He is a man in his mid-forties, black-bearded, richly dressed in the Jewish manner. I ask him what I can do for him. I am amazed when he tells me he wants permission to take and bury the body of Jesus. After only six hours, how can the man be dead? To verify the fact, I send for Paronius as the centurion in charge of the execution.

Wrapped in his soldier's cloak, the man stands before me. Am I imagining things, or is there something different about his appearance, an unusual pallor on his deeply tanned face? A lack of the usual self-assurance in his bearing? If so, I intend to find out the reason why...Of course, after what has been happening here today, I suppose we all look and act different.

I ask, "When did Jesus die?"

He says, "Just before the earthquake."

"How can you be so sure?"

He answers, "The usual signs—pallor, loss of breath, lack of movement. And for an extra precaution, about an hour later, I had a soldier drive a spear into Jesus' side."

"With what result?"

"If he wasn't dead before, he must be now. The proof—look at me."

The centurion throws back his cloak and displays his uniform. It is spattered with blood. Jesus' blood. I shrink back involuntarily. He says it squirted everywhere—a regular torrent of blood. Strange enough, but this blood was mixed with water. *Water.* Claudia's dream is on my mind, and I feel queasy. I find myself glancing at my hands, rubbing them as if I am still washing them. I have been avoiding the unpleasant sight of my centurion in his soiled uniform. I make a conscious effort to look at him directly. I tell him to assist Joseph in the burial—and then go to the baths. I hope he did not notice when I winced at the sight of him. I tell him I will call on him tomorrow for a complete report. As an afterthought, I tell him to take note of the location of the burial site. I am not sure why I said it. I then dismiss him, and he leaves with Joseph.

I shall put this Jesus affair out of my mind until tomorrow. Perhaps Claudia will feel better when she wakes up now things are back to normal. But then I will have to tell her Jesus has died. Of course it was to be expected. Yet now his death is official, I hate to face her. Jesus must have bewitched her from afar, for she truly believes (as he seems to have believed) that he was the Son of God....

Our household appears to have returned to normal. Claudia is still sleeping. I send for an aide to see what he has been able to learn about the results of the earthquake. There are the usual salutations, and he inquires about my wife's health. I tell him she is not well—the disturbing events of this day have affected her. He gives me the usual condolences.

I say to him, "What have you found out about the earthquake?"

"Your Excellency, there was considerable damage. It caused a fissure which ran clear across the city. The tremor was so severe just south of us, in the Temple area, that it burst the gates open. The guard on the walls reported that though they were unable to see well in the unusual darkness, they detected some disturbance within the Temple, perhaps in the Sanctuary itself."

"I'll bet no outsiders will ever learn the full details. Did the quake do any damage in the area east of the Temple?"

"It caused rocks in the hillsides to crack and slide. It made some graves split open in the cliffs beside the Brook Kidron."

I thank him for his information and I dismiss him.

CHAPTER 5

A Most Un-Roman Weakness

Supper is late because of the afternoon's disturbances. It must be nearly six when the servants lay the table and start to bring in the food. I inquire about Claudia, and Eunice tells me she is starting to rouse. Before I can eat, I must do my unpleasant duty. I have had some wine, but I have had no food since breakfast. So I hastily drain another cup to fortify myself and go in to Claudia. She is now awake. I sit beside her on the edge of the bed. She looks at me listlessly.

I say to her, "Claudia, I have something to tell you."

She says, "I know. Jesus is dead, and you are the one who killed him."

I was expecting to see again the wild-eyed prophetess with the streaming hair. I was expecting to hear a strident voice pronouncing my doom. But my wife is speaking quite matter-of-factly in a tired little voice. It is most unsettling.

I try to take her hand, but she pulls it away from me. "But Claudia...."

She says, "Don't touch me, you murderer!"

I say, "You have got to let me explain!"

She says, "I don't want to hear your explanations, you promise-breaker!"

I come completely unhinged—I simply fall apart. The words and the wine are taking their effect. When she turns her back to me, I do something I have never done before. I seize her roughly by the shoulders and roll her over and force her to face me. She starts to open her mouth, but I gag her with my hand. I will regret this later, but in my towering passion I enjoy the expression in her eyes, the look of a frightened animal. I am not so drunk that I yell and rouse the servants and lose all control. I am just drunk enough to say things which have been on my mind for a long time and express feelings which I have repressed because I was ashamed of them.

I hiss through my teeth, "*You will* listen to me, Claudia. For once, *you will listen to me*. I am going to tell you some things you won't like to hear, but *you will* hear them. I will be sorry for this tomorrow, when I am cold sober, but now I am just drunk enough to speak my mind. *And you will hear me out.*"

"This God of the Jews—I defy him! From the very first day in this land, he has set himself against me, foiling all my plans, constantly subjecting me to defeat and humiliation. I do not deny his existence, but I defy him. These people are hard enough to understand, but their God is completely incomprehensible. I never know what he is going to do next. He causes whatever I do to work out for my worst interest. And here in this place, right next to the Temple where he is most imminent, I feel his power most strongly. And I am afraid. Day and night I remain fearful. It is an un-Roman weakness, and I will not admit to it tomorrow when I am sober, for I will be ashamed. I am a brave man as men go and a good soldier, but I fear this God of the Jews. He is my invisible Enemy. I cannot resist him and I cannot escape from him. Even if eventually I must bow my knee to him, I will not bow my heart. In my heart I will continue to defy him.

"This God is not like the gods of other nations, content to dwell apart from men. He makes everyone's business his business. He is impossible to satisfy. Even his own people are afraid of him. They must make constant sacrifices to pacify him. He is insatiable. If they do not surrender to him everything—all they are and all they have—his wrath breaks out against them, and he allows their enemies to punish them.

"Your Jesus believed he was the Son of this angry God. Well, I would hate to be the Son of a God like that, a God who refuses to defend his own offspring—even worse, a God who demands the death of his own Son! For I am convinced that Jesus went to his death making no defense because he thought his God wanted him to die.

"This unnatural Father-God used me to condemn his own Son. He frustrated all my attempts to save his Son's life. He pushed me into a corner with no way out except to submit to the Jews and give the order, 'Let him be crucified.' What kind of a God is that? He is the image of the father-god Chronos of the barbaric Greek myths, who devours his own children. I want nothing to do with a God like that.

"One way or another, this God is out to get me, to destroy me. He destroyed his own Son through me, and now he will seek to destroy me through his Son. I don't know how he will do it, but he will do it. He will not rest until he does it. I hate him and I fear him. I will run from him as long as I can. And when he finally catches up to me and he brings me to my knees, I will die defying him."

At last I run down. I remove my hand from Claudia's mouth. She says nothing. There is no longer any fear in her eyes, only dumb amazement. I feel empty, drained of all emotion. I realize I am hungry.

I say to her, "Claudia, I am going to eat my supper. You can join me if you like. I am going to drink as much as I want to. And when I am so drunk I can't feel anything, I will come to bed. Don't worry, I won't touch you. I will be too drunk to notice you and too drunk to care."

CHAPTER 6

My Husband Has Blood on His Hands

Pilate fell into the bed beside me hours ago. He was very drunk, as he said he would be, and he let me alone, as he said he would. He went right to sleep. When he got up a few minutes ago, I pretended to be sleeping. Actually I have been awake for a long time, just lying here thinking. I have a lot to occupy my mind. I must make some decisions before morning comes.

I have never before seen my husband as he was today. I hope I will never see him like this again. I am emotionally exhausted. Today I went from apathy to fear to horror and shock and pity, all in a few minutes' time. And then tonight, his terrifying outburst. I never dreamed he was so prejudiced, not only against the Jews, but against their God. I never dreamed he felt such dread and hatred toward Jesus' Father. If he had not been drinking heavily, he would never have let me see this side of him.

If only my husband could put faith in the place of fear! Yet what draws me toward the Lord drives him away. But Pilate needs me. Who knows? Eventually through me he may come to God. And I need him. I have lost my Jesus and his promise—my only hope of becoming a mother. My Pilate is all I have left.

I thought I knew my husband before tonight; I really know him now. I know his rage and pain, his fear, his insecurity and frustration. Though tomorrow he may wear his governor's face and assume his governor's stance, he is unsure of himself and everybody else except me. My Pilate is self-centered, dictatorial, pompous, prejudiced, insensitive and abrupt. He is also affectionate, honest, just, loyal, hard-working and conscientious. He is all of these things, both the bad and the good

He feels insecure because he is alone. Except for me, my Pilate stands alone. He has no friends to talk to and confide in. He has no gods, and he has rejected the only God who has the power to help him. I want to draw closer to God, but he wants to run away from him.

And to think that today I rejected my husband! I drew away from him in body and mind and spirit. And without me to turn to, he had only wine for comfort. I need to make up with him, for his sake and mine. Since I know this, why do I recoil when he touches me? It is because of Jesus, the one who was to bring us closer together. He has driven us apart through no fault of his own. His blood is on my husband's hands. How can I let him touch me as a husband when he has on his hands the blood of the Son of God?

I remember my dream and the stone bearing Pilate's name which fell on Jesus and crushed him. It did not just fall of itself—it was pushed by others. I think of Pilate's acts today, forced by others. I remember the awful earthquake in my dream, and I think of the real quake today which stopped just short of the Antonia.

Perhaps it was just a warning. Was Pilate spared for a reason? Is there hope for a man with the blood of God's Son on his hands?

Perhaps that is what Jesus meant when he said to my husband, "He who betrayed me has the greater sin." Perhaps when they were flogging him and he looked up and saw me in the window, that is what he would have told me if he had had the chance. Perhaps he would have told me not to lose hope, for this is not the end.

I can only imagine the crucifixion. I am glad I did not see Jesus hanging on the cross with my natural eyes. What I did see was bad enough. I shall never forget this picture: Jesus below my window, stripped and tied to the whipping post—Jesus looking up at me—Jesus with the thongs like stinging serpents wrapping themselves around him, drawing blood—Jesus' blood on the stones of the courtyard—Pilate standing by, with that smug look on his face. How could I ever forget it, Jesus' blood on Pilate's hands? No matter how often he washes them, there will still be blood on my husband's hands.

CHAPTER 7

Don't Touch Me

I have to get up near morning to attend to a pressing physical need. I can blame the wine for it. I feel wretched, thoroughly sick, in my head and in my stomach. And I am sick at heart. I am embarrassed about what I have said and done. When I get back in bed, I feel Claudia stirring beside me. With a painful effort, I turn over and attempt to put my arm around her. She moves away from me and murmurs, "Pilate, please don't touch me—not tonight."

I say, "Just the other night you wanted me to touch you."

She hesitates. "That was before—before...."

She has touched a raw nerve. "Before I killed your precious Jesus." It bursts out of me without any inner warning.

There is a moment's silence. Then she says, "After what happened today, I can't bring myself to let you touch me—not yet."

She has hurt me. I flash back at her, "If you won't even let me put my arm around you, how is this 'Unknown God' of yours going to give you a child? Maybe you expect to lay an egg...."

I never get the chance to complete my ironic comparison with Leda and her swan-god and the hatching of those heavenly twins, the Gemini. And I regret that I said anything, for she starts to sob uncontrollably. She will not permit me to comfort her. Finally she drops off to sleep, but I lie here wakeful until the dawn. I have had a very bad night. And I am anticipating a miserable day.

CHAPTER 8

A Detailed Report

By eight o'clock I am in my office, tackling a pile of documents. I have an enormous hangover and even the rustle of papers hurts my head. At least there are no cases coming up today because of the Passover Sabbath. No activity in the Temple. No crowds in the streets. All the Jews are celebrating the festival in their homes. The danger of an uprising seems to have passed. In spite of what happened yesterday, it seems as if everything will work out all right.

The routine tasks I am doing have a soothing effect. At a time like this, papers are easier to handle than people. But my tasks leave my mind free to wander. In the back of my head, there is something which puzzles me, a growing uneasiness, hard to put into words. The things my wife has been saying are completely illogical to a man. After ten years of living with the woman, this does not surprise me. But how can she claim to worship this Unknown God of hers—the one who has promised to give her a child—and also believe Jesus was the Son of God? It would not make sense, even to another woman, unless—and this is unthinkable—the Unknown God and Jesus' God are one and the same, *unless the priest she saw on Monday was actually Jesus.* Yet I would swear it was not. I have sized up the man through many second-hand reports and a few first-hand investigations, especially those two private interviews I had with him. And I would swear Jesus was not the lying priest who took advantage of Claudia's credulity. That was just not Jesus' style—his *modus operandi*.

But why worry? Nothing will come of it. If it was Jesus, he is dead and gone. If it was a cultish priest, Claudia will never see him again. A year will pass and she will bear no child. Her heart will be broken again. Let her keep her little secrets and hold on to her pitiful illusion as long as she can. She will soon find out the truth—she has been deceived again. I promised to ask no questions and I will keep my word. I always keep my word—unless I have no choice in the matter, like yesterday. Yes, I keep my word, unless I am given no choice....

At nine o'clock I send for Centurion Paronius. He gives me a full report on Friday's three crucifixions. Except for the breaking of the legs, the first two were just routine; I ask no questions.

I feel a little awkward today in the presence of the centurion. He has served under me for some years now, but I do not know him well. I make it a point not to get familiar with my under officers, those below the rank of tribune. It is a wise policy for many reasons. But yesterday I let my guard down in front of this man. I had been drinking, and I was taken aback at the sight of Jesus' blood. I know he must have noticed my surprised reaction, and today I am embarrassed. But perhaps he is, too. After all, was not his bravado a little overdone? Perhaps the bloody experience shook him up more than he wanted to admit.

Today I can stand to look at Paronius, for he has bathed and his uniform is clean. Today we are both calm and rational, relatively speaking. Except for my hangover, everything is back to normal. I ask him to tell me about the crucifixion of the third man, Jesus of Nazareth, starting at the beginning. I interrupt his account with questions and comments. Of course I need the information for my year-end report, but I am interested in every detail that will shed light on the extraordinary circumstances of this last crucifixion. I want to find out who Jesus really was.

"Centurion, if you were so sure he was already dead, why did you give the order to drive a spear into his side?"

"Just routine precautions, Excellency, because the apparent death had occurred after only six hours. I wanted to take no chances of burying a man who was still alive."

"I approve your thoroughness. In spite of appearances, he must have been still alive, or he would not have bled."

"Sir, I have seen hundreds die, and I know the signs of death. I would have sworn the man was dead. When the spear pierced his heart, none of us expected the jet of blood and water to come from a dead body. Why it happened, I can't explain. I leave this to the learned physicians."

I ask Paronius for details about the darkness, about the earthquake. He says the darkness came on gradually for no apparent reason. The sun's light simply failed. But the earthquake came suddenly, without any warning. It seemed to start right there at the Place of the Skull, almost beneath their feet. Rocks fell and everyone was thrown to the ground, but no one was seriously hurt.

I have asked about everything except what I really want to know. I am about to dismiss my officer, and it is now or never. I try to sound casual as I remark, "One of the accusations against Jesus was his claim to be the Son of God. It is my considered opinion that he actually believed this about himself. Did you observe any evidence of such a delusion in his behavior?"

"Yes, Excellency. I heard him call on God, addressing him as 'Father' in several instances. The first time was while we were nailing his hands to the crosspiece. He called on God, saying, 'Father, forgive them, for they do not know what they are doing.'"

"Extraordinary. I see what you mean. What else did he say?"

"The Jewish leaders were taunting him. They were saying, 'If you are the Son of God, come down from the cross.' One of the robbers crucified beside Jesus jeered at him, 'Yes, if you are the Messiah, why don't you prove it by saving yourself and us?' The other thief said to his comrade, 'Don't you even fear God when you are dying? We are getting our just desserts, but this man has done nothing wrong.' Then he turned to Jesus and said, 'Remember me when you come into your kingdom.'"

"How did Jesus answer?"

"He said, 'I solemnly promise you, today you will be with me in paradise.'"

"Then he must have persisted in this God-fixation right down to the end, for apparently—even on the cross—he got at least one man to believe it."

"I am sure he died believing he was the Son of God."

"Centurion, what do you yourself believe about him?"

After a slight pause, Paronius answers, "I believe the man was innocent."

"Innocent of being the King of the Jews?"

"Yes, sir, in any political sense."

"But what about the claim of divinity? Who was he, centurion?"

Another hesitation. Then Paronius says, "As I told you before, sir, at the moment Jesus died, the earth shook beneath us, and we all fell to our knees. I was struck with awe at what I considered to be God's answer. And I said, 'Truly this was the Son of God!'"

"Do you still believe it?"

"At that moment, I was expecting the world to fall apart around me as a punishment for what we had done. But then the sun came out and nothing more happened except...."

"Except for your blood-bath."

"Right, sir. It shocked me because it took me by surprise. But after that, everything returned to normal."

"Now, who do you think he was?"

"I am not so sure. But perhaps time will tell."

"One way or another. I assume you supervised the burial as I requested?"

"I obeyed your orders, sir. From a distance I watched the Jews prepare the body and lay it in the tomb. And I fixed the spot well in my mind for future reference. I left just before sunset, following the burial party."

I say, "Then we have heard the last of this Jesus."

He says, "I hope so, sir."

CHAPTER 9

A Request Denied

We were wrong. At ten o'clock I receive a most unusual delegation from the chief priests and Pharisees. Unlike yesterday, they seem unconcerned about defilement although this is for them a high holy day. They are eager to speak to me in private inside the fortress.

They say to me, "Sir, we remember that this imposter said, while he was still alive, 'After three days I will rise again.' So give orders to have the tomb safeguarded until the third day, to prevent his disciples from coming and stealing his body and then telling everyone he has risen from the dead. If that happens, we'll be worse off than we were at first."

I want no part of it. I gave orders for the death of their so-called imposter most grudgingly, and I have washed my hands of the whole affair. From now on, I refuse to become involved. This is their concern, not mine.

So I say to them, "You have your own Temple Guard; that should be sufficient. Go, make the tomb as secure as you can. Good luck and goodbye."

I think they are surprised and offended when I dismiss them so summarily. But I have a splitting headache today and I will put up with no nonsense. How unreasonable can they get? If they were so concerned, why did they not tell me last night? But I suppose these Jews would not do anything which is not strictly religious on the night of their *Seder*, even if the world should come to an end. At any rate, this is bound to be the last I will hear of Jesus from them.

Rather strange I should have had no previous reports about this business of Jesus' claim that he will rise on the third day. Perhaps Joanna has written about it to Claudia. I will ask her at lunch—if we are on speaking terms again. It will be her decision.

CHAPTER 10

I Did the Best I Could

I decide to stop work at noon. If all the people of Jerusalem are having a holiday, why not their governor? Perhaps if I take it easy this afternoon, I shall be completely well by Sunday morning, ready to finish the cases I left off Friday at noon.

Claudia is at least approachable. She even shows some concern about my health. Although my stomach turns at the sight of food, I recline with her at the table. She eats more than she usually does at noon; she is making up for the meal she missed last night. A bit of bread, the first I have had today, is all my stomach will accept. But I do feel like talking, and Claudia seems willing to listen. She accepts my apologies about my conduct last night. She says she is glad it happened, as painful as it was for both of us, because it cleared the air between us. She says now that she realizes how I feel, she is able to be a better wife to me.

I say, "Now you can understand why I hate to come to Jerusalem, why I brought in those gilded shields. In this stronghold of the Jewish God, I feel helpless without the symbols of the power of Rome. I feel his evil influence behind everything which happens to me here. Even when I win, I win only by the skin of my teeth—take the aqueduct affair. I know I lost yesterday."

"Who won, then? The Jews?"

"I had to back down and accede to their requests. But they had to grovel before the might of Rome and shout, 'We have no king but Caesar!' They had to admit they had trumped up the charge of high treason against Jesus. To secure his death, they had to demand the release of a real insurrectionist, Barabbas, a man whose past activities were a danger to society. I know I lost, but I am not so sure anybody won."

"It seems to me as if everybody lost, except maybe Jesus."

"How do you mean that?"

"He was the only one who was true to what he believed in, right down to the end."

"But he was the only one who lost his life."

"He was the only one who refused to compromise his convictions. In my way of thinking, that makes him the real winner."

"Claudia, I've told you, I did all I could. I fought for Jesus' life. I used every trick I could think of. At first I thought I was battling just the priestly party. But it soon became apparent that I was also fighting against the will of the people. In that crowd of hundreds, there were only a handful who were willing to speak up for Jesus when I gave them a choice for freedom between Jesus and Barabbas. A ruler who defies the will of the people doesn't stay in power long. Still I was willing to take the risk and set Jesus free until one of those shrewd priests noticed the ring on my finger. When he said, 'If you turn this man loose, you are not Caesar's friend,' I knew I was beaten."

"All because of a mere ring? You are over-simplifying."

"Because of what that ring stands for. Claudia, it stands for everything I have attained in life—my property, acquired and inherited, my chances for advancement, my reputation, my liberty, perhaps my life itself."

"You are exaggerating. Surely turning loose one harmless prisoner could not cause so much trouble for you."

"Think about it, Claudia. You know how unsure I am about my standing with Tiberius since Sejanus' execution. You know about the consequent change in official policy. As Caiaphas and his clan inform me at every opportunity, I must foster the Jewish religion and protect its traditions. Well, in the first place, if I had turned Jesus loose, he would probably never have made it back to Galilee. Although they would have disclaimed it, the priestly party would have hired someone to do away with him. In the meantime, Caiaphas would have sent a delegation to complain to Tiberius about my failure to uphold the Jewish laws, and in a few months I would be standing before the emperor, trying to refute their charges.

"They would claim, just as they told me they would, that I am no friend of Caesar's because I turned loose a dangerous revolutionary, and doddering old Tiberius would believe them because of my past record. The ring which marks me as *amicus caesaris* would be torn off my finger. I would be cast into prison and tried before the Senate. If found guilty, I would be either fined heavily or exiled, or in the worst possible case, strangled. My body would be denied decent burial and thrown down the Steps of Mourning into the Tiber. Would you want that to happen to me?"

"No, of course not, but you are over-reacting."

"I haven't finished yet. I haven't told you yet what would happen to you. As my wife, you would probably choose to accompany me into exile. Of course we would forfeit all our property and live out our lives on some remote island, far from family and friends. And if I should be executed, all our property would be likewise confiscated, and you would pass the rest of your days in poverty and disgrace. Would you want that to happen to you?"

"If you had died for what you really believed in, I would honor you and accept whatever shame and hardship I must undergo as a tribute to your memory. And I would do so cheerfully."

"You would undergo hardships cheerfully? You have never done without anything you needed in all your life, and as for shame—your family has been respected for generations. Far from honoring my memory, you would end up cursing me."

"I would never curse you. I would thank God daily for having given me such a noble husband."

"I may not be the hero you would like for a husband, one who would put duty above everything else; but I can give you a better life than some unrealistic visionary. I want the good things for both of us. And I was unwilling to hazard everything we have attained for—please forgive me—a poor Jewish carpenter-turned-traveling teacher. I repeat, I did the best I could for him. But in the last extremity, I had no choice."

"Are you telling me you sacrificed Jesus to protect yourself and me?"

"I suppose I am."

"What if some day you should find out he really was the Son of God?"

"I should spend the rest of my life regretting my action."

CHAPTER 11

A Puzzling Prediction

"I just remembered something, Claudia—something I need to ask you. Has Joanna ever written you anything about Jesus' claim that after three days he would rise again?"

"No. Why do you ask?"

"A little while ago some of Caiaphas's men came here to enlist my aid. They wanted some Roman soldiers to seal Jesus' tomb and guard it for three days. They said he had predicted he would rise again in three days; they feared his disciples might steal the body and then tell everyone he had risen, in order to gain popular support."

"Did you promise to help them?"

"Certainly not. I told them to seal the tomb themselves and use their Temple Guard. Rome has no interest in the body after the criminal is executed. I delivered the body to a Jew; therefore the protection of the tomb is a Jewish affair."

"I wonder why Joanna never told me about this saying if Jesus really said it. She wrote me she was worried about his visit to Jerusalem this time because he had been talking about his death, but she never mentioned his coming back to life after three days."

"It seems odd to me that his enemies should know about this

claim and not his friends. Perhaps the priestly party misinterpreted something he said."

"What I overheard outside the temple indicated that they understood him perfectly. This is why they were out to get him, because he prophesied they would kill him and God would punish them for it."

"Perhaps his friends themselves misunderstood. You said they failed to understand him at the time."

"Yes, he had to explain his story in detail before they realized what he had been talking about."

"Under such circumstances, I don't think Caiaphas and his men have anything to worry about. Let them seal the tomb themselves. Tomorrow morning will be three days by the Jewish reckoning. And of course nothing will happen."

"Of course, but...."

"Claudia, this is reality. There is life and there is death, and death is final. This is no mythical tale of Isis and Osiris. Come down to earth. Your Jesus is dead and I am sorry. But it is time to stop grieving about *him* and to start thinking about *me*. He was just a man you heard a lot about and saw only a few times. I am your husband of ten years, and I am still alive. By the way, when are you going to let me touch you again?"

"I will let you know."

"If I put my arm around you tonight, will you push me away?"

"When I feel I am ready, I will put *my* arm around *you*."

"Oh, before I forget it—we are invited to the Hasmonean Palace for dinner Tuesday night. Apparently my gesture of deference to Herod has paid off. I want you to wear your prettiest outfit—the one with the silk shawl. But don't get too close to Herod; the man has roving eyes."

"And hands. Now don't worry; Herodias will take care of that."

I will just have to wait. At least Claudia and I are talking to each other again. Tonight will be better than last night, and we will both get some sleep.

CHAPTER 12

Another Tremor and an Empty Tomb

When I rise Sunday just before dawn, I detect a slight earth tremor. I steel myself, expecting more to follow. I feel a momentary flash of guilt and fear, remembering Friday's quake and its implications. But nothing more happens.

Less than an hour later, in my office, I have an early visitor. It is an officer of the City Guard. He has with him a soldier who was on duty at the western gate during the last watch of the night. The officer tells me he believes something strange has happened at the tomb of the Nazarene, for this soldier has just witnessed a very odd thing. I proceed to question the auxiliary.

He says, "It was just before dawn, Your Excellency. During the change of the guard, several men came running toward us through the gate. When they hurtled into us, I grabbed one of them, but the others escaped into that maze of alleys."

"Did you follow them?"

"Some of us tried to follow them, but in the darkness before the dawn, it was a hopeless case. They were running scared, as if they'd seen a ghost. Would have been hard to catch them in broad daylight."

"Were you able to find out anything from the man you seized?"

"Yes, Excellency. They were Temple guards, like him. After he bumped into me, at close range I recognized the uniform."

"What did he tell you when you questioned him?"

"I seized him by the throat and demanded to know his business. He was trembling like a frightened rabbit. The man was hysterical, and nothing he said made sense."

"Then you were unable to get any information out of him?"

"On the contrary, sir. After I threatened to turn him in to my superiors for questioning, he decided to cooperate. He told me he and his comrades of the Temple Guard were on duty at the tomb of the Nazarene. He said a little while before dawn, when they were standing watch, an earthquake shook the place, and an angel all in white rolled away the stone and sat upon it."

"Wait a minute. To tell you a fantastic tale like that, the man would either have to be mad or else very drunk. Could you tell if he had been drinking?"

"He seemed completely sober, only frightened to death by what he said he had just seen."

"Was that all he said he saw?"

"No, sir. He said when the angel rolled the stone away, they could see the tomb was empty."

"Wait another minute. Are you telling me they were guarding an *empty tomb*?"

"Yes, sir."

"How did the man explain this?"

"Excellency, he was in no condition to explain anything. He blurted out his story, that was all. He said when they saw no body inside the tomb, some of the guards fainted dead away. He said when he and his companions bumped into us, they were running toward the High Priest's house to tell him what had happened."

"Officer, what action did you take when this soldier reported to you?"

"I wrote down the name of the Temple guard and then I turned him loose."

"You didn't think I might want to question the man myself?"

"Sir, with all due respect, I believed my soldier had got the truth out of him...."

"The truth? That fantastic tale, the vagaries of a Semitic imagination?"

"Excellency, I am convinced the man believed his own story. But when he saw me, be became fearful, and he promptly lost his tongue. I was unable to get anything out of him. If I had brought him to you, he would probably have said nothing. And besides, sir I remembered your orders not to interfere with the Temple Guard in the performance of its duties."

"Ha! This would be more like 'in its dereliction from its duties.' But Caiaphas would have considered such meddling with his affairs an undue provocation. You did the right thing."

I dismiss the officer and his auxiliary. I sit back and ponder for a moment. Well, what am I to make of all this? I decide to check it out first-hand. So I call for Paronius. He leads me to the site just outside the city wall on the north where he supervised the burial. We see the stone, which has been rolled away. And as the man said, the tomb is empty. For a moment we are both speechless.

Then I say to my centurion, "Can you figure out some logical explanation for what has happened? What about that stone, for a starter?"

He says, "It couldn't have been easily dislodged; it took several men to push the stone in place. Perhaps the earthquake did it."

I add, "And perhaps the guards imagined the angel when they saw the stone rolled away by no human hand. These Jews are so superstitious."

Paronius adds, "They must have been thrown to the ground by the impact, like the auxiliaries and myself the other day. Don't be too hard on them, sir. It is easy to imagine anything at such a time. And what with the empty tomb...."

"Yes, what about that...Paronius, how do you explain the empty tomb?"

"Sir, I am at a loss to explain it. All I know is this: It was occupied when I left it Friday night. What happened after that? Your guess is as good as mine."

"I intend to find out if I can. Let's go back for now."

We return to the city. This time I decide to play it smart like

Caiaphas. I will not go looking for answers; I will sit back and wait while he stirs around. Perhaps if I do, the answers will come to me....

On Monday morning my aide reports to me that the city is full of rumors and crowds are starting to gather around the burial site. People are saying Jesus has risen from the dead after three days according to his prophecy. By Jewish reckoning, Friday night to Sunday morning is exactly three days, as I remarked to Claudia before all this happened. It is just a coincidence, I tell myself. Just an extraordinary coincidence. There has to be some logical explanation for all of this. I continue with my duties as governor. And I wait and I wonder.

CHAPTER 13

Two Impossible Explanations

It is early Monday afternoon. I receive a messenger with a letter from Caiaphas. I scan it hurriedly and write a brief answer, which I dispatch to him by the waiting messenger. Then I study the letter more closely. It is the High Priest's explanation of what happened at the tomb. It is not very convincing to me. It is not very flattering to the efficiency of the Temple guards at the tomb. (In fact, if they had been Roman soldiers, they would all have been executed for such an offense.)

Caiaphas says his men fell asleep on guard Saturday night. While they were sleeping, Jesus' disciples came and stole away the body. They did not discover the theft until after they were awakened by the earthquake, which caused the stone to roll away, revealing the empty tomb. Caiaphas says the man who was detained by the City Guard has since denied the outrageous lie he told about the angel. He invented it because he was afraid of being punished for sleeping on duty. He and the other guards who were at the burial site are now in agreement as to what really happened.

The High Priest goes on to say that he, Caiaphas, is deeply concerned because of the way this wild tale is spreading, lest it cause unrest in the city. He requests me to cordon off the area around the tomb and to issue a warrant for the arrest of the grave robbers.

I wrote my brief answer, tongue-in-cheek. For the second time I said, "You have a guard of soldiers; that should be sufficient. Go, make it as secure as you can." I underscored the last part to make sure the High Priest got the point. I did not deign to answer his second request. Grave robbery is not a capital offense, and I do not intend to make it my business.

I settle back in my chair and reflect rather pleasurably on Caiaphas's apparent discomfiture. He had me sweating on the judgment seat; let him sweat now. This is an internal matter of no concern to Rome. I determined that the living Nazarene was no threat to Roman authority, despite Jewish fabrications; then why should the dead one be...?

It is now early Tuesday morning. I have been wrestling all night with the problems which confront me. The Temple guard's babble about an angel—ridiculous, the ravings of a superstitious Semite. The High Priest's explanation of the same—preposterous. How could a detail of fifteen men all be asleep on guard at the same time? How could it be that none of them heard the noise the disciples must have made when they supposedly rolled the stone away and then rolled it back in place? For according to the now-official story, they did not discover the theft of the body until the earthquake revealed the empty tomb.

If Caiaphas was going to concoct a story, why did he not say the body must have been stolen Friday night, when the tomb was left unguarded? That would have made the tale more convincing...No, he could not have said this, for his men would have discovered the theft Saturday morning when they sealed the tomb. Surely they would have checked to see whether the body was still inside, since Caiaphas was so concerned about it. There would have been no point in sealing an already empty tomb. And if they had found it empty on Saturday, Caiaphas would have reported the theft immediately.

I keep wandering in circles; I am right back where I started with my conjectures. Although this second explanation leaves out supernatural intervention, it is just as illogical as the first one.

I must make some move of my own if I hope to learn the truth. It will do no good to send for the Temple guards who were involved. Undoubtedly Caiaphas has paid them well, and they will stick to the official version of the story...I know what I shall do: I shall call for Joseph of Arimathea. After all, he was a witness to the burial. He seems to have been a follower of Jesus, or he would not have asked for the body and buried it in his own tomb. Whether or not he can resolve my doubts, I believe he will answer my questions honestly. I promptly dispatch a courier to bring Joseph to me....

The councilor seems elated, eager to communicate what he knows. He is almost too cooperative. I ask routine questions at first to verify hearsay evidence.

"Joseph, were you one of the followers of the deceased Jesus of Nazareth?"

"I was a secret believer but not an active follower."

"Did you have any contacts with Jesus or his active followers?"

"Only occasional contacts through a disciple named John."

"Why then did you offer to give the body burial?"

"I sought to make amends because I had not come out openly for Jesus while he was living."

"Is it true you buried Jesus in your own tomb?"

"Yes, Excellency, the tomb was one I had prepared for my own burial."

"Then you are quite familiar with the site of the burial and would know if the empty tomb is the same one you buried Jesus in?"

"Yes, sir. Yesterday morning when I heard the tomb was empty, I went there immediately. I am ready to swear it is the same tomb in which we buried the Master."

"That removes any possibility of false identification of the grave site. Now let us proceed to the burial itself. Joseph, were you present at Jesus' presumed death and did you witness the subsequent spear thrust which reportedly caused the emission of much blood and water?"

"Yes, sir, I saw Jesus die, and about an hour later, I saw the soldier thrust the spear into his side."

"Did you consider it a wound sufficient in itself to cause a man's death?"

"It was a wound to the heart, sir. The soldier knew his business.

It would have dispatched any man."

"When you prepared the body for burial, did you inspect the wound?"

"Yes, Excellency. It was a very deep wound, right under his left breast. It was large enough for a man to put his hand in."

"Did you verify the death by any other observations?"

"The body was becoming stiff, and there was no breathing. Our law requires certain tests with a downy feather placed under the nose before we can pronounce a person dead and proceed with the burial."

"Then you are positive the man Jesus was dead when you buried him?"

"Positive, Your Excellency."

"Then there is no possibility that he could have lain in the tomb unconscious for two days, revived on the third day, pushed back the stone, and issued out of the tomb?"

"Sir, a bloodless corpse does not revive, except by a miracle of God."

"Do you believe this was a miracle?"

"Yes, sir, I do."

"And what basis do you have for this belief?"

"Sir, Jesus appeared to some of the women and to the disciples. He told them to go before him to Galilee, where he would meet them."

"Did Jesus have a twin brother whom they might have confused with him?"

"Jesus had several younger brothers and sisters but no twin."

"Is it possible they may have seen a ghost?"

"At first the women and the disciples thought it was a ghost. But after the men inspected his wounds and watched him eat some of their food, they became convinced he was a living man."

"Have you yourself seen Jesus since the alleged resurrection?"

"No, Your Excellency."

"Is there a possibility that Jesus' disciples have hatched up some clever plot to deceive the public into believing he has risen from the dead so as to gain a following?"

"Sir, Jesus' resurrection was the last thing any of them were expecting. Most of Jesus' disciples did not believe God would let him die. When they saw him die, they were too depressed and disillusioned to undertake any concerted action. They would not believe the women's stories until after they had seen Jesus for themselves."

"Joseph, you have the reputation for being a man of sober judgment. Yet you seem to believe the unbelievable. Tell me, when you found the tomb empty, before you heard the women's story, did you not once think of the possibility that the body had been stolen by grave robbers?"

"It did cross my mind, sir, until I saw the graveclothes...."

"This is the first I have heard anything about graveclothes. Tell me more."

"I found the shroud neatly folded at one end of the slab on which the body had been laid, and at the other, neatly rolled, the cloth which had covered the head. Grave robbers in their haste would never have done such a thing. They would have seized the body and carried it off along with the wrappings."

"Then, in your opinion, who could have done it?"

"Jesus himself."

There is no need to question this man any further. He thinks he knows all the answers, but all I am left with is more questions. I wish Joseph well and I thank him for his assistance. Then he leaves.

There is one more thing I could verify, if I chose to do so. I could summon the Temple guard whose name I have on file. I could ask him whether or not the guards checked the tomb before they sealed it on Saturday. But I do not choose. In the first place, the man has already lied at least one time, and he would probably tell me what his master Caiaphas wants me to believe. In the second place, I told Caiaphas that these are internal matters in which Rome will not intervene. And in the third place, as long as I do not actually check this out, I leave myself a loophole for skepticism. At least now I can tell myself the body must have been stolen Friday night and the stupid guards sealed an empty tomb.

Whichever explanation I consider—the one the Temple guard told my soldier or the High Priest's official version—it shows the Temple guards to be a flighty, undependable lot, capable of making gross oversights and coming to unjustified conclusions. It is highly possible that they did not check the tomb before they sealed it. It appears they did nothing else right.

If I should find they actually saw the body in the tomb before they sealed it on Saturday morning, I would have no other choice than to believe the stories told me by my soldier and Joseph of Arimathea. They go together. And to believe such a supernatural explanation, I would have to descend to the level of a superstitious Jew or a gullible woman.

CHAPTER 14

Rumors of a Resurrection

I have felt miserable since Jesus' death, but now I am getting better. All over town people are saying Jesus is alive, and I have hope again. The city has been teeming with rumors ever since the earthquake tremor Sunday morning. Pilate has been very close-mouthed around me about what is going on. I suppose he does not want me to become overwrought. All he has told me directly is that the body of Jesus is missing. When I questioned him this afternoon, he had to tell me about the contents of the letter I saw him reading.

But no matter—I have heard all the details of the story from the servants. Eunice heard from one of the auxiliaries the original version told by the Temple guard. Hannah says people are flocking to the gravesite to gawk and wonder, and the crowds are increasing every day. This morning I caught a glimpse of a strange man coming out of Pilate's office. I learned he was Joseph of Arimathea, the rich Jew who buried Jesus in his own tomb. I wish I could have talked to the man. He would surely be able to tell me if Jesus is alive.

I do not believe the story which is circulating about Jesus' disciples stealing his body. It sounds like something Caiaphas would concoct to hide the truth. I can hardly wait until tonight, when we are to eat dinner with the Herods at the Hasmonean Palace. I feel sure of meeting Joanna there. She will certainly be able to tell me if what I am hearing about the resurrection is really true. And if it is true, will Jesus fulfill his promise? Or did the death sentence by my husband cancel out the promise? Joanna will know if anybody knows. At least I have grounds for hope, but the suspense is killing me.

Now that I feel better, I am paying more attention to Pilate. He seems different from the man I knew before, more withdrawn and preoccupied around me. He is not in deep depression, as he was on Friday and Saturday. I do not notice him washing his hands all the time or rubbing them absent-mindedly or studying them closely, as if to discover some uncleanness on them. He is not drinking as heavily as he was on Friday. Yet something is on his mind. Perhaps it is the problem of the missing body. This is no problem for me because I want to believe Jesus has come back to life. But it is a great problem for Pilate because he refuses to believe the dead can live again.

From some of the things he lets slip, I know his mind is attacking the problem from every angle. I know he got a letter from the High Priest this morning. I saw him with the letter in his hand, and I overheard him muttering, "I wonder how much he paid them." Of course I asked for an explanation, and he showed me the letter. Then he remarked at lunch how Caiaphas must think he is rather gullible to accept such a far-fetched story. He said, "How could all those guards be sleeping at the same time, and why did none of them hear the disciples when they stole the body?"

The High Priest must be the source of the second story which is spreading all over town. People are laughing and sneering at the inefficiency of the Temple guards, but many tend to accept this explanation. Unlike the first story, it does not require a complete change in their materialistic way of thinking. But Pilate is too irreligious to accept the first story and too realistic to accept the second. He is a man who wants everything explained in a way which will satisfy his natural mind. And so now he is just as miserable in his own way as I have been in mine.

I wonder if he is really looking forward to our dinner with the Herods. After all, he doesn't particularly enjoy the company of Antipas, and he can't bear Herodias. Perhaps he is hoping, as I am hoping, to hear something that will cast light on the empty tomb and the missing body. Of this I am sure—we cannot both find a satisfactory answer.

CHAPTER 15

After Herod's Banquet

It is late Tuesday evening. Pilate and I have just left the Hasmonean Palace and are on our way back to the Antonia. We are sitting side by side in our carriage. Pilate is in a mellow mood and I am in high spirits. I'm bursting to share with my husband the things I learned about Jesus, but I must be careful not to reveal too much.

Pilate has said nothing yet. Good food and good wine must be taking their effect.

I say, "Don't fall asleep on me, Pilate. I want to talk about the party."

He says, "You enjoyed it, then? I thought you would."

I say, "Very much. It was nice to get out of our cramped quarters at the Antonia and socialize with someone else besides the servants."

He says, "I was proud of how you looked tonight wearing your birthday jewelry and that new silk shawl."

"All the ladies liked my shawl and wanted to feel of it."

"Probably all the men, too. I'm surprised Herod didn't try. He couldn't keep his eyes off you."

"Herodias took care of that by reclining between us. And she couldn't keep her hands off the shawl, even after they brought out the appetizers. You saw how she kept stroking it and fingering those silken fringes."

"Claudia, I wanted to tell her how much the shawl cost. But at least she wiped her hands first."

"And then she said, 'I simply must find one like it the next time I go shopping in Rome or Antioch.' She kept stroking my arm."

"Well, at least it wasn't Antipas."

"She said, 'It looks and feels so sensuous; what is it made of? Is it silk?' And I answered, 'Yes, it's silk.'"

"Ha! The woman can't bear to be outdone. You heard her bragging about how she was going to buy enough yards of silk to make herself a complete outfit. Claudia, you heard her say, 'I want to feel the touch of silk next to my skin.' That was when I got an irresistible urge to give her the putdown she really deserved."

"You were wicked, but you were wonderful!"

"I could say I'm sorry, but I'm not. I thoroughly enjoyed telling her, 'Can you believe anything so beautiful could be spun from the gut of a spider?'"

"I knew what you were doing, and I could hardly keep a straight face when I saw hers start to twitch. And then when she grabbed the napkin and—Pilate, your timing was perfect. Did you know she had her mouth full of a jellyfish appetizer at the moment?"

"No, I suppose I was just lucky. I hoped it was something gooey. But I was too busy making up the spider story as I went along to notice such details."

"You were quite convincing with your tale about your learned Greek in Caesarea who has traveled all over the Orient and has told you the true story about the making of silk."

"I was in good form, explaining how the Chinese squash the spiders and extract a viscous fluid from their guts, how they draw it out into strands, spin them into threads, and weave them into cloth...."

"In the dark of the moon, accompanied by fearful spells and incantations...."

"Perhaps I overdid it a little."

"You were almost too good. Herodias was shifting around uneasily as though she could feel the spiders crawling all over her. I could almost feel them myself."

"I think I fixed her—she won't be talking again about buying anything made out of silk any time soon. Now are you going to give another of your lectures about my lack of social graces?"

"No, Pilate. I have stopped sympathizing with the delicate sensibilities of any woman who would have a man's head carried in on a platter at a banquet. And I must admit, tonight I did enjoy that expression on Herodias' face. But to change the subject—how was the men's after-dinner session? The usual drinking and off-color jokes?"

I do not wait for his answer and I add, "I hope you stayed sober enough to forego your usual anti-Jewish ones."

He says, "I kept myself under control. When I am around Herod, I need all my wits about me. In spite of his friendly overtures, I don't really trust the man. And remember, this is the Holy City, where Herod must keep up appearances. The drinking was moderate, and there wasn't much joking. We were all discussing more serious things like religion and politics. They go together here in Jerusalem. We talked about Barabbas and how my show case unexpectedly fell apart, about the unpredictability of crowds...."

"And about Jesus?"

"Herod favored us with a comic description of Jesus' demeanor when he appeared before him. He is an excellent mimic. To be polite, I felt as I had to laugh, but my heart wasn't in it."

"I hope not, Pilate. At least you had the grace to feel guilty."

CHAPTER 16

Joanna Takes Her Stand

We have reached the courtyard of the Antonia. We go upstairs and prepare to retire. I am eager to resume our conversation. I say to Pilate, "Don't you want to know what we women talked about?"

Pilate says, "Not especially. Silk shawls and fashions, I suppose?"
I answer that our conversation was similar to the men's.
He says, "You talked about Jesus too?"
"Almost exclusively. Herodias was most spiteful. I think she wanted to goad Joanna into making a public statement of her faith. She wanted to embarrass her and lower her in the esteem of the other guests."
"In other words, Herodias was acting in character."
"She said, 'Really, Joanna, you should have been present when we entertained your prophet at our holiday breakfast. In spite of all those miracles you say he has performed, he refused to do a single trick for us. And in spite of all those pearls of wisdom which you claim have fallen from his lips, he wouldn't say a single word.'
"I could see Joanna's eyes snapping in anger. However, she said gently, 'Jesus does not perform to amuse the mighty, but to serve the lowly. That is why he would not.'

"Herodias sneered, '*Would not or could not?* Without his prearranged deceptions, he could not. My Antipas revealed him as the pitiful imposter he is.'"

I pause for effect.

"Ha!"

Pilate is getting into bed while I am taking off my make-up. Since he makes no further comment, I go on with my story.

"I saw Joanna pulling on her napkin nervously. She said, 'You are mistaken, Mistress. You and Lord Herod are mistaken.'

"Herodias tossed her head and smirked, 'Really, Joanna! If he were not an imposter, would he have died on a Roman cross?'

"Then Herodias looked at me, and I know my face must have turned all shades of red. 'What do you say, Lady Claudia? Your husband must believe this Jesus was an imposter, or he would not have crucified him.'

"I blurted out, 'My husband had no choice. He wanted to release Jesus, but he was afraid it might cause a riot.'"

"Good for you, Claudia. You told it like it is. What did Herodias say to that?"

"She went back to picking on poor Joanna. She said, 'There, you see—Joanna should be grateful to be freed from her delusions. This Jesus held her spellbound. He made her believe he had healed her eyes. She went off with him and his followers. She spent more time with him and his uncouth disciples than she did with us. And heaven knows how much of Chuza's money she has thrown after him!'

"Herodias smiled and sighed. Shaking her head, she turned to the rest of us. She went smugly on: 'Poor Joanna, she is still deluded. Tell them, Joanna. Tell them how this Jesus has risen from the dead. Although everyone else eventually saw through his sham, even after his death *some people* will still believe.'

"Joanna stood up. She was very white and she kept clenching and unclenching her fists. Looking around at us, she said, 'I am not deluded. Lady Herodias, it is you and your husband who are deluded. I have seen and I have believed.'"

I pause for a moment, expecting some comment from Pilate in the bed, but all he says is "Well?" At least the man seems to be listening intently. So I resume.

"All our eyes turned to Joanna. She told us how she and several other women went to Jesus' tomb early Sunday morning, bearing spices for the anointing. They were wondering how they should get inside the tomb, but when they arrived, they saw the stone had been rolled away. Fearfully, one by one, they went inside. They came out looking as though they had seen a ghost, and they ran away."

"Aha! Just like the Temple guards."

"Yes, at least to begin with. Joanna said, 'When I got inside the tomb, I saw a young man in white sitting on the right side where we had left the body. But the body was not there. The young man said Jesus had risen and we should go tell all the disciples. I ran back to the house and tried to tell what had happened; but I was too upset to express myself clearly, and they didn't believe me.'"

"No wonder those men refused to believe a tale like that. How did Herodias react to it?"

"She made some snide remark which wasn't very funny, and we tried to ignore her. We encouraged Joanna to continue. She told us how Jesus appeared in person to some of the other women and later, to all the disciples, after which they all believed. She said he had promised to meet them in Galilee. And then...."

"Well?"

"I just wanted to make sure you were listening. Then Joanna looked triumphantly around the group. She said, "So you see, Jesus was no imposter, for God has affirmed him by raising him from the dead. And I am not deluded no matter what some may say.'"

Having reached the climax of my story, I pause to size up its effect on Pilate. He says, "You women are so gullible, so simple-minded. I can see Joanna has you believing with the others that Jesus has risen from the dead. No man of sober judgment would let himself be hoodwinked so easily...Claudia, when are you going to get into bed?"

"Right now." I crawl in on my side, making sure to leave some space between us. He makes a comment about this which I choose to ignore. I pick up my story, reminding him how men also saw and believed.

"What about the man who came to see you, Joseph of Arimathea?"

"He doesn't count. These pious Jews don't count. However

well-balanced they are in other things, they are all half-mad when it comes to their religion. Show me a Roman man who believes in him! It will never happen. You'll notice he appears only to a few Jews who were his followers. Nobody else can see him. Does this tell you anything?"

"It tells me you and I are different. I don't have to see to believe."

"Obviously not. But I will not believe in a risen Jesus unless he appears to me."

"Perhaps he will."

"Perhaps. But if it makes you happy, go ahead and believe. It's better for you than bathing in the Tiber in the dead of winter. It's better than running after cultish priests. And I can learn to put up with it if—Claudia, you looked wonderful tonight, and if I weren't so sleepy...."

Pilate dozes off, but I am too excited to go to sleep for a long time.

CHAPTER 17

The Promise Renewed

If he had given me any indication of being convinced by Joanna's testimony, I might have told my husband the rest of my story. I wanted so much to tell him what Jesus has done for me. I wanted to tell him what God is going to do for me because of Jesus. But I could see this was not the right moment.

Lying here beside my sleeping husband, I relive what happened just after Joanna made her stand. The memory is so precious that I want to hug it and hold it close to me, over and over....

When Joanna finished speaking, she sat down in her place. Herodias tried to turn the conversation to other things. She realized Joanna had got the last word on the previous topic.

My heart was beating as fast as it did last Monday when I went to the south steps of the Temple and met Jesus for the first time. I said to Herodias, "Will you excuse me? I feel ill. I was indisposed over the weekend, and I would like to lie down."

Herodias purred, "Why, you poor dear! Joanna, take Lady Claudia to the ladies' room and make her comfortable."

I knew she would call on Joanna to help me. We have tried to keep our friendship a secret, and she has no idea that we are more than casual acquaintances.

Joanna took me to another room. She helped me to a couch and she arranged some cushions around me. She brought me a cup of water. With my feet propped up and a blanket over me, I recovered quickly. Now we were alone, we felt free to talk and act like the friends we could not be while around Herodias. We fell on each other's necks.

I said, "It's wonderful to see you with your vision restored and to know Jesus did it."

Joanna said, "Thanks for defending me in front of my mistress. That took courage."

"She is quite intimidating, isn't she? But did you notice? After you finished your testimony, she had nothing else to say. She could see how the other women sympathized with you and not with her."

"Enough about Herodias. I want to hear about *you*. Claudia, did you get to meet Jesus? Did he heal you?"

"Yes, last Monday was the day which changed my life. Let me tell you everything that happened..." I proceeded to tell her all about the meeting and the healing and the promise.

Joanna was as excited about it as if she were my own mother. She said, "When the baby is born, you must let us know, so we can visit you in Caesarea, Chuza and I. Now I have my sight back, thanks to Jesus, I can travel around with my husband again."

I said, "Joanna, wait a minute—slow down. Before I can let myself get really excited, you must help me straighten out a few things. When Jesus made me this promise last Monday, I was disguised as a Jewish woman. Could he have known then that I was Pilate's wife?"

"It's quite possible, for the Spirit revealed many things to him. Why do you ask?"

"Because now I wonder if he would have made such a promise if he had known who I was."

"Jesus once said God is no respecter of persons. It would not have mattered to God who you were, and neither would it have mattered to Jesus."

"At the time, could he have known Pilate was going to condemn him?"

"It's entirely possible—in fact, practically certain. Since Sunday morning, the disciples have been reviewing everything Jesus said.

A Stone Laid in Zion

Now in the light of his resurrection, they are beginning to understand things he said which for some reason were dark to them before—things they couldn't understand and things they refused to accept. Jesus himself has explained to some of his disciples the prophecies which speak of him in the Scriptures. It seems he warned them about this very thing while we were on our way to Jerusalem."

"What did he say?"

"He told them he would be delivered to the chief priests and scribes and they would condemn him to death. He said they would deliver him to the Gentiles to be mocked and scourged and crucified. And he told the disciples plainly that he would be raised on the third day."

"It seems quite clear to me. Why couldn't they understand?"

"I don't know, unless for some reason the Lord was hiding it from us until now. But the point I am making, Claudia, is this: When Jesus made you the promise, he probably knew who you were and who your husband was. And since Pilate was the only one with the power to crucify him, he had to know about that too. He had to know what Pilate would do later. Of course God, who knows everything, knew these things all along. It was God who made the promise through Jesus. God told him what to say to you, and God will fulfill his promise."

I started to cry. I said, "Are you telling me God will do it for me, even after what has happened? Are you saying God will give a son to the wife of the man who killed his own Son?"

Joanna patted me and soothed me. But her words were far more comforting than her hand. "I am telling you that when the Lord God of Israel makes a promise, you can depend on it. The psalmist has said, 'The Lord is faithful to all his promises.' What exactly did Jesus promise you?"

"He said, 'A year from this day you shall bear a son.'"

"Did Jesus state any conditions for the fulfillment of the promise?"

"He said I must believe in him if I hope to receive. And when I tried to thank him, he said to thank the God of Israel and give him all the glory."

"That sounds just like Jesus. So if you obey his words, you do not need to worry. God will fulfill the promise whatever Pilate may do."

"I fear he will not believe...."

"Perhaps he will, after God fulfills the promise. Then you can tell him about the God of Israel, and he will see there is nothing too hard for the Lord."

"Joanna, if you only knew the depth of his bitterness against the God of Israel! I'm afraid if I told him, he might reject both me and the baby. We have an ancient custom among my people that the newborn child may be cast out for any reason by the father. Once he accepts him, however, he is legally bound to rear him and educate him."

"Then wait till after he accepts the child. But sooner or later, Claudia, you will have to tell him, for his own good and yours, as well as the baby's. And the sooner the better. Perhaps the reason God is giving you this child is to draw Pilate to him. It is your responsibility to tell your husband."

"But back in Caesarea, I feel so alone!"

"Pray, Claudia. Get your women who believe in Jesus to pray with you. God will show you a way to do anything he wants you to do for him. And when you pray, ask everything in Jesus' name. The last night they ate together, Jesus told the disciples to do this. We Jewish believers will be praying for you too...."

CHAPTER 18

Going Home Tomorrow

We are going home tomorrow. What a pleasant prospect! Although it is getting late—and except for the night-light, this room is completely dark—I feel as if I am looking at a beautiful sky at dawn, expecting the sun to rise at any moment. God's promise has been renewed. My life has been renewed. There is hope for me. There is even hope for Pilate. But in one sense, it is all up to me....

I will make a start. Pilate has been asleep for nearly an hour. I wonder if I can rouse him just enough to let him know I am ready to be a wife to him again.

We are lying back to back. He is snoring a little. I turn over and snuggle up to him. He makes contented grunting noises. Then he rolls over and puts his arm around me and nuzzles in my neck like a rooting pig...Now he's snoring again. I wonder if he even knows what has happened....

How sweet it is to make up! But it will be even sweeter a few months from now when I am lying like this with his arm around my middle, and I feel our baby move inside my body. Then Pilate will be able to feel his son pushing against his arm. We will both feel the precious life moving within me. I must find a way to tell him about the precious Giver of that little life-to-be. I must find a way....

Printed in the United States
69481LVS00006B/85